In the Name of God and Country

IN THE NAME OF
GOD AND COUNTRY

Reconsidering
Terrorism in
American History

MICHAEL FELLMAN

Yale University Press
New Haven & London

Set in Adobe Caslon type by Keystone Typesetting, Inc., Orwigsburg, Pennsylvania.
Printed in the United States of America.

Library of Congress Cataloging-in-Publication Data
Fellman, Michael.
In the name of God and country : reconsidering terrorism in American history / Michael Fellman.
p. cm.
Includes bibliographical references and index.
ISBN 978-0-300-11510-9 (alk. paper)
1. Terrorism—United States—History. I. Title.
HV6432.F446 2009
363.3250973—dc22

2009017156

A catalogue record for this book is available from the British Library.

This paper meets the requirements of ANSI/NISO Z39.48-1992 (Permanence of Paper).

10 9 8 7 6 5 4 3 2 1

For Santa,
Once More and Always

Contents

IN THE NAME OF GOD AND COUNTRY

Introduction

"Through the terror caused by murders and threats, the colored people are thoroughly intimidated. . . . [They] are disfranchised [and] are to be returned to a condition of serfdom—an era of second slavery."[1] With this letter, Adelbert Ames, the New England–born "carpetbag" Republican governor of Mississippi who had attempted to bring African Americans into the political process, thereby provoking southern white men to acts of racial violence, confessed to his wife in October 1875 that he had lost political control of his state to a well-organized white-supremacist terrorist movement. Coming in the aftermath of the Civil War, the bloodiest conflict fought on American soil, such acts might seem to be aberrations, unfortunate byproducts of a particularly violent period of American history. But Governor Ames's experience was far from unique: in fact, violence aimed at inspiring terror in order to impose political objectives has never lain far beneath the surface of American life.

Most of us, historians included, seek to distinguish the civilized from the savage and to put the savage into a small corner of practices conducted only by our enemies. Americans want their creation legends to be beautiful and uncontaminated—"life, liberty, and the pursuit of happiness," the "city upon a hill." They do not want to view the United States as grounded in organized political violence against alien "others"—people whose social and religious practices may not fit white Christian norms—and rarely acknowledge the lengths to which individuals and government alike have been willing to go in order to repress such peoples when they appeared to be threatening. Americans prefer to see terrorism as external to the "American way," as exceptional. And this desire to compartmentalize and strictly delimit terrorism because of its anti-human horrors has made it difficult for Americans to understand terrorism fully. Tragically, terrorism is more pervasive and complex than many would like to acknowledge. The narrow conventional definition of terrorism as political violence visited on the state by non-state individuals and organizations blinds us to the wider means through which terrorism is experienced.

What then if we erase artificial lines and look at terrorism as a mutual exchange of intimidating violence, a process central to state and society building—as more usual than unusual? Looking at the United States as a nation built, like other nations, to considerable degree on terrorist exchanges helps explain terrorism by demonstrating the ways in which it has remained a "normal" process, practiced by those with great power in concert with those with less power. (By describing the process as normal I do not mean to condone or trivialize it or in any way to reduce the horrors of the terrorist exchanges discussed in this book. But Americans will gain little comfort by seeking to separate themselves from terrorism as something that is only practiced by bad people from distant lands using alien ideologies. To understand terrorism in its historical as well as contemporary contexts we must also look into the patriotic American soul through the lens of history.) *In the Name of God and Country* challenges the fundamental belief that modern states possess an always-legitimate monopoly on the uses of power and that terrorism, by contrast, results only from individual or group invasions on the state. Rather, terrorism comes in two forms, revolutionary and reactionary, and it is engaged in by both non-state and state actors. The idea of a "just" or "civilized" war, for example, in practice more rationalization than description, applies only to certain aspects of warfare between modern states. *War* is a polite term in contrast to *terrorism;* it refers to legal boundaries. But when war becomes illegal, it merges into war crimes and terrorism. And terrorism is the more primal form of warfare, the means of social domination to which states as well as non-state actors frequently revert when they drop the mask of legality.

Terrorism frequently occurs in violent exchanges between outside and state forces. Specialists in terrorist studies often refer to "insurgent" or "agitational" versus "enforcement" terrorism. In this study I use respectively the terms *revolutionary* and *reactionary* terrorism, words that define the polarities and the reciprocal nature of the exchange. In addition, there is an inextricable relation between ad hoc terrorism from below (that is, from common citizens or alien civilians) and the reaction such terror prompts in the state. This significant dialectic reveals that terrorism played a central part in the development of the American state in the late nineteenth century, the most significant epoch in the consolidation of national governance and national expansion.

Terrorism by elements of the people or the government, or both, is often justified defensively as a prophylactic against impending terrorism imagined to be in the works and contemplated by others. We might call this the preemptive strike based on the projection of fears onto those who threaten us. From the beginning of the American state (and before), terrorism has pervaded American war making, social transformation, and political development, obliterating many conventional fine distinctions of morality, including those between combatants and noncombatants. When organized armies engage in what they know to be illegal activities, they blur the distinction between terrorism and war—between war and war crimes. In practice, belief in "civilized" warfare often amounts to a self-deluding nicety.

Terrorism in American history is ultimately related to wider patterns of social inequality and domination—especially, though not exclusively, to divisions of race and class. These are recurrent themes, whether in terrorism adopted by revolutionaries confronting the state in what terrorism experts call "asymmetrical warfare," in terrorism practiced by those wanting to assert their social privilege, or, in certain instances, in terrorism initiated by the state itself. Within the Protestant Christianity so central to American culture in its formative history lay a core of moral absolutism and self-righteousness that served to justify political violence in the minds of its perpetrators. In turn this assurance of divine sanction was often a causal factor in the occurrences of terrorism. In this sense terrorist exchanges within the United States or in American imperialist activities abroad often have been holy wars. The pattern of terrorism as war crimes in late- nineteenth-century society set a template, with the colonial war in the Philippines serving as a prefiguration—both in practices and in rationalizations—for Vietnam and Iraq.

I am a historian rather than a political theorist or social scientist, whose main concern would be to construct a morphology of terrorism of the sort I discuss in the Note on Terms.[2] As such, I explore the nature of terrorism through analysis braided into narrative—the onrushing drama inherent in terrorist exchanges is best served, in my opinion, by a narrative methodology. Underlying my study is a belief that dominating forces used terrorism to suppress the people they accused of revolutionary activities and that the uses of political violence have been motivated by religious certitude coupled with psychological anxiety, with the larger goal of instilling fear—terror—in the hearts and minds of ordinary people in order to defeat political challenges to the status quo. In this sense, *In the Name of God and Country* might best be seen as a post–September 11 reflection on the nineteenth-century past through the lens of historical casework, an effort to discern longer-term historical patterns that underlie the terrorism with which American society has engaged with so much fear, anger, and persistence.

Although my case studies commence in the 1850s, before that, indeed from the inception of the European incursion into North America, terrorism characterized relationships with the native peoples, creating a new landscape of violence. This struggle amounted to a race war, of the sort that would be mounted later against alien peoples in distant lands that Americans would one day colonize by armed force. *In the Name of God and Country* reconstructs the nineteenth-century structures that would be applied in the twentieth century and beyond, but the original colonial and anti-British revolutionary struggles helped create the forms the actors in my case studies used when confronting their enemies.

It is conventional to separate terrorism from war, with the latter defined as somehow more civilized, even more morally and legally controlled by shared rules, and thus more limited and separate from the savagery of uncivilized, terrorist fighting. Perhaps the most important codifier of this distinction was Hugo Grotius, who lived through the horrors of the Thirty Years' War when the slaughter of Christians by other Christians devastated Germany. When fighting Christians, Grotius insisted in *De Jure Belli et Pacis* (On the Laws of War and Peace, 1625), soldiers must constrain themselves with Christian morality. Writing at the height of the English Civil War, in a text available to the first English settlers of North America, Anthony Ascham also sought to define the legal and religious limits of civilized warfare. Thus, he argued, it ought to be the rule that "to cut off a few nocent, wee are not to cut off multitudes of Innocents, such as are Weomen and Children (as in sieges, and other depopulations) of whom the one is to be spared for sex, the other for want of age." But neither Ascham nor Grotius confronted the issue of how Christians should combat non-Christians.[3] And from the time of Grotius to the Iraq War, the civility that was supposed to be applied to wars among white Christians frequently has disintegrated into the double edge of savage terrorist actions within wars otherwise conducted by mutually agreed-upon rules of engagement. In those places, all bets were off.

In many ways the desire to separate Christian warfare from savage fighting—in fact, the whole idea of placing moral and legal constraints around warfare, in considerable measure by restricting the legal use of organized violence to states presumably acting under civilized constraints (a rather circular set of assumptions)—is illusory. Although Americans, like others, are horrified when their adversaries ignore civilized warfare, they tend to avert their eyes from the terrorist behaviors of those licensed by their own state or religious faith, seeking to isolate them as rogue agents acting outside "normative" moral and legal bounds. When the enemies are, by Americans' definition, uncivilized, unchristian, and undemocratic, the constraints of civilized warfare and civilized behavior tend to disintegrate rapidly. Dissidents and aliens—"others"—simply do not merit the protections due the civilized. Under sufficient duress Americans can make others of even Christian republican enemies. The same military act in the same war committed by a Christian (or by a Unionist), when committed by a Muslim (or by a Confederate), suddenly becomes terrorist, thus meriting the most brutal countermeasures. In short, a double standard escalates terrorist activity during war.

Colonial warfare, in which Western, "white," Christian nations conquer non-Christian, "primitive," nonwhite peoples, attests to this double standard. Such struggles to subdue or displace whole populations have always included savage treatment of noncombatants. Such was the nature of precivilized warfare, the archeologist Lawrence Keeley argues in *War Before Civilization*, and such was the case later when purportedly civilized nations conquered racial others to seize their land and rule them. Slaughter occurs in civilized armies, Keeley contends, when commanders lose control of their soldiers, who are acting from "primitive" motives such as "avenging combat losses of previous or fictive enemy atrocities." Even more tellingly, he suggests, "Slaughters of noncombatants can occur as a matter of policy, when the policymakers themselves are consumed by ethnic hatred or when they make a calculated attempt to use state terrorism to cow a conquered populace."[4]

It is central to my argument that "regression to the primitive" is that point at which "civilized war" (in this instance Christian) can devolve into terrorism. Such terrorism is most commonly unleashed when fundamental ideological values or religious beliefs are challenged and therefore need to be reasserted by the conqueror in an alien and alienating environment that must be colonized and changed from unrecognizable savagery to "civilized" form. Fear of the threatening other drives the conquerors into a frenzy of violence well beyond the norms of war. Any means to subdue the threatening enemy are justified, if not on the surface of avowed policy then by new and brutal practices that become actual policy.

When they first crossed the Atlantic Ocean to plant fragile colonies in the "wilderness," Christian European colonizers immediately began a protracted colonial war against the indigenous populations who sought to resist their encroachment. In the eyes of the European settlers, the Indians were heathens living in a state of wild unconstraint. They appeared threatening in peacetime because colonists feared that they themselves might lose their religion and their social constraints, turning into the Indian other; these aliens were even more threatening during violent clashes because they fought by savage means best combated by counter-savagery—red terrorism by white terrorism.[5]

In *The Name of War: King Philip's War and the Origins of American Identity,* which should be read alongside Peter Silver's *Our Savage Neighbors: How Indian War Transformed Early America,* Jill Lepore describes a horrific terrorist conflict in 1675–76, filled with torture, massacre, and the mutilation of men, women, and children on both sides. The spark was the execution of an Algonquian leader by New England colonists. In the violence that followed, English losses were at least eight hundred, and thousands more fled their lands. During the yearlong conflict, the Algonquians destroyed more than twenty-five English towns, over half of the colonizers' settlements, almost pushing the English back into the sea. Looking at the vast pollution of this invasion, the Quaker dissident Edward Wharton said at the time that the attackers had made "a burdensome and menstruous cloth" of English settlements, fouling them in order to throw the English off the contaminated land.

Both sides fought their ferocious campaigns as holy wars. When the Algonquians and their other Indian allies fell upon Goodman Wright, he held out his Bible before him to ward them off. After they killed him, as another colonist reported, they "rippe[d] him open and put his bible in his Belly" for other settlers to see. To spread chaos and create panic, the Algonquians dotted the countryside with burned houses, barns, and crops; killed whole families; mutilated corpses, "with some Heads, Scalps and Hands cut off from the Bodies of some of the English, and stuck upon Poles near the Highway, in that barbarous and inhuman Manner bidding us Defiance." And they frequently scattered leaves of "newly torn Bibles . . . in Hatred of our Religion." One colonist accurately summarized the cultural meanings intended by the Indians: "Our Enemies proudly exault over us and Blaspheme the name of our Blessed God: Saying, Where is your O God?"

For their part the New Englanders rallied to their religious banner, acting out their belief in biblical retribution: such savages merited not Christian forbearance but slaughter. Joshua Moodey preached to a New England militia company, "Take, kill, burn, sink, destroy all sin and Corruption, &C which are *professed enemies to Christ Jesus,* and [do] not spare or pity any of them." In another sermon, John Richardson asserted that vengeance "is an ordinance appoynted by God for subduing and destroying the Churches Enemies here upon Earth." By killing Indians, colonists would be God's instruments, purging the land of "the perfect children of the devil."

With these convictions, the colonists launched their reactionary terrorist campaign. By March 29, 1676, when the forces of the Wampanoag leader King Philip (Metacom) had nearly been destroyed by a series of raids that killed women and children as well as men, a band of Narragansett attacked and destroyed Providence, center of Roger Williams's Rhode Island, the only colony consciously constructed to make good and peaceful neighborhoods with the Indians. When Williams challenged the leaders of this band as to why they had returned kindness with destruction, they replied that Williams had forced his strange religion upon them and that, in any event, as Williams recorded their words, "God was [with] them and had forsaken us for they had so prospered in Killing and Burning us far beyond What we did against them." In white-hot anger, and justifying the English part in the spiraling devolution into terrorist retribution and chaos, Williams, usually the most tolerant of Puritans, replied that God was on the side of the English. "God has prospered *us* so that wee had driven the Wampanoogs with Philip out of his Countre and the Nahigonsiks out of their Countre, and had destroyed Multitudes of them in Fighting and Flying, in Hungr and Cold etc.: and . . . God would help us to consume them." This was the language not of Christian war but of ethnic cleansing and slaughter.

When it came time a decade later to sum up the meaning of the mutual slaughter, the early Puritan historical chronicler the Reverend William Hubbard concluded that the fighting, by colonists as well as Indians, had been "Massacres, barbarous inhumane Outrages [rather] than Acts of Hostility or valiant Atchievements." Groping for adequate language, Hubbard concluded that such mutual savagery failed to "deserve the Name of a War." He held to the belief that Christians ought to practice civilized warfare—limited acts of hostility leading to glory while maintaining honor. What he had seen of the colonial maelstrom in which he had been immersed, however, led him to seek a new word for the realm of primitive destructiveness his people had entered with the Indian people. That new word for "barbarous inhumane outrages" was *terrorism*, though it had not yet been invented.[6]

If King Philip's "war" had been an isolated event it might have lost its hold on the memories of the English settlers. But for the next eighty years, such colonial slaughters were frequently repeated, climaxing along the settler frontier during the French and Indian War of 1754–63. There, as the historian

Matthew C. Ward describes the conflict, Indians armed and supported by the French devastated vast reaches of western Virginia and Pennsylvania, killing at least fifteen hundred white settlers, capturing approximately two thousand more, and driving huge numbers back toward the eastern seaboard. As had been the case in previous Indian "wars," bands of Indians struck isolated settlements, burning all, torturing women and children as well as men, and then decorating the crossroads with mutilated corpses, the better to spread panic. After word of the slaughter passed to other settlers, a militia captain reported to the Pennsylvania authorities, "shocking Descriptions . . . given by those who had escaped of the horrid Cruelties and indecencies committed by these merciless Savages on the Bodies of the unhappy wretches who fall into their Barbarous hands [have] struck so great a Pannick and Damp upon the Spirits of the people, that hitherto they have not been able to make any considerable resistance or stand against the Indians." Instead, as other reports indicated, "terrified to death" with every account and rumor, thousands of settlers fled east in "confusion and Disorder." These were "not the idler and the vagrant . . . but the honest and industrious, men of worth and property."

Farther east, furious that the authorities were not protecting them (particularly in Quaker Pennsylvania)—the organized armies having marched elsewhere to attack French forces—mobs of young men organized themselves into gangs in order to massacre local Indian bands, some of whom were peaceful Christians. In December 1763, in Lancaster County, Pennsylvania, the "Paxton Boys" butchered six Conestoga and later finished off the fourteen survivors of their raid by storming the local county jail, dragging the prisoners out, and lynching them. Their numbers swelling to five hundred, the raiders, announcing that they intended genocide of all the Indians they could lay their hands on, marched on Philadelphia in a successful effort to force the authorities to forgo legal retaliation. Clearly this race war had entered the realm of systematic war crimes.

Although a truce ended this round of hostilities in the backcountry—a treaty drawing a line beyond which British civilians would not be allowed to advance, thus spelling out something of an Indian victory—mutual practices of terrorist, criminal war would continue until almost the end of the nineteenth century, activities that did not "deserve the Name of a War."[7]

In addition to this long, bloody, and deeply ingrained tradition of colonial terrorism, the Declaration of Independence and the American Revolution, those legendary foundational blocks of the American nation, were secured quite often (although not exclusively) by terrorist assaults against British colonists who did not join the rebel program. The term "American Revolution" itself emphasizes the abstract and universalistic libertarian ideology, added to the resistance to tyranny that with it led up to the Declaration of Independence, as the highly moral cause and purpose of the Revolution. Militarily the same founding legend has focused almost exclusively on the revolt against the distant British Crown that sent troops across the Atlantic to suppress the rebellion. But in the part of the story that relatively few historians have emphasized, this same struggle was equally a civil war, marked by terrorist activities on both sides. The high-minded assertions of life, liberty, and the pursuit of happiness, of equality and freedom from tyranny, were secured not only at Valley Forge, Saratoga, and Yorktown in a just war against the red-coated enemy. Securing independence also required a widespread and nasty internecine struggle in which armed bands of civilians called militias grappled to destroy the enemy's legitimacy by conducting terrorist campaigns. American revolutionaries fought to drive the Tory enemies into silent acquiescence with their cause at the least, if not to banish them from the nation altogether, branding British North American Loyalists (their term for themselves) "enemy aliens," a category created by Congress on October 6, 1776, just as the American nation began. Loyalists in turn considered the American Patriots (to use the revolutionaries' term) rebels and traitors to legitimate English authority. On both sides, ideology turned fellow American colonists into dangerous outsiders fit to be purged.

After the Declaration of Independence, the states all passed laws demanding oaths of allegiance from suspect civilians, renunciation of British authority, and acceptance of the legitimacy of the new nation. Those who refused—and by the calculation of the revolutionaries themselves a third of the populace remained loyal to the Crown and another third indifferent or neutral—faced escalating punishments: the stripping of civil liberties (including jury duty and the right to purchase or sell land), confiscation of property, jailing, mental and physical torture, exile, and in at least sixty-five instances, execution. Many revolutionary and loyalist militias—essentially self-constituted armed bands that were usually legitimated after the fact by one set of authorities or the other—set to savaging those people they construed as the enemy. They seized property, terrified undecideds into choosing sides, and pushed into flight those who did not. In Westchester County, New York, "Skinners" and "Refugees" on the rebel side and "Cowboys" on the British and Loyalist side created what amounted to a free-fire zone at a considerable distance from the opposing official armies, and this pattern was repeated at many other places in the new states. Loyalist gangs marauded in New Jersey, Long Island, the Dismal Swamps of Virginia, along the western frontier of that state, Bucks County, Pennsylvania, the Eastern Shore of Maryland, and, on a larger scale, in the Carolinas late in the war, where these terrorists were called Scoffelites.

In all these places, Patriot gangs counterattacked civilians they deemed British sympathizers. Again we see a pattern and form of revolutionary terrorism at the edges of organized and uniformed warfare carried out by disorganized, armed bands of male civilians terrorizing anyone they defined as the reactionary terrorist enemy. This military borderland, where war bleeds into terrorism and revolutionary and reactionary terrorism collide, gave birth to what became a permanent member of its own subset; this separate but powerful kind of war encompassed the demonstrative intimidation of civilians redefined as enemies. Terrorism accompanied civil war in the less celebrated and more inglorious events in the founding of the American nation.

Several examples demonstrate the intensity of the terror induced in civilians. In each case it is clear that the purpose was to terrorize by example and by inference a far greater number than the individuals chosen for special treatment. In New Cambridge, Connecticut, in 1777, seventeen members of the local high Tory Anglican church (who had split from their evangelical coreligionists over the Revolution and been imprisoned for treason) petitioned the Connecticut General Assembly for release from their confinement, "while our Farms & Familys [are] laying waste & Suffering." They denied disloyalty to the state and "humbly & earnestly" begged to be allowed to take an oath of allegiance, thus conclusively renouncing their previous loyalty to the Crown. Most were released, but to make a fearsome example for all such congregations, one of their leaders was tried, convicted of treason, and hanged.

That same year a lusty shoemaker in Richmond, Virginia, insisted on huzzaing for King George in defiance of a North Carolina militia led by General Francis Nash that had entered town. The soldiers took him down to the James River to teach him a lesson, much as later American captors would use the "water cure" in the Philippines and "water-boarding" in Iraq. According to an account written by one of the militia, "The soldiers tied a rope around his middle, and seesawed him backwards and forwards until we had him nearly drowned, but every time he got his head above water he would cry for King George.... His wife and four likely daughters crying and beseeching their father to hold his tongue, but still he would not." The militia then tore open their captive's featherbed and pried open a tar barrel, "into which we plunged him headlong." Pulled out by the heels and rolled in feathers, "still he would hurrah for King George. The General now ordered him to be drummed out of the West end of town, and told him expressly that if he plagued him any more in that way he would have him shot. So we saw no more of the shoemaker." And in 1778, when the British Army withdrew from Philadelphia, two collaborators from the Quaker community, the carpenter Abraham Carlisle, who had kept a gate to the town during the occupation, and John Roberts, a miller who had served as an enlistment officer for the British, were convicted of treason. Despite a petition for clemency signed by most of their jurors, 5 clergymen, and 387 Philadelphians, they were hanged to demonstrate to the local pacifist Quaker community just how disloyalty that was acted upon in even peaceful ways would be punished by revolutionary terrorists in the new American nation.[8]

Terrorism bled into political domination and warfare from the inception of America, forming deep traditions of political violence that were available when necessary during the Revolutionary War and creating models of terrorist action played out in later cases, in the nineteenth and twentieth centuries and beyond. This book, however, does not seek to survey every element of the history of terrorism throughout American history. Rather, I shall consider five prescient cases of American terrorism that were both historically significant in themselves and representative of wider patterns, revealing the underlying currents of terrorism intrinsic to the formation of modern American society. As we shall see, race and class dominion enforced by terrorism lie at the core of these cases and their characteristic Americanism, in the violent collision and repression that lay along those great and perpetual fault lines in American society. Most important, I hope to shed light on the masked figure in the shadowy corner of the room—the terrorist—and refine our understanding of types of terrorism: revolutionary, reactionary, and state-sponsored.

These cases cover the period from the late 1850s to the turn of the twentieth century, the decades of most rapid transformation of American society into the modern forms in which Americans still live. In 1859 the United States was still a loose congeries of states—indeed, it was not clear whether the United States, weakly coordinated both politically and economically, was a plural collection of states or a unified nation. That was the primary constitutional issue of the Civil War, the result of a second declaration of independence by the majority of the slave-holding states. By 1902 and the conquest of the Philippines, where my historical discussion ends, it was clear that the

United States was not only a nation but one growing in central authority and thrusting abroad in imperialist ways that continue to the present. It is my contention that these developments would not have occurred without terrorist exchanges within the country itself that led to the consolidation of national power, sometimes in response to anti-state terrorist threats, sometimes during war, sometimes with the state or quasi-state forces initiating the terrorism. I conclude with a coda arguing that these historical cases created the political template for modern-day American terrorism following September 11, when a terrorist attack elicited state responses that violated both international treaties and the basic civil rights guaranteed by the United States Constitution.

In each chapter I focus on a great national event in which the ownership of primary American moral and social values—republicanism and Christianity—were combated violently. In each instance, this struggle was based on staking a claim to the legitimate use of vengeful violence as the central means to intimidate, eliminate, or convincingly suppress the other. Although the uses of power were frequently one-sided, each episode led to a serious ideological debate over the ownership of social truth. Each party asserted that it served the higher ends of American virtues—those without power who were fighting for some idea of justice and those empowered enough to use demonstrative violence insisted that by this means would they purify the nation. Together both sides fought over higher truths: each understood the other perfectly well, and each believed that its side was good and the other's evil. The various others were depicted as alien, contaminated, subversive, dangerous; they were less than human and fit for expulsion, displacement from public legitimacy, suppression, exile, jail, torture, death, and mutilation. By contrast, those claiming legitimacy insisted that they represented progress, truth, liberty, and freedom, and that preemptive terrorism or counterterrorism was necessary to expunge the insidious forces of corruption from the nation.

In four of the five cases, these terrorist truths were played out first in the streets and countryside and then in a courtroom or a Senate hearing committee room, and every element of the terrorist acts and the reactions to them carried intentional ideological freight. Conflicting interpretations of those acts, amounting to alternative versions of the purification of America, were deployed in an attempt to claim ownership of the fundamental values of the nation. For the moment debate was allowed between the powerful and the unpowerful, as dissenting versions of social values had their day in court. These courtrooms and hearing rooms, frequently stacked to the advantage of the powerful, ultimately justified the state power gained through terrorist actions—but they also left a record of the voices of those ground under by political violence.

CHAPTER 1

John Brown
Slavery and Terrorism

One hot summer day in 1859, the New York journalist Frederick Law Olmsted was riding with an overseer on a large Mississippi cotton plantation:

We were crossing . . . a deep gully . . . when the overseer suddenly stopped his horse, exclaiming, "What's that? Hallo! Who are you there!"

It was a girl lying at full length on the ground at the bottom of the gully, evidently intending to hide herself from us in the bushes.

"Who are you there?"

"Sam's Sall, sir."

"What are you skulking there for?"

The girl half rose but gave no answer.

"Where have you been all day?"

The answer was unintelligible.

After some further questioning, she said her father accidentally locked her in, when he went out in the morning.

"How did you manage to get out?"

"Pushed a plank off, sir, and crawled out." . . .

"That won't do—come out here." The girl arose at once and walked towards him; she was about eighteen years of age. A bunch of keys hung at her waist, which the overseer espied, and he said, "Ah, your father locked you in, but you have got the keys." After a little hesitation the girl replied that these were the keys of some other locks; her father had the door-key.

Whether her story were true or not could have been ascertained in two minutes by riding on to the gang with which her father was at work, but the overseer had made up his mind about the facts.

"That wont do," said he, "get down on your knees." The girl knelt on the ground; he got off his horse and struck her thirty or forty blows across the shoulders with his tough, flexible rawhide whip . . . well laid on as some people flog a baulking horse, but with no appearance of angry excitement. . . . At every stroke the girl winced and exclaimed "Yes, sir!" or "Ah, sir!" or "Please, sir!" not groaning or screaming. At length he stopped and said "Now tell me the truth." The girl repeated the same story. "You have not got enough yet," said he, "pull up your clothes—lie down." The girl without any hesitation drew closely all her garments under her shoulders and lay down upon the ground with her face toward the overseer, who continued to flog her across her naked loins and thighs. . . . She now shrunk away from him, writhing, groveling and screaming "Oh, don't sir! Oh please stop, master! please, sir! please, sir! oh, that's enough, master! oh Lord!, oh master, master! oh God!, master, do stop! oh, God, master, do stop! oh God, master, oh, God, master!" . . .

It was the first time I had ever seen a woman flogged. I had seen a man cudgeled and beaten in the heat of passion, but never flogged with a hundredth part of the severity used in this case. . . .

[I rode away from the scene.] The overseer laughed as he joined me and said, "She meant to cheat me out of a day's work—and she has done it too." . . .

"Was it necessary to punish her so severely?"

"Oh yes, sir" (laughing again). "If I hadn't punished her so hard she would have done the same thing to-morrow, and half the people on the plantation would have followed her example. Oh you've no idea how lazy these niggers are. You northern people don't know anything about it. They'd never do any work if they were not afraid of being whipped."[1]

It is not melodramatic to say that slavery is begun through kidnapping and perpetuated through violence. As this Mississippi overseer was willing to demonstrate to his northern guest, slavery was maintained, when need be, through severe corporal punishment. Not only did the overseer compel a young black woman to strip naked before him so that he could beat her loins, he continued the punishment until the sound of her screams carried to other slaves working the nearby fields. He intended her to bear scars and for her thrashing to serve as an example to all the slaves. This overseer knew how to play the role of omnipotent master through coolly targeted (not random or angry) physical force in order to maintain the efficiency of slave labor. The beating was not personal but political.

When he wrote his book for northern readers, Olmsted would have understood that they would recoil from the erotic and sadistic components of the actions of the overseer, and also from the blasphemy of his assumption of the position of master and God over the supine body and spirit of this young woman and all her people, including her father, who could not come to her defense. To an increasing number of northerners (though they were still a minority), these mortal sins made slavery an evil institution. Therefore, when one talks of John Brown as a terrorist, which I shall do, this context must be kept in mind. The horrors of slavery corrupted a whole nation: slavery was an institution grounded in absolute authority and systemic submission. It was maintained through ever-present coercion, including physical violence, that had to appear perpetual and unyielding to appeal or change.

In 1859, what was an American citizen to do about slavery? Most Americans took pleasure in the profits of the southern cotton field and northern cotton mill, bought the cheap but excellent cotton clothes available in every shop, and tried not to think about the means of production. (How many of us give much thought to our own cheap clothes, produced under near-slavelike conditions in factories far away?) But if they were eager consumers, white Americans were also, North and South, mainly evangelical Christians who believed that they were personally answerable to God for the sins they committed or omitted to contest, and who also believed that their nation was devoted to individual and social freedom—to life, liberty, and the pursuit of happiness, in the totemic words of Thomas Jefferson, America's most famous slaveholding revolutionary ideologue.

Many in the South urged kind treatment of slaves, whom they believed to be perpetually childlike and subhuman, coupling belief in racial inequality with Christian duty. Some felt guilty, arguing that slavery was a necessary evil that would die in time, while others, including an increasingly powerful and vocal leadership, argued that slavery was a positive good that heightened economic productivity, served the interests of properly paternalistic owners, and even enlightened the slaves, whom they were educating, slowly but surely, in civilized white values.

In the North, the majority accepted slavery as a fact of life and a correct racial ordering, while others urged that it be limited, with their part of the nation kept free of blacks as well as of slaves. A smaller band of militant abolitionists, who condemned the institution as a great moral evil, sought to separate from it and destroy it, deeply outraged by the institution on Christian and republican grounds. Some abolitionists withdrew from politics as invariably corrupted by compromises with the slave power, while others believed they could turn politics to antislavery ends.

But what did abolitionists *do* about slavery? Well, in June 1859, John Brown (fig. 1), an aging, enraged white abolitionist, stood up in the middle of

Fig. 1 John Brown (Library of Congress, Prints and Photographs Division, LC-USZ62-106337)

a session of the New England Antislavery Society and rudely interrupted yet another verbal denunciation of the evil Moloch of slavery. "Talk! Talk! Talk!" he shouted. "That will never free the slave. What is needed is action!—Action!"[2] And he meant it. Brown took action farther than had any other abolitionist, right into the belly of the slave South.

Brown is often viewed—and judged—as though his acts and personality could be divorced from context. But as had been the case with Nat Turner and other violent black rebels, slavery drove him to self-destructive terrorism in part because no one else was confronting the horrific evil through direct action. He personally felt the plight of the slave and the essentially undivided force of the master class. Moreover, at Brown's trial after the raid on Harpers Ferry it became clear that Brown and the southern ruling class understood each other perfectly. Believing the southern system to be grounded in political violence, he sought to use violence to expose and destroy it. For their part, Brown's southern judges saw in him the point man of a slave rebellion joined with an abolitionist invasion, both physical and moral, that had to be destroyed to secure their Christian commonwealth. His act and their response were as crucial to the onset of the Civil War as the attacks on September 11 were to the greatly heightened War on Terror, including the invasion of Iraq. Brown shook the nation.

Although Brown's terrorism needs to be conceptualized within the terrorism of slavery, this should not lead us to the simple conclusion that he was a "freedom fighter," as though his acts in themselves had no questionable moral dimensions and consequences because of the greater immensity of the evil he was fighting. Brown took innocent lives, apparently with relish, in the name of his beliefs. Extremists sometimes cut to the central point of a cultural contradiction, but this never makes them "good" extremists. Brown's personality and behavior were indeed extreme, and even though slavery was horrendous he presents issues that cannot be reduced to good versus evil. In tandem with the state he terrorized, a state that destroyed him in the name of white liberty and black enslavement, Brown was an elemental force that drove a wedge through a society built on contradictions. Brown and the slaveholding class together created a terrorist dynamic that accelerated the split of one nation into two warring peoples.

Brown's personal road to revolutionary terrorism was long and hard. Born in 1800 with the new century, John Brown became a committed, full-time terrorist only in 1855. As I shall demonstrate, he experienced a second and equally dramatic self-transformation, from terrorist to martyr, only after his capture in 1859, a role that lasted for the six weeks until he was hanged. This brief final phase created the John Brown of legend, a heroic edifice he consciously constructed while awaiting death at the hands of his enemies. Rhetorically, he removed himself from violence, almost repudiating terrorism while seeking the moral high ground during his trial by a state intent on killing the terrorist and claiming righteousness for itself.

For the first fifty-five-year stretch of his sixty years, John Brown was a man of burning religious zealotry and single-mindedness of purpose, often adrift in a world that did not bend to his imperious demands on it. He experienced fifteen business failures (a few such failures were common enough in the boom and bust of the antebellum United State but fifteen was exceptional); he was a domineering, angry man who struggled for self-control and self-containment. He was deeply opposed to slavery nearly his whole life, but there was nothing inevitable about his marching off to his antislavery war. Yet whatever jerks and turns he had made before his climactic vendetta, he always cast himself as the central actor in grand drama: he never committed to half-measures but pursued his changing goals with obsessive energy.

This energy was based not on optimism about the future for himself or his nation but on the need to find a stoic well for action despite the chaos of a terrible world. Unlike most abolitionists, whose faith was based on a belief in the benevolence of God and the ever-expanding reformist potentiality of humankind, or members of other Christian sects like Methodism that stressed the human capacity for free will, Brown was a rock-ribbed Calvinist, a devourer of the sermons of Jonathan Edwards, a man seized with a sense of sin. Sinfulness not only was without, as represented by the institution of slavery, but within: acting meant the scourging of self as well as of others.

Brown traced the boyhood origins of his tormented adult self in a letter of July 15, 1857, to Henry Stearns, the twelve-year-old son of George Luther Stearns, a Boston abolitionist who had become one of Brown's financial backers. Brown's first memories were of being taken to the wilderness of Ohio when he was five, learning to drive cows and ride horses, hanging around Indian encampments, dressing his own leather from squirrels, wolves, dogs, and cats, and rambling in the "wild new country finding birds and squirrels." But even before this idyll of boyhood well-being could be convincingly constructed, loss and grief set in; his self-education occurred in "the School of Adversity," as Brown put it to Henry Stearns. Brown feared that Henry might laugh at this melodramatic description, but in Brown's bruised memory his childhood had presented loss after loss—"sore trials to John." (Brown wrote his tale in the third person, the better to objectify and moralize from personal experience.) The boy had few earthly treasures, and so, at six years old, when he lost a yellow marble, the first he had ever seen, which an Indian boy had given him, "it took years to heal the wound; & I think he cried at times about it." Five months after this loss he caught and tamed a little bob-tailed squirrel, which he also lost, "& for a year or two he was in mourning." Brown next described his boyhood self as a liar who could not take criticism, "to screen himself from blame or punishment," because he had never been encouraged to be open about his actions or, of course, about his sense of loss and of being wronged. These losses, the fifty-seven-year-old Brown concluded, "were the beginning of a severe but much needed course of discipline which he afterward was to pass through," teaching him that the "Heavenly Father sees it best to take all the little things out of his hands which he has ever placed in them."

These painful earliest memories were filtered through Brown's memories of his mother's death when he was eight, a not-so-little loss that he had taken as "complete & permanent" abandonment. His father soon remarried a "sensible, intelligent [and] estimable woman, yet he never addopted her in feeling, but continued to pine after his own mother for years." He believed this inconclusive mourning had cut him off from women and his own warmer nature, as well as from any trust that this world might provide dependable nurturance.

While in his early teens, Brown boarded with a "very gentlemanly landlord," who also owned an intelligent and kind slave boy about his own age. "The Master made a great pet of John" while the "negro boy (who was fully if not more his equal) was badly clothed, poorly fed [and] beaten before his eyes with Iron Shovels or any other thing that came first to hand." This contrast brought Brown to reflect on the "wretched, hopeless condition of Fatherless & Motherless slave children," who had no one to protect and provide for them. "He sometimes would raise the question: is God their Father?"[3]

Brown dated his own abolitionism from this early experience. The narrative of his early and profound identification with the degraded motherless and fatherless slave boy, when he himself was separated from his father having long since lost a mother for whom he continually grieved, was written with searing emotional authenticity. He was as one with his slave double, his feelings of brotherly solidarity made more intense by the false praise coming from his hypocritical master, a false father who may have elicited feelings parallel to those Brown's natural father aroused in him.

Also authentic was Brown's insistence that early loss prepared him for a lifetime of grief and humiliation. Among his many business failures was a bankruptcy in 1842, about the same time that he served a brief sentence in prison for threatening grievous harm to a former associate—an example of the considerable anger that he tried to contain, sometimes unsuccessfully. Chasing fortune and fleeing misfortune, in common with many Americans of his day, Brown frequently pulled up stakes and moved huge distances, sometimes with his family, sometimes without. When it came to homes, he had no fixed address; in matters of religion he held tenaciously to his unchanging faith in an inscrutable and punishing but absolutely powerful and just God.

Most significant, in his adult life Brown, a strict but loving father, lost nine of his twenty children at birth or in early childhood, including four at once in September 1843, when they were killed by cholera or perhaps typhoid fever. Later three of his grown sons died in battle under his command in Kansas and at Harpers Ferry. On August 11, 1832, his first wife, Dianthe, died, probably of heart disease, shortly after giving birth to a son who had died four days before she did, her seventh child in twelve years of marriage. After her death, Brown wrote to his father that he was so numb he could feel nothing: "We are again smarting under the rod of our Heavenly Father."[4] But he married sixteen-year-old Mary Day nine months later, much as his father had hurried into a second marriage when John was eight.

In 1843, long away from his family and homesick while pursuing wealth (or at least economic survival), Brown learned that his daughter Ruth had accidentally scalded her younger sister Amelia to death. He wrote to his "dear afflicted wife and children": "One more dear little feeble child I am to meet no more till the dead small & great shall stand before God. This is a bitter cup indeed, but blessed be God a brighter day shall dawn." Three weeks later, responding to a mournful letter from Mary, Brown eloquently expressed the well of stoicism and energy that kept him at the Lord's work despite terrible reversals of fortune. "I have sailed over a somewhat stormy sea for nearly half a century, & have experienced enough to teach me thoroughly [to] buckle up & be prepared for the tempest. Mary let us try to maintain a cheerful self command while we are tossing up & down, & let our motto still be Action, Action; as we have but one life to live."[5]

It is almost inconceivable for us, when so few of our children die young, to imagine the pain of these unpredictable and seemingly continual losses or to understand how those living in fear of Calvin's angry and inscrutable God could have charged themselves up to go out into the world with renewed enthusiasm. Perhaps the Calvinist faith in ultimate heavenly reunion and the idea that the Lord had a plan and humankind a duty to obey the unknowable almighty counteracted the gloom of repeated mourning. The faithful could be righteously active rather than passive or self-serving if they were coursing the hound of heaven, if they were using the fragile resources of their human natures on this earth to try to discern and most energetically strive to attain ultimate goals that they saw only through the glass darkly. If there was little joy otherwise, there could be joy in suffering faithfully for God. This required an almost superhuman damping down of rage in order to live under the rule of such an apparently punishing Being, but it also could provoke powerful action when one worked through the outlets provided for human choice.

Moreover, Brown's deterministic Calvinism was tempered by antinomian and perfectionist views held in common with many other abolitionists and religious reformers of his day. Antinomianism, an anti-clerical Protestant heresy with a long life, held that in matters of faith each soul was in direct communication with God outside any church or minister's discipline. If believers then gained a powerful conviction of assurance that they had been saved, the potential for righteous action grew exponentially as the saved believed they incorporated truth. In this mode, Brown wrote to his family in 1839 that they must not "get discouraged . . . but hope in God and try to serve him with a perfect heart." Orthodox Calvinists never would have believed that the human heart could be made perfect before the millennium arrived, never would assert that one could attain perfect assurance of salvation on this earth, but Brown came to be convinced that the tossing tempests would be short run, and he knew with unorthodox conviction that salvation was to be his. Moreover, he believed it was God working through him rather than his own impulses that compelled him to action—he came to the certainty that he acted as God's instrument, his prophet. In this absolutist formulation, spiritual submission would be synonymous with action, and God would be responsible for the actions of his truly enlightened servants, actions that they should commit with zeal and totality lest they be incompletely true to the word given them.[6]

Something of the powerful emotional expression of suppressed anger coupled with the demand for God-like action can be found in one of the most striking documents concerning Brown's family life. In the retelling of the story years later by Brown's oldest son, John Brown, Jr., when he was about ten his father tired of admonishing him about his faults, and began keeping an account book of his son's moral lapses.

John, Jr.
For disobeying mother . . . . 8 lashes
    " unfaithfulness at work 3   "
    " telling a lie 8   "

Finally, one Sunday morning, Brown told his son that the day of reckoning had come. "He showed my account, which exhibited a fearful footing of *debits* [and] had no credits or off-sets, and was of course bankrupt. I then paid about *one-third* of the debt, reckoned in strokes from a nicely prepared blue-beech switch, laid on 'masterly.' Then, to my utter astonishment, father stripped off his shirt, and, seating himself on the block, gave me the whip and bade me 'lay it on' to his bare back. 'Harder!' he said; harder, harder!' until he *received the balance of the account.* Small drops of blood showed on his back where the tip end of the tingling beech cut through. Thus ended the account and settlement, which was also my first practical illustration of the Doctrine of Atonement. I was then too obtuse to perceive how justice could be satisfied by inflicting penalty upon the back of the innocent instead of the guilty; but at that time I had not read the ponderous volumes of Jonathan Edwards's sermons which father owned."[7]

Brown rarely used corporal punishment, and he clearly thought through this instance with coolness and calculation before he acted. It is noteworthy that the explanation for the punishment was economic—from a father who was often failing at business. But even more striking was the studied reversal of paternal power in which, there on the block, son became father and father son, slave became master and master slave. The understanding of the consequences of a perceived moral evil was to be taught in all its ramifications when the father atoned for his infliction of pain on his guilty son by taking pain from him in turn for his own sins, thus learning from suffering while he taught lessons of obedience with the ultimately divine rod he and his son were wielding as God's stewards. Love and pain, punishment and redemption were conjoined not separate. Knowledge was of a bare and brutal justice. Accounts would be settled through righteous violence.

Always deeply concerned about family politics, as he aged Brown shifted his focus increasingly to the politics of antislavery. By the late 1840s, he had begun to interpret his drive in the world of business in a larger abolitionist context. Thus as he prepared to go to England to sell masses of others people's wool on the market there—hoping to displace slave-grown cotton as the clothing material of choice, a scheme that proved to be a disaster—Brown wrote to the noted antislavery congressman Joshua R. Giddings, "I wish to manage the business in such a way as to benefit the abolitionist cause to which I am most thoroughly devoted; whilst at the same time I wish to encourage American Tallent & industry." He gave Giddings the opportunity to invest in this plan in order to demonstrate that Giddings too was "American to the core; as well as an abolitionist."[8]

At the same time he was evolving this exercise in venture capitalism as a form of abolitionism, Brown was planning to move to upstate New York to settle among a black colony that the wealthy philanthropist Gerrit Smith had created. He wrote to his father, "I can think of no other place where I think I would sooner go; all things considered than to live with those poor despised Africans to try, & encourage them; & show them a little so far as I am capable how to manage." Brown moved his family in May 1849 to North Elba, near Lake Placid, deep in the Adirondack Mountains, a remote place that would remain his home base until the end, though he ventured far afield from there. He befriended the black settlers, treating them as equals in the field and at the dinner table.

However committed he was to his black brothers and sisters, Brown still had something condescending in his attitude, and he would never entirely expunge his sense that he was the necessary father figure to lead the benighted blacks from slavery to freedom. In a richly ironic and elegant essay, "Sambo's Mistake," written in 1847 for the *Ram's Horn*, a black abolitionist newspaper in New York, Brown assumed, with the editor's knowledge, the voice of an irresponsible free black in order to construct the sort of message of self-improvement frequently preached by free black leaders to their flocks. Instead of being concerned with buying "expensive gay clothing nice Canes, watches, Safety Chains, Finger rings, Breast Pins," smoking tobacco, and reading "silly novels & other miserable trash," "Sambo" explained that he should have denied his pleasures and served his race: "I have always expected to secure the favour of whites by tamely submitting to every species of indignity contempt & wrong instead of nobly resisting their brutal aggressions from principle" and assuming full responsibilities as a citizen and head of family. When appropriating this black voice, Brown wrote not to mock racial inferiors but to encourage the blacks' assumption of independence and full citizenship.[9]

Although somewhat abstracted from contact with blacks in this parable,

Brown was increasingly led by his form of paternalism to be willing to mingle his blood with theirs, his suffering with theirs, much as he had with his son when using the blue-beech switch. Brown created a concrete manifestation of this identification in his "Words of Advice" to the United States League of Gileadites, an organization of free blacks he helped form in Springfield, Massachusetts, in 1851. As were many other northerners, Brown had been incensed by the passage of the Fugitive Slave Act, on September 18, 1850, part of the political compromise of that year, that allowed slaveholders' agents to come north and compel northern tribunals to seize escaped slaves and return them to the South without a jury trial. "Union is strength," Brown declared in his manifesto. He insisted that blacks should arm and join together to attack any slave catcher who showed his face in Springfield. "Do not delay one moment after you are ready; you will lose all your resolution if you do. Let the first blow be the signal for all to engage; and when engaged do not do your work by halves, but make clean work with your enemies." If caught and hauled before the courts, Brown urged, the prisoners should "stand by one another . . . while a drop of blood remains; and be hanged, if you must, but . . . make no confession."[10] Although no other branches of the league were formed and this one never acted, it is notable that Springfield blacks subscribed to Brown's leadership and apparently accepted his identification with them as sincere.

The Springfield covenant marks the overt inception of the career of Brown the engaged warrior—until his dying day he would believe that his task was to lead a black army against the monster of slavery. A revolution was necessary, Brown believed, and only liberating political violence by the slaves themselves could accomplish this end, liberation in action that would unleash an inner revolution in the slave personality, releasing the free man from the servile slave. Assuming the mantle of leadership, Brown tied his deepest and most burning emotional and physical energies as well as his religious conviction to the cause of the most downtrodden of Americans; in this manner he expressed his belief that only terror could throw off terror. He and his followers would use power against power in a dramatic showdown with evil.

To believe that such a goal was attainable, Brown had to act in the belief that blacks were not merely willing but eager to fight for their liberation, even if fighting meant death. Few abolitionists, black or white, appeared willing to sign up for such a project. In 1856 the antislavery journalist William A. Phillips interviewed Brown about his theory of the necessary and cleansing power of black insurrection. Brown told Phillips about "Spartacus and his servile war, and was evidently familiar with every step in the career of the great gladiator," Phillips reported. Brown discussed the tactical mistake Spartacus had made by waiting in place to improve his army when he either should have struck immediately at Rome or retreated to the mountain vastness of northern Italy to fight a guerrilla war while gathering and training an irresistible army. "I reminded him," Phillips later recalled, "that Spartacus and Roman slaves were warlike people in the country from which they were taken, and were trained to arms in the arena." "The negroes," on the other hand, Phillips continued, voicing a standard, demeaning stereotype, "were a peaceful, domestic, inoffensive race. In all their sufferings they seemed to be incapable of resentment or reprisal." "You have not studied them right," Brown replied, "and you have not studied them long enough. Human nature is the same everywhere." While seeking to build liberationist interracial brotherhood, Brown, in company with other radical abolitionists, frequently quoted Lord Byron: "Hereditary bondsmen know ye not! / Who would be free must themselves strike the blow."[11]

During the 1850s, in concert with his closest circle of supporters, Brown evolved a theory of black redemption through organized violence that helped prepare the ground for his terrorist activities. Perhaps the clearest statement of this ideology came in an article entitled "Physical Courage" that the zealous young minister Thomas Wentworth Higginson published in the *Atlantic Monthly* in 1858. In this essay, Higginson created a typology of forms of courage. First was "the spontaneous [and] innate courage of the blood," found in such "heroic races" as Arabs, Afghans, and Scots Highlanders. For less bloodied peoples, "habit and discipline" were needed to give "steadiness," the second form of physical courage. Third was "magnetic, or transmitted" courage, innate but dependent on emulation in order to emerge. Women and Africans appeared to be passive in the face of injustice, but they were capable of passing, though desperate action, "from cowering pusillanimity to the topmost height of daring." The key ingredient for this combustion was the right leader, who could express the "element of inspiration, something superadded and incalculable, when all other forces are exhausted." Lit by such fire, "desperate courage makes one a majority." Though he never mentioned him by name, Higginson clearly was thinking of John Brown, the man who had promised to act with superadded inspiration to lead blacks into the conclusive war of liberation.[12]

To serve his revolutionary task, Brown married his Christian faith to the traditional concept of American liberty in his definition of the inevitably violent struggle for black freedom. In the late 1850s he told Franklin Sanborn, another young Bostonian supporter, "I believe in the Golden Rule and the Declaration of Independence. I think they both mean the same thing; and it is better that a whole generation should pass off the face of the earth—men, women and children—by violent death, than that one jot of either should fail *in this country.*" Black men must first become soldiers and then, having seized their freedom, full citizens. "When they stand like men, the nation will respect them. It is necessary to teach them this." Neither would it take thousands of men to set the revolution going. "A few men in the right, and knowing they are right, can overturn a mighty king, break slavery to pieces in two years." God's time of judgment was imminent, and Brown was ready to seize his (self) appointed role as prophet, teacher, and military leader of the black revolution. He had long been prepared to abandon everything when the end time should sound, he told the journalist Richard Hinton in 1858: "Whenever the time should come [I will] be ready; that hour is very near at hand, and all who are willing to *act* should be ready."[13]

In 1859, as he approached Armageddon, Brown composed "A Declaration of Liberty by the Representatives of the Slave Population of the United States of America," in which he revised the fundamental document of American revolutionary republicanism, melding libertarianism with Christian liberation in order to prepare and justify slave rebellion:

> When in the course of human events, it becomes necessary for an oppressed People to Rise and assert their Natural Rights, as Human Beings, as Native and Mutual Citizens of a free Republic, and break that odious yoke of oppression, which is so unjustly laid upon them by their fellow countrymen, and to assume among the powers of Earth the same privileges to which the Laws of Nature, and nature's God entitle them; A moderate respect for the opinions of Mankind, requires that they should declare the causes which incite them to this Just & worthy action. [The history of American slavery is] a history of injustice and cruelties inflicted upon the Slave in every conceivable way. . . . It is the embodiment of all that is Evil, and ruinous to a Nation; and SUBVERSIVE of God. . . . We will obtain these rights or die in the struggle to obtain them. We make war upon oppression. . . . Nature is mourning for its murdered and Afflicted children. Hung be the Heavens in Scarlet."[14]

Emotionally and ideologically, during the last decade of his life Brown was preparing himself to set the match to the powder keg. He was uncertain of his future tactical direction, but he had laid the religious, political, and emotional groundwork to do whatever was necessary to propel the black revolution into being.

By compromising with slavery while the nation expanded, the government provided the field for action. In 1854, Congress passed and President Franklin Pierce signed the Kansas-Nebraska Act, which opened those western territories to settlers, leaving it up to them to decide whether the territories should be organized as free or slave. This principle of "popular sovereignty" guaranteed a westward rush of settlers from both north and south, all of them using as much force as they deemed necessary to define the future of the trans-Mississippi West. In the mid-1850s, Kansas, the southern portion of the territory, became a sectional battleground, a precursor to the civil war to come.

Among the earliest emigrants from the North to Kansas were four of Brown's sons, convinced that they were entering the next battleground against the spread of slavery. Their father hesitated for several months before joining them, citing business and family pressures as well as his sense that he was aging. But then Brown set off for Kansas in 1855, ready for action, in part as an agent of Massachusetts antislavery forces, who had organized the Massachusetts Kansas Aid Committee to provide men and arms for the struggle.

From this point on, for the last five years of his life (until his final radical transformation during his trial) Brown would remain a professional revolutionary terrorist. One of his central roles was to raise funds in order to purchase guns to smuggle into the territory, together with men and supplies. On the ground in Kansas he rallied public opinion, exhorting men to battle. And he formed a company of twenty-six young men, including his sons, making them sign a covenant he composed swearing that they would behave with decorum and in every instance obey the orders of John Brown, Commander. Brown drilled the men and led them in political and religious discussions, preparing them to act as the shock troops of the struggle against what he called the "loathsome embrace of the old rotten whore" of the proslavery forces.[15] This legion would serve as his revolutionary vanguard, a small band of dedicated terrorists who would trigger the destruction of the tyrannical slave system. Here was born a classic case of revolutionary terrorism, political ideology linked to a plan for direct and violent action.

Of no one was it truer that the personal was political than John Brown. He had fused a boiling inner anger with a carefully formed outward political project, working through a band of disciples whom he had trained to be the perfect extensions of his will. He could bide his time, but there was always great urgency in his preparations for days of action. The journalist William A.

Phillips, interviewing Brown in Kansas, perhaps put it best in his now famous observation: "He looked upon passing political movements as mere preliminaries or adjuncts to more important events in the future. With him men were nothing, principles everything. . . . He was always an enigma, a strange compound of enthusiasm and cold methodic stolidity—a volcano beneath a mountain of snow."[16] He was Old Brown by now, the aged, tightly wound, and perpetual zealot, ready to strike.

The first blows that fell in May 1856 were all at the hands of Brown's enemies. On May 21, Congressman Preston (Bully) Brooks caned antislavery advocate Senator Charles Sumner almost to death on the floor of the Senate over an insult to Brooks's cousin Senator Andrew Butler of South Carolina. Also on the twenty-first, proslavery settlers pillaged and burned much of Lawrence, the free-state center of Kansas. When Brown heard about this attack, he was already in the field, marching on slaveholding territory, and could not return in time to help repel the invaders. He was incensed that the Lawrence men had not fought more vigorously, believing that if such terrorist actions went unanswered slavery would triumph in Kansas. Only graphic political violence could answer political violence.

Brown turned his band southward, by May 24 reaching Pottawatomie Creek, where several proslavery families had settled. None of these families held slaves, and although they annoyed their antislavery neighbors verbally, it was not clear that they posed any personal threat to free-state forces. None of the men had been at Lawrence.

Brown and his band lay in wait much of the day on the twenty-fourth. Then Brown told the men to sharpen their cutlasses on a hand-turned grindstone, and they realized that he meant business. One of them went to Brown urging caution. "Caution, caution, sir. I am eternally tired of hearing that word caution," Brown responded; "it is nothing but the word of cowardice." Several of the band attempted to dissuade Brown from the actions he was obviously premeditating. To end their talk, Brown insisted that it had become necessary "to strike terror into the hearts of the proslavery people."[17]

Around midnight, when their targets would be asleep and defenseless, Brown's band struck, seizing five men from three cabins, dragging them to the woods, and hacking them to death with their swords. Some reports suggest they also continued to mutilate the bodies after death, but in any event this was a calculated terrorist action against unarmed civilians, done to broadcast the message that the free-state forces were willing to act with as much brutality as it might take to drive their enemies from Kansas. And the swords had been swung with planning and pent-up anger. Two of Brown's sons and two of the other men did the killing, but Brown planned and directed the attack, probably shooting a bullet into the corpse of one of the slain, the more thoroughly to consummate by personal participation the grisly violence he had instigated.

Brown never admitted in public that he was the author of the Pottawatomie massacre, although he fled the scene and, after some more fighting that summer, returned to Boston to escape the retribution he expected. The night after the event, John's son Jason, who had not been at the creek and who held to nonviolence, confronted his father at a farm where the band had set up temporary camp. Jason asked, "Did you have anything to do with the killing of those men on the Pottawatomie?" His father replied, "I did not do it, but I approved of it." In shock, Jason reproved his father: "I think it was an uncalled for, wicked act," to which Brown responded, "God is my judge. It was absolutely necessary as a measure of self-defense, and for the defense of others." Writing a few weeks later to his wife and children still in North Elba, Brown neither affirmed nor denied the act. He claimed that he had taken horses and prisoners, and that "we were immediately after this accused of murdering five men at Pottawatomie, and great efforts have since been made to capture us." And then, much as he had told Jason soon after the event, he wrote to Mary, "God, who has not given us over to the will of our enemies, but has moreover delivered them into our hand, will, we humbly trust, still keep and deliver us. We feel assured that He who sees not as men see, does not lay the guilt of innocent blood to our charge."[18]

Brown's service to an all-powerful God, his sense of vocation as a prophet of the Lord, as an instrument in God's hand, was crucial to his terrorism: that John Brown did not perform his acts, God performed them through him was something Brown knew with towering certainty. It was God who determined that the men at Pottawatomie Creek were guilty, thereby instructing Brown to set the hands of his armed men to killing them in defense of God's higher ends. By this route—justice flowing down from an avenging God—was violence justified . . . and politicized. By executing the guilty, slavery-contaminated men, God's band would terrorize all others like them, driving them from a territory that God wanted to be a free state. This was political cleansing of the contested land through the propaganda of the deed, revolutionary terrorism in the name of God.

Arrested in 1859 after the Harpers Ferry raid, Brown told his captors that he had killed no one at Pottawatomie and that any killing he did in Kansas was only in self-defense or fair fights. He had not confessed even to his wife, and he never confirmed to his backers, exactly what he had done. But he knew that the rumors that he *might* have such blood on his hands added to his reputation as a man of conviction and action among the people who might fund his future activities. He did not admit to guilt in part because he felt no guilt, or at least deeply repressed any guilty feelings beneath ideological certitude. Within his ideology, his task was justice, not murder. In addition, and perhaps more important, he had a practical reason for his denial: he could not openly avow his deed and avoid arrest. He wanted to remain free to carry out further actions. And as we shall see at his trial at Harpers Ferry, John Brown never entirely admitted that he was a terrorist, even though he consciously planned acts of terror. Such a limiting and negative self-definition would have made his task seem less than sanctified. To liberate the enslaved, he needed to carry on with his work, with *His* work, the consummation of a pure and holy destiny. Brown conceived of himself as an instrument of truth; political violence was his means to God-sanctioned ends. Such self-abnegation is atypical of terrorists, most of whom are only too eager to strut their egos. Brown sublimated his mighty ego within his belief in the divine wrath he served.

Revolutionary terrorists in even the most sanctified causes need money and backers in order to carry on. News of his military triumphs in Kansas provided Brown with a calling card among antislavery forces: here was the man who struck real blows against the hated institution, answering violence with violence. Swashbuckling and secretive in equal measure, he presented himself as a man of destiny planning an unknown but deadly mission. Back east he came to call himself Osawatomie Brown, or Old Osawatomie, after another of his military engagements in which his band defeated an armed proslavery Missouri unit, a more honorable affair than Pottawatomie, and he often used a variety of dashingly piratical aliases, among them Isaac Smith, Nelson Hawkins, and Shubel Morgan, when plotting his attacks.

Old Osawatomie inspired and wound up a band of wealthy, well-born, and largely young Bostonians, the Secret Six, who backed him with sympathy, guns, and money, and his renown spread increasingly among antislavery cadres. He was well known in black abolitionist circles as well, to which few white abolitionists ventured, having formed deep personal as well as ideological bonds in particular with James McCune Smith and Frederick Douglass. These two black men, along with Brown and Gerrit Smith, with whom Brown long had worked, formed an interracial circle of radical abolitionists, all of whom longed for a final reckoning with slavery.[19] Many abolitionists were losing faith in the possibility that moral suasion would ever destroy that horrid institution, and direct action became an increasingly enticing alternative. Brown both frightened and thrilled such people with his rough-hewn manliness and his overtly destructive intent.

On the lam from federal marshals after Pottawatomie, Brown hid on the third floor of the Beacon Hill mansion of Judge Thomas Russell, a man not widely known for abolitionist views who thus could provide a safe house likely to escape the attention of suspicious federal marshals. Russell's wife later recalled this visit: "The first time that I went up to call John Brown, I thought he would never open his door. Nothing issued but an interminable sound of the dragging of furniture. 'I have been finding the best way to barricade,' he remarked when he opened at last. 'I shall never be taken alive you know, and I should hate to spoil your carpet.'"

One evening, when she was alone with Brown in the parlor, Mrs. Russell related, "He drew from one boot a long, evil-looking knife, then from the other boot he extracted two smaller knives. Then he produced a big pistol, and a smaller one." He spilled the cartridges into her hands, telling her, "'now don't be awkward or they all fire off.'" She sat "stiff with fright" as he cleaned and reloaded his guns, she recalled. "I think he really, seriously wished to make sure his defenses were in good condition; also it amused him to see the effect on me."[20]

Brown was toying with Mrs. Russell, who certainly knew of his reputation, whispered around Boston, for political violence, which had heightened his influence on others, especially genteel abolitionists. His previous actions lent credence to his image as a man of special powers, the leader of a cult on the road to a collision with the institution of slavery that more timid abolitionists hated but feared to attack themselves. This backwoods romantic revolutionary was the perfect Byronic surrogate for their aggressive desires.

Sharing the specifics for future action with few others, Brown nevertheless took to the road to raise funds and recruit participants. By early 1857 at the latest, he had evolved a scheme to move a force along the Appalachian Mountains from Virginia down to Alabama and Mississippi. He imagined initiating this action with a small, disciplined band of about twenty-five men, who would make a raid into Virginia, where between two and five hundred slaves would join them immediately in a dash on the federal arsenal at Harpers Ferry, after which they would head south, guns bristling. Slaves rushing off their plantations on either side of the mountains to join him would continually augment his compact army. Vague about what he would do to the slaveholders—when he talked of them he said he would hold them hostage—

or non-slaveholding whites, whom he said he would protect, Brown planned to create armed colonies in the mountains where the liberated slaves would be schooled in skilled trades while making free states of their colonies. In 1858, Brown went so far as to write a constitution for his new states, which he shared with escaped slaves living in Canada when he made a recruiting trip that year.[21] Creating a vanguard to set off a violent chain reaction that would destroy the old order and forge the new was a classic, grandiose design for unleashing revolutionary terrorism.

During the last three years of his life, Brown traveled widely among abolitionists in the North to raise funds for his revolutionary project. He reckoned that he would need around twenty-five thousand dollars to purchase arms, several hundred rifles and pistols and a thousand pikes. And he would need expense money to set up an advance camp somewhere near Harpers Ferry. Of course, he did not share this plan but instead relied on his reputation and considerable charisma to garner donations. He had already established a network of contacts by serving as a conduit among the groups that had financed the militants in Kansas, and now he promised to strike an even more telling blow, asking potential funders to trust him on the basis of his past performance. On January 24, 1857, he told a meeting of the National Kansas Committee at Astor House in New York with mystery and grandiosity: "I am no adventurer. You all know me. You are acquainted with my history. You know what I have done in Kansas. I do not expose my plans. . . . I will not be interrogated; if you wish to give me anything, I want you to give it freely. I have no other purpose but to serve the cause of liberty."[22] Fundraising proved difficult.

Sometimes Brown would speak in churches to only scattered applause and no donations. He repeatedly wrote pleas for funding to the newspapers, often to little avail. His wealthy friends sometimes helped out, probably more out of admiration for the man himself than for his vaguely defined projects, but he had to dun them repeatedly, and he found the process wearing and discouraging. Those who gave money often wanted concrete plans for reassurance, but at the same time they were afraid of being implicated in a failed scheme, and so did not really want to know what he was doing. Because he was queasy about violence, Gerrit Smith, the richest of the lot, wanted to know nothing specific, but despite misgivings he continued to fund an admired friend whose whole meaning was violence, while avoiding thinking about what might be the result of that help.

Such was the life of this professional terrorist among abolitionists who were ambivalent about violence, even though they knew that nothing else was likely to destroy slavery: on the contrary, slavery was continuing to spread. Some refused to give Brown funds; others paid with closed eyes and ears. Despite their longings for peace, they conducted a furtive romance with terrorism, enough to keep the committed terrorist going. He appealed to their Christian and libertarian convictions, and they supported his goal and, in practice if not always in profession, his means.

At times along this apparently endless road, Brown gave in to self-pity on a grand scale. While holed up in Judge Russell's house, just before heading back to Kansas in April 1857, Brown sent a paragraph to the newspapers titled "Old Browns Farewell to The Plymouth Rocks, Bunker Hill Monuments, Charter Oaks, and Uncle Thoms Cabbins." "He has left for Kansas," Brown began in the third person he often used to heighten his image (and perhaps to distance himself from his own voice). "[Brown] has been trying . . . to secure an outfit . . . the means of arming and thoroughly equipping his regular Minuet [*sic*] men, who are mixed up with the people of Kansas, and he leaves the States with a feeling of deepest sadness; that after having exhausted his own small means . . . suffered hunger, cold, nakedness . . . lying on the ground for months in the most sickly . . . places . . . hunted like wolves . . . in order to sustain a cause which every citizen of this 'glorious Republic' is under equal obligation to do; and for the neglect of which every man, woman, and child; of the entire human family has a deep and awful interest . . . when no wages are asked; or expected; he cannot secure, amidst all the wealth, luxury and extravagance of this 'Heaven exalted,' people; even the necessary supplies of the common soldier. 'How are the mighty fallen.'"[23]

Brown simultaneously appealed to patriotism and mocked it. He wanted to rescue the United States from itself, save the cause of freedom from the institution that made American nationalism hypocritical. What if his prophecy were not enabled to be fulfilled? The people, even the abolitionists, would have failed him—he knew what was for the national good even if few shared his vision. And such knowledge amid general indifference frustrated and angered him.

Rarely did Brown give in to such negativity. Usually he caught himself up by reminding himself that the bright day was certain to dawn, and soon. He was a man of towering faith in his mission and his ability to follow it to the end. "Certainly the cause is enough to live for, if not to — for," Brown wrote a potential recruit in 1858. "God has honored [few] with any possible chance for such mighty and soul-satisfying rewards. . . . I expect nothing but to endure hardness; but I expect to effect a mighty conquest, even though it be like the last victory of Samson."[24] On he would march to the end, even if he were misunderstood, even if few marched all the way with him. However grandly romantic his language might have sounded, he meant what he said, and he was willing to die for the cause, not as a suicide bringing others down with him but as a prophet willing to pay for principle with his blood. In our own day we can find echoes of religious sacrifice among both Islamic terrorists and Christian terrorists like Timothy McVeigh.

In 1858, Hugh Forbes, a British soldier of fortune Brown had recruited to train his legion, threatened to betray the whole project, forcing Brown to postpone his plans. To reinforce his credentials and continue to act against slavery, he returned to Kansas in late 1858. There on December 20 he led his band on a spectacular raid into Missouri, where they freed eleven slaves, and his men killed a slaveholder. As before, Brown expressed no guilt for "executing" a man whose hands were washed in the blood of slavery. His reputation thus solidified, Brown found more funds coming his way.

Returning east, Brown finalized plans for his raid. Finally, on July 3, 1859, calling himself Isaac Smith, he rented a dilapidated farm in Maryland, seven miles from Harpers Ferry. His men began arriving, as did guns and money, until there were twenty-two men—including five African Americans—two hundred rifles, and an equal number of pistols all packed together in the little farmhouse.

In late September, still gathering arms and men, Brown wrote to his close friend and comrade Frederick Douglass, pleading with him to pay the farm a visit, and then arranging a rendezvous at a stone quarry near Chambersburg, Pennsylvania. When they met Brown argued, "Come with me, Douglass. . . . I want you for a special purpose. When I strike, the bees will begin to swarm, and I shall want you to help hive them." Brown described his final plan, which Douglass later recounted: they would seize the town and the federal arsenal, an act that "would serve as notice to the slaves that their friends had come, as a trumpet to rally them to their standard." So augmented, his force would be impossible to dislodge, Brown insisted. Such arguments convinced Douglass to the contrary; he told Brown "that he was going into a perfect steel-trap . . . that he would be surrounded at once and escape would be impossible." Guided, as he later recalled with irony and shame, by "my discretion or my cowardice," Douglass resisted Brown's blandishments, although an escaped slave, Shields Green, who had accompanied Douglass to the meeting declared, "I b'leve I'll go wid the ole man."[25]

In their hideout, Brown had trouble convincing his own band that they were not marching into a steel trap. After heated discussions, he threatened to resign his command, and such was his hold over them and his persuasiveness about the indispensability of their mission that they chose to follow him. And so on the evening of October 16, with three men left behind to guard the arms at their base, the other eighteen saddled up and rode down with Brown to confront the slaveholding nation.

That night Brown's men fanned out through Harpers Ferry, seized the federal arsenal, almost without resistance, posted guards on the bridges into town, and went up into the hills to cut the telegraph lines and raid nearby plantations. The raiders brought back slaves and white hostages, including Colonel Lewis W. Washington, the great-grandnephew of George Washington. By mid-morning on the seventeenth, when word of the attack spread, local farmers and militiamen began gathering to fire on Brown's men, most of whom retreated into the sturdy brick fire-engine house next to the arsenal, taking eleven white hostages and a number of black men with them. Several of Brown's men, who had been detached on other duties, were killed, though a few escaped. During the day, as many as ten different militia companies from nearby towns marched toward town, five arriving by that afternoon. President James Buchanan ordered three artillery companies and a detachment of ninety U.S. Marines under the command of Colonel Robert E. Lee to rush to Harpers Ferry.

The next morning, the Marines, who had arrived around midnight, battered down the engine-house doors, burst in, and killed most of Brown's remaining men. Lieutenant Israel Greene, leader of the storming party, thrust his light dress sword at Brown, but it did not penetrate his body the way a heavier sword would have done. Greene then beat Brown unconscious with the hilt. All told, during the raid seventeen men lost their lives, including ten of Brown's company, among them his sons Watson and Oliver, who died by his side in the engine house the night before the Marines stormed in. Thirty-six hours after Brown's band seized the arsenal the attack was crushed. Most significant from the vantage point of Brown's plan, no slaves had joined the army of liberation (although a few might have served temporarily at the edge of town).[26]

Brown had failed to trigger the spontaneous and massive rebellion he was certain would come to pass. Slaves feared the likely outcome of this violent assault on slavery: the terrible retribution of reactionary terrorism they would suffer should they join Brown in what appeared to be an utterly reckless and even suicidal action. In any event there were not a lot of slaves in the area, nor did mere news of the event set off the wider uprising Brown anticipated. Although many historians have tried to explain why Brown stayed in a static position where he was seemingly destined to be destroyed, the simplest explanation may be the most convincing. He had no fallback position in mind, so certain had he been that local slaves would flock to him, allowing his augmented army to take to the hills. Therefore he waited far too long for the unwelcome and unanticipated truth to emerge.

Yet there is a second, noncontradictory explanation for his stasis, one Brown himself made in a letter to a friend the evening before he was to be sentenced. "It is solely my own fault" that I am a "prisoner in bonds," he wrote, and "in a military point of view, that we met with disaster. I mean that I mingled with our prisoners and so far sympathized with them and their families that I neglected my duty in other respects. But God's will, not mine be done. You know that Christ once armed Peter. So also in my case he put a sword into my hand, and there continued it so long as he saw best, and then kindly took it from me. I wish you could know with what cheerfulness I am now wielding the 'sword of the spirit' on the right hand and the left."[27]

In this rendition, notwithstanding that he had killed other slaveholders in cold blood and without apparent regret, Brown had hesitated to pursue his bloody terrorist goals when innocent lives were under his control (a reversal of the Stockholm syndrome, in which hostages identify with their captors). He would not execute his hostages; neither would he embark on a larger and even bloodier campaign. In this manner Brown expressed his own underlying ambivalence about the terrorist killer he had become. Given the chance, he had gladly shifted from war to peace even in the middle of making war; immediately after his capture he expressed real relief that he had not killed his hostages at the start of what could only have turned out to be a homicidal as well as suicidal rampage. In Brown's almost instantaneous reconstruction of his motives, even before he was captured, the act of staying put marked his sudden conversion to man of peace. Out of the humane side of his nature he had hesitated to produce a second Pottawatomie or something even worse, and this ambivalence might have served in part to paralyze him into remaining in the engine house.

Without doubt, for whatever combination of reasons, the tactics of this terrorist action were a disaster. Had he been shrewder, or even operated off earlier plans, Brown might have established a base in the Virginia mountains and then pounced on Harpers Ferry in a lightning raid, seizing arms and going back to the hills to spread terror.[28] But tactical considerations had always counted for less than the ideological conviction that the slaves, ever on the brink of revolution, would gladly join him, like Israelites following Moses (an analogy he sometimes employed). Revolutionary terrorism such as Brown's is grounded in the religious faith that a hugely inspirational deed will trigger cascading political violence that will overturn the old order in a revolutionary Apocalypse. Such terrorists believe that the hearts of the oppressed are pure and that they need only the right example to provoke them to unleash their inner revolutionary potential.

To quash the terrorist uprising, the state brought overwhelming physical force to bear in the form of both Virginia militia units and the United States Marines. And then, the day after Brown was captured, Virginia's governor Henry A. Wise showed up to direct Brown's punishment. The state acted precipitously, rushing Brown to trial on October 25, before he had recovered from his severe wounds and before he could secure adequate counsel, and hanged him on December 2. Wise later claimed that he had acted with such overwhelming force to prevent a lynching, but, particularly given his ambitions for the Democratic presidential nomination in 1860, what he really wanted was to appear decisive. The raid had produced a wave of panic not only in Virginia but throughout the South. The worst fear in southern white society was the possibility of a slave insurrection. Better to string up the bogeyman before such a rebellion ensued and before he could be rescued by what Wise and others believed to be a large-scale abolitionist conspiracy. Reactionary terrorism was the immediate response to revolutionary terrorism.

In this context of massive and almost hysterical state-repressive reaction, through his words rather than his actions Brown turned his trial into a national forum about the morality of slavery. The courtroom became the stage where despite the best efforts of the state to dominate the proceedings, Brown debated fundamental American values with his prosecutors before the press and, through it, to the whole nation, which, indeed, was listening. He gained significant control over who would define the meaning of his raid by reversing his image from bloody-minded terrorist to martyr for the freedom of even the lowliest Americans, crushed by a violently repressive social system and state. Not by the raid itself but by his management of the response to the raid, Brown turned what had begun as terrorism into an act of atonement. Before his captors and their rigged courtroom he presented an elemental morality tale of his own creation, which his enemies abetted by their reactions to him. By so doing he heightened the political meaning of his raid, accelerating the already smoldering sectional crisis over slavery. He initiated a process that led directly to southern secession fifteen months later, following the election of a northern antislavery party perceived in the South to be an extension by other means of the inner intention of John Brown's attack.

It was Brown's eloquence that allowed him, a solitary and wounded prisoner arraigned by the angry state, to control the trial during the last six weeks of his life. He re-created himself as playwright and lead actor in the drama of slavery and freedom. Suddenly he came into total focus—he now knew for certain the meaning of his life and his death; he knew God's design and his own instrumentality, and he knew how to be heard.

Even on the night of his capture, as he lay on a litter wrapped in bloody bandages Brown clearheadedly confronted his puzzled and angry interlocutors, led by Governor Wise and accompanied by several reporters. As he had after Pottawatomie, he denied that his goal had been terrorist, thus in effect repudiating his terrorist means. "I claim to be here in carrying out a measure I believe to be perfectly justifiable, and not to act the part of an incendiary or ruffian, but to aid those suffering great wrong." Far from wishing to do harm to his hostages, he in fact had allowed himself to dally and be captured because of his "desire to spare the feelings of my prisoners and their families and the community at large." He had not killed a single man "except directly in self-defense," just as he claimed had been the case in Kansas. When one of the bystanders asked Brown upon what principle he justified his treasonous acts, he answered, "Upon the golden rule. I pity the poor in bondage that have none to help them; that is why I am here; not to gratify any personal animosity, revenge or vindictive spirit. It is my sympathy with the oppressed and the wronged, that are as good as you and as precious in the sight of God." Having seized national attention, and aware that the press would report his every word, Brown shifted his self-definition away from the violent means he had used, through which he knew he had failed and which were now as nothing, to a Christian, egalitarian prophecy of fundamental American truth.

After his military defeat, then, Brown reframed his motives. Before the act he had been a revolutionary terrorist keen for a bloody reckoning with slavery. In jail he refashioned himself as a martyr, and his eloquence more than made up for what amounted to self-denigration. It was an extraordinary act of legerdemain and a highly political transformation. The terrorist persona was no longer useful; the suffering servant of God was. Brown reversed his terrorist project: he used his own impending political murder, which he knew his captors intended, to elevate his cause while casting them in the role of the true terrorists.

At the same time that he seized the moral high ground, Brown was quite willing to address, in a highly ironic fashion, the deepest fears of southern whites about the dark side of what he represented. Pressed to reveal a larger conspiracy of backers who had sent him to Harpers Ferry, he replied, "No man sent me here; it was my own prompting and that of my maker, or that of the devil, whichever you please to ascribe it to. I acknowledge no man in human form." Brown knew, as did his captors, that the world was divided into good and evil, and he knew he was inverting their version of those shared values. If he represented their deepest fears, he was glad to use the power their anxieties offered, pleased to have them enter the debate over the most elemental moral meanings in American life. He communicated effectively with his captors and beyond them with the American public.[29]

The dramaturgy of the trial, broadcast to the nation by dozens of newspaper sketch artists and reporters, was electric. On one side was the state of Virginia, assembled at the Jefferson County courthouse in Charlestown, Judge Richard Parker presiding from his high bench, with a local jury and a prosecution determined to have his hide, state-appointed defense attorneys with whom the defendant would not speak, and guards bristling with guns. On the other side was John Brown lying wounded on a pallet, unable to mount a legal defense. Preparing to condemn and execute their hated prisoner after the mere semblance of a trial, those exercising overwhelming state power embodied organized terror in the eyes of much of the national audience eagerly reading about the proceedings. And in this setting prisoner Brown was now the victim, bleeding like a beaten and supine but ever-defiant slave. The state keened for the avenging destruction of the revolutionary avatar, and Brown knew it. He sought to make it clear that reactionary terrorism was let loose on the nation, erasing the ideal of freedom for all Americans. He consciously shifted the mantle of "true terrorist" from himself to the violent, slave-enforcing state. This would provide a courtroom melodrama of the highest order—the Christian, libertarian conclusion to Brown's revolution, unleashing powerful imagery that would vastly deepen the meanings of his puny act of physical rebellion. The Commonwealth of Virginia joined with him to create a terrorist event that became, as he had hoped, one of the catalysts of a civil war fought over the issue of slavery.

As the trial opened, Brown struggled to his feet and complained that his ears were still ringing from the blows Lieutenant Greene had administered, preventing him from hearing the proceedings. As he had been "promised a fair trial," he requested "a very short delay . . . and I merely ask this, that, as the saying is, 'the devil may have his due,' no more." Later during the proceedings, he would again complain that he was not being granted a fair trial, as he lacked counsel of his choosing and the right to call witnesses. Brown acknowledged the image in which the white South had cast him as the very devil placed on trial, even while demonstrating through his calmness, modesty, and desire for fair play his assertion of himself as the figure of justice at this trial. The judge denied his requests, and the case rushed on.

Generally, Brown remained silent and almost indifferent to the proceedings. When one of his counsels attempted to introduce a defense of insanity, however, noting the madness of many of Brown's relatives and implying that Brown's whole strategy could only have been the product of an unhinged mind, Brown immediately rejected it. "If I am insane, of course I should think I know more than all the rest of the world. But I do not think so. I am perfectly unconscious of insanity, and I reject, so far as I am capable, any attempt to interfere in my behalf on that score." Brown wanted to serve his cause, not save his skin. He was, of course, convicted.

On November 2, before he was sentenced, Brown was given the opportunity to make a statement. He immediately stood up, and in a ringing, deliberate manner, offered his message to the world. He opened by asserting, "I never did intend murder or treason, or the destruction of property, or to excite or incite the slaves to rebellion, or to make insurrection." He had only wanted to free the slaves. And he concluded his statement similarly, with a denial that he had intended to start a "general insurrection." This rationalization was a lie and an apparent repudiation of terrorism. But it also was a political reformulation, a redirection intended to broaden his popular appeal in the North. What he actually might have believed was less significant to him than his underlying identification with the slaves. Brown looked past his carefully premeditated violent plans, the better to focus on his (that is to say the Lord's) ultimate ends. The goal was freedom rather than destruction, even though he had always believed that only destructive means could spring slaves from their terrible iron cage. This was a classic revolutionary terrorist rationale, but Brown delivered his blood-laden message with biblical eloquence.

The core of Brown's statement was his declaration of identification with the downtrodden of the earth, an assertion that he was serving universal human freedom.

> Had I interfered . . . in the behalf of the rich, the powerful, the intelligent, the so-called great . . . and suffered and sacrificed what I have in

this interference, it would have been all right, and every man in the Court would have deemed it an act worthy of reward rather than punishment. This Court acknowledges, too, as I suppose, the validity of the law of God. I see a book kissed, which I suppose to be the Bible, or at least the New Testament, which teaches me that all things whatsoever I would that men should do to me, I should do even so to them. I endeavored to act up to that instruction. I say I am yet too young to understand that God is any respecter of persons. I believe that to have interfered as I have done, as I have always freely admitted I have done in behalf of His despised poor, is no wrong, but right. Now, if it is deemed necessary that I should forfeit my life for the furtherance of the ends of justice, and mingle my blood further with the blood of my children and with the blood of millions in this slave country whose rights are disregarded by wicked, cruel, and unjust enactments, I say let it be done.[30]

This speech produced an electric effect across much of the North—here was the core of Christ's message delivered by an Old Testament prophet, a saint marching forth from the holy land, willing, even eager to die for human freedom. In the month remaining to him, Brown preached this gospel of liberation in dozens of letters written from his jail cell. Shortly after his death, Wendell Phillips remarked, "Having taken possession of Harpers Ferry, he began to edit the *New York Tribune* and the *New York Herald* for the next three weeks."[31] Nearly all his correspondence to his family and friends was published, as well as the trial record. In all he said and wrote, Brown continued to issue a King James rendition of the higher calling he had preached so eloquently before the court.

While he was imprisoned awaiting execution, his admirers understood how brilliantly Brown had captured the moral and political high ground during the trial, and how the Virginia authorities had played into his hands. "Nothing could his enemies do, but it redounded to his infinite advantage," Henry David Thoreau told a Concord, Massachusetts, audience. "They did not hang him at once, but reserved him to preach to them. . . . No theatrical manager could have arranged things so wisely to give the effect to his behavior and words."[32]

Henry C. Wright, a veteran abolitionist, agreed with Thoreau and Phillips about Brown's definitive performance as the martyr for American slavery. For the two months after the raid, Wright concluded, "John Brown, the friend of the slave, edited every paper, presided over every domestic and social circle, over every prayer, conference and church meeting, over every pulpit and platform, and over every Legislature, Judicial and Executive department of government; and he will edit every paper, and govern Virginia and all the states, and preside over Congress, guide its deliberations, and control all political caucuses and elections, for one year to come."[33] As later generations of revolutionaries would say was their goal, Brown had dramatically illuminated the contradictions of the slaveholding libertarian republic, forever altering the discourse about the inescapable problem lying at the core of American values. In this sense he was an immensely successful revolutionary terrorist.

Brown realized, with wry good humor, that he could win a huge victory with public opinion in the North despite the fact that his terrorist excursion had been a catastrophe, or even *because* he unconsciously or consciously had decided not to indulge in a bloodbath. On November 10, he wrote to his wife, "I have been *whipped* as the saying is; but I am sure I can recover all the lost capital occasioned by that disaster; by only hanging a few moments by the neck; & I feel quite determined to make the utmost possible out of the defeat." His death would be an act of propaganda that would reap a harvest far greater than would his continuing to live in jail. As he put it to his brother Jeremiah, "I am worth inconceivably more to hang than for any other purpose."[34] Ultimately he was right politically—his hanging was in a sense the first death of the Civil War, that vast killing field where slavery was finally destroyed.

Governor Wise considered clemency on the grounds of insanity and even might have recognized that hanging Brown would make a hero of him, but it was inconceivable for Wise to commute the sentence when the whole white South was howling for Brown's blood, desperate to crush any threat of future rebellion. So the state proceeded with the execution, through its actions elevated the meaning of Brown's death. By giving him a pulpit and then making him a martyr, Wise and the authorities ceded to Brown much of the contested high moral ground, and he took advantage of his opportunity with unwavering eloquence.

In his prison letters, Brown addressed a broad public that was as deeply immersed as he in the symbolism offered by evangelical Christianity. His correspondents understood him when he claimed to be on God's mission, and perhaps in their hearts they wished they were courageous enough to emulate his identification with the central figures of their Bible as he faced death. Not merely did Brown resign himself to his fate; he embraced it. He repeatedly wrote to others that he was happy, not despondent, joyous, not downhearted. As he explained to a clergyman friend in a letter of November 15, "I have been a good deal disappointed . . . in not keeping up to my own plans; but I now feel entirely reconciled to that event: for God's plan, was Infinitely better; no doubt: or I should have kept to my own." An all-knowing God was defining his actions. "Had Samson kept to his determination of not telling Delilah wherein his strength lay: he would probably have never overturned the house."[35] Brown had often referred to Samson while he planned his terrorist route; perhaps this was the way he had reconciled himself from the first to the possibility of failure. Temporary defeat placed him in a position to inaugurate ultimate victory through lighting the fuse that would start a chain reaction of explosions and destroy the hated old order.

As he faced death, Brown was Samson and Moses; he was Peter, and he was Paul. "I think I feel as happy as Paul did when he lay in prison," he wrote to another clerical friend on November 23. "He knew if they killed him it would greatly advance the cause of Christ; that was the reason he rejoiced so."[36]

And, of course, he was Jesus. He urged his family to submit to his fate and not to feel degraded because of it. "Remember, dear wife and children all, that Jesus of Nazareth suffered a most excruciating death on the cross as a felon, under the most aggravating circumstances." And in a less inward-turning reading of his death to come, he told a reporter for the Charlestown paper on November 23, "I am entirely ready [to meet death]. I feel no shame on account of my doom. Jesus of Nazareth was doomed in like manner. Why should not I be?"[37] Even Governor Wise noted that this was the gamest man he had ever met, and for those sympathetic to the plight of the slaves, here was the letter-perfect martyr, arisen from their Bible.

The last time Brown wrote home was to reassure his family that his death at the hands of a blood-drenched state would be politically meaningful and religiously sanctified. "I am writing the hour of my public murder with great composure of mind, & cheerfulness; feeling the strongest assurance that in no other possible way could I be used to so much advance the cause of God & of humanity; & that nothing that either I or all my family have sacrificed or suffered: will be lost. . . . I have no doubt but that our seeming disaster: will ultimately result in the most glorious success."[38]

As he prepared to hang, Brown refused the ministrations of southern clergymen, believing them all corrupted by their service to slaveholders. He wanted his benediction to come from humble blacks, the people for whom he was dying. He wrote to Mary Stearns, the wife of a Boston abolitionist supporter, "I have asked to be spared from having any mock; or hypocritical prayers made over me, when I am publicly murdered: & that my only religious attendants be poor little, dirty, ragged, bare headed, & barefooted Slave boys & Girls; led by some old grey headed Slave Mother." Almost certainly this letter was the origin of the legend that John Brown kissed a slave baby as he was being led to the tumbrel that would carry him to the gallows. He would certainly have kissed that baby if one had been available; through his intense and richly symbolic language he had prepared the ground for further legends to be woven into his legacy.[39]

Brown handed a note to one of his guards on the morning of his execution: "I John Brown am quite certain that the crimes of this guilty, land: will never be purged away; but with blood. I had as I now think: vainly flattered myself that without verry much bloodshed; it might be done."[40] Remission of national sin would demand universal bloodletting—warfare far deeper and more prolonged than the slave revolt he had sought to ignite. Brown was certain that his blood, like that of his sons and his men, was only a preliminary shedding, and he had convinced northerners and southerners alike that he was prophetic about the approaching Armageddon. His terrorism and his martyr's death, played out with the full cooperation of the state of Virginia and the Buchanan administration, marked out and illustrated the moral passion that underlay the larger terrors that were to come.

At the hanging ground, fifteen hundred Virginia militiamen guarded the scaffold, so frightened were the authorities that the abolitionists would stage a violent and massive rescue effort, and so eager were they to demonstrate the power of the slave South. Among the armed men, in a borrowed uniform, stood John Wilkes Booth, who hated everything about Brown's ideals and yet could not help but admire Brown's composure as he stood alone awaiting his execution surrounded by the hatred of all gathered to witness his fall.

The shrewd generalship with which Brown outflanked the whole state apparatus of Virginia created the ground on which others could amplify the legend he made of himself. By his elegantly expressed bravery he opened up the rhetoric of the abolitionist cadre and extended their cause to vast new audiences. Taking their cue from him, they moved to canonize him even before his death, a process that would swell after the execution.

This use of Brown, initiated by the captured terrorist himself, was a conscious strategy, not an intuitive outpouring. Thomas Wentworth Higginson, in particular, understood that in order to widen Brown's appeal, abolitionists would have to play up his character and play down his terrorism. Brown himself could be made right even for those who believed his actions wrong. Interpreted this way, Higginson argued, Brown's death could do "more than Sumner or Kansas to re-awaken antislavery agitation."[41] This might have seemed a bit cold-hearted on Higginson's part had not Brown himself construed the potential meaning of his execution within the same political framework.

Even Ralph Waldo Emerson, a sometimes tepid outrider of abolitionism who had been no special admirer of Brown's in the past, spoke out with unusual forcefulness and praise while Brown faced his death. On November 8, before a Boston audience, he referred to Brown as "that new saint, than whom nothing purer or more brave was ever led by love of men into conflict and death—the new saint awaiting his martyrdom, . . . who, if he shall suffer, will make the gallows glorious like the Cross." Emerson predicted that Brown's hanging would expand the antislavery family to include, "almost every man who loved the Golden Rule and the Declaration of Independence." From Rome, where he was dying of tuberculosis, Theodore Parker, the most prominent of the Secret Six, proclaimed, "The Road to heaven is as short from the gallows as from a throne."[42] To those who howled for Brown's blood, his supporters replied, "Was not Christ crucified?"

Brown's resolute calmness as he marched up the gallows steps reinforced his image as a martyr in a traditional American context. Even William Lloyd Garrison, a committed pacifist, joined the chorus of praise for the new saint. On the evening after Brown's execution, he told a packed interracial meeting at Boston's Tremont Temple that although he was an " 'ultra' peace man—I am prepared to say: 'Success to every slave insurrection at the South.' . . . Rather than seeing men wearing their chains in a cowardly and servile spirit, I would as an advocate of peace, much rather see them breaking the head of the tyrant with their chains." Affirming Brown's insurrectionary spirit as well as his martyrdom, Garrison went on to connect his actions with the revolutionary tradition in America. "Give me, as a non-resistant, Bunker Hill, and Lexington, and Concord, rather than the cowardice of servility of a Southern slave plantation."[43]

Others linked what they believed to be Brown's heroic individualism with a long American tradition of fighting for national liberty. Writing in his journal, Henry David Thoreau decided that Brown was the truest transcendentalist of all, a "man of action and rare common sense" but "above all a man of ideas and principles." Brown had acted out the higher-law beliefs Thoreau shared with him. As he told an audience in Concord, Brown personified "a wisdom and nobleness, and therefore an authority, superior to our laws." As did Garrison, Thoreau believed that Brown was a throwback to a more heroic republican era. "He died lately in the time of Cromwell, but he reappeared here." He was the true descendent of the Puritan stock that had settled New England seeking religious liberty. A portrait of Brown ought one day to be hung alongside historical paintings of the "Landing of the Pilgrims and the Declaration of Independence," in some future national gallery when slavery would be no more. "We shall then be at liberty to weep for Captain Brown. Then and not till then, we will take our revenge."[44]

In this collective abolitionist portrait Brown was the liberty-loving Puritan hero of warm heart and steel principles who had come back to restore antislavery manhood. Such a purely masculine figure could spark a new, true antislavery revolution. Two days after Brown's execution, Moncure D. Conway, son of a Virginia slaveholder, an Emersonian transcendentalist, and a Unitarian minister, told his Cincinnati congregation that Brown's soul was like a phoenix. "Out of the ashes of our martyr a Revolution must come. It may creep [at first] but at last its free pinion will strike the air . . . until the progeny of Freemen arise to crown America's destiny." Then shall Americans "be baptized afresh to the cause of LIBERTY, HUMANITY AND GOD." Brown provided the perfect combination of Christian holy manliness, American revolutionary zeal, and abolitionist righteousness.

When he preached Brown's eulogy at North Elba on December 8, 1859, Wendell Phillips linked the gallows in Virginia to Bunker Hill, the overthrow of George III to the coming emancipation in the South. In fact, Phillips dated Virginia's inexorable emancipation to Harpers Ferry. "True, the slave is still there. So when the tempest uproots a pine on your hills, it looks green for months,—a year or two. Still, it is timber, not a tree. John Brown has loosened the roots of the slave system; it only breathes,—it does not live,—hereafter."[45] Onward, Christian soldiers.

African Americans immediately embraced Brown's insurrectionary meanings as much if not more than his saintliness. At the same Tremont Temple meeting where William Lloyd Garrison foresaw the violent overthrow of slavery, J. Stella Martin, minister of the Joy Street Baptist Church in Boston, told the throng, "I endorse his end, because every single instinct of our nature rises and tells us that it is right." After all, "Fourth-of-July orators sanctioned the same thing" when they commemorated Concord and Bunker Hill, "the only difference being, that in our battles, in America [revolutionary] means have been used for *white* men and that John Brown has used his means for *black* men." Martin criticized Brown for having said at his trial that he had not intended to shed blood. "In not shedding blood, he left the slaves uncertain how to act." If anything Martin would have preferred more terrorism and less martyrdom, a root-and-branch revolution; all the same he honored Brown for his deep identification with blacks and his willingness to fight and die for their freedom.[46]

While Brown awaited execution, and at considerable risk to himself because he was a well-known Brown confederate, Charles H. Langston affirmed his militant support for Brown the terrorist at a mass meeting before fourteen hundred at the Melodeon in Cleveland and later in a letter to the Cleveland *Plain Dealer*. Langston went so far as to link Brown to "Gen. Nat Turner. . . . [Brown] admired Nat Turner as well as George Washington," and he quoted the Bible and the Declaration of Independence to argue that Brown was righteous not only for his "lofty . . . humane and Godlike" character but for his insurrectionary actions. "Does not the Bible plainly say . . . 'He that stealeth a man and selleth him or if he be found in his hand, he shall surely be put to death'?" Did Jefferson's declaration of the right to rebel and Patrick Henry's avowal "Give me liberty or give me death" mean "liberty for proud 'Anglo Saxons' and chains and fetters" for the rest of mankind? "I think they must have had a higher, a nobler idea of man and his inalienable rights." In a white society that he believed to be unalterably racist, Langston celebrated a man and a deed that assaulted mainstream racism with so much drama and self-sacrifice. While the revolutionary fathers had failed to extend liberty to African Americans, and subsequent generations had reinforced slavery, John Brown now had extended freedom to them with his heart, his words, his blood, and his life. "So wide-spread and well nigh universal is the feeling of negro-hate in this country, that I had nearly made up my mind never to find one of the dominant race true to the principles of brotherhood." But, Langston said, now he had found one truly American white man: Brown was a "lover of mankind—not of any particular class or color, but of all men. . . . He fully, really and *actively* believed in the brotherhood of man. . . . He is the only American citizen who has lived fully up to the Declaration of Independence."[47] Black leaders believed that redemptive terrorism, the best means to overthrow the terrors of the slavery system, was embedded in American republican, African American, and biblical traditions. If Harpers Ferry proved to be the precursor to an antislavery war, so much the better.

Even though they were far more conservative than the radical abolitionists and miles apart from engaged African Americans, many members of the Republican Party also found themselves both horrified and impressed by John

Brown's terrorism and his martyrdom. They were gradualists who wanted to stop the *spread* of slavery as a first step in the ultimate strangulation of the peculiar institution. But if they ever hoped to be elected to national office they had, of course, to deny and denounce support for anarchist destructiveness such as Brown's. Most condemned Brown as a madman, yet there was something about him that they could not denounce entirely.

Salmon P. Chase, a veteran political antislavery leader from Ohio who was running for the Republican presidential nomination, wrote about Brown's character and the implications of his actions, "Poor old man! How sadly misled by his own imagination! How rash—how mad—how criminal thus to stir up insurrection which if successful would deluge the land with blood and make void the fairest hopes of mankind!" However, if Chase denounced the sinful actions he could not help praising their perpetrator, almost despite himself, thereby demonstrating the effectiveness with which Brown and his radical supporters had moved the antislavery argument into new territory. Chase admitted to having been stirred by Brown's "unselfish desire to set free the oppressed—the bravery—the humanity toward the prisoners which defeated his purposes! . . . Men will condemn his act and pity his fate forever." And then Chase projected a future in which the South would be visited with the just fate Brown had enunciated: "How stern will be the reprobation which must fall" on proslavery politicians and upon "slavery itself, which underlies it all." Divine retribution might be inevitable, Chase asserted, writing in the passive voice that left unclear what action would bring about this change and obscured his own potential involvement. But sometimes, he implied, historical fate was speeded along by human agency, even if by a madman who was, in the final analysis, an ally to the broader antislavery cause.[48]

In private, some Republicans voiced their belief that Virginia's trial and execution of Brown demonstrated that sectional war was fast approaching, the sooner the better. In this vein, William H. Herndon, Abraham Lincoln's law partner, wrote to Senator Charles Sumner, "Two such civilizations as the North and the South cannot co-exist on the same soil. . . . To expect otherwise would be to expect the Absolute to sleep with and tolerate 'hell.' . . . Let this natural war—let this inevitable struggle proceed . . . till slavery is *dead—dead—dead.*"[49]

Even the cautious and moderate Illinois Republican Abraham Lincoln could not deny Brown serious consideration, demonstrating how indelibly the terrorist had reset the national agenda. In his speeches Lincoln frequently discussed Brown, always calling him wrong, sometimes calling him insane—

"an enthusiast broods over the oppression of a people till he feels commissioned by Heaven to liberate them . . . which ends in little else than his own execution." In the face of attacks from Democrats, Lincoln repeatedly denied that a single Republican had supported Brown. On December 5, 1859, he told a Kansas audience, "Old John Brown has just been executed for treason against a state. We cannot object, even though he agreed with us in thinking slavery wrong. That cannot excuse violence, bloodshed and treason. It could avail [Brown] nothing that he might think himself right." Within this speech, Lincoln could not quite bring himself to rule Brown out of the antislavery community, though he insisted that Brown was no Republican. He qualified his negative comments, as he had a few days earlier when he had said that Brown "has shown great courage, rare selflessness," something even Brown's southern captors had acknowledged, although, Lincoln still insisted, Brown's actions were both "wrong" and "futile."[50]

Lincoln frequently used John Brown as a kind of warning, as he did in his famous Cooper Union address on February 27, 1860, when he said that if "the peaceful channel of the ballot box" did not succeed, should the Democrats manage to use Brown to defeat the Republican Party, antislavery sentiment would not disappear but would find another channel, and the number of John Browns would multiply. To northern listeners, this formulation promised a conservative means to advance antislavery goals, but southerners would have noted the lack of outright condemnation of Brown's agenda and, indeed, the muted threat of the future employment of Brown-like methods should the normal and peaceful path of political change be permanently blocked.[51]

In these subtle but telling ways, when he was spinning out his response to the political problems Brown presented the antislavery Republican Party, Lincoln avoided disavowing the man who was willing to go to the gallows out of hatred for slavery, a hatred that deep in his soul Lincoln shared. He found a use for Brown the terrorist as a bogeyman with which to warn voters about the consequences of not employing Republican moderation to rid the nation of slavery, and yet in so doing, with whatever criticisms he made, he lent force to the legacy of Brown the martyr.

The North was by no means united in praise of John Brown, however. At many meetings called by his supporters, anti-abolitionists packed the halls, shouting their contempt at the speakers. In Philadelphia, at a noon meeting held on December 2, about the time Brown was executed, the Reverend Theodore Tilton, editor of the New York *Independent,* aroused both cheers and hisses when he proclaimed, "Today the nation puts to death its noblest citizen." Tilton compared Brown to Saint Paul, who was thrown to the ground by God and then arose, "converted and transformed." So, by extension, did Tilton now wish the whole corrupt nation to be "struck down upon its knees by the sudden glory of God bursting out of heaven," that it would be "humbled in the dust until it shall rise repentant." Hearing this vivid and familiar biblical metaphor, the polarized audience exploded into both applause and catcalls. Two weeks later, when he rang out in defense of Brown, Wendell Phillips was shouted down in New York, with hisses, derisive laughter, and cries of "Treason, Treason."[52]

Just two years earlier, Chief Justice Roger B. Taney, in the *Dred Scott* decision, had defined the Constitution as the basis of a purely white republic. Taney had written in his eight-to-one majority opinion that blacks were not citizens but a "subordinate and inferior class of beings" who had "no rights which the white man was bound to respect," and who therefore "might justly and lawfully be reduced to slavery for [their own] benefit."[53] Now at pro-union meetings, northern conservatives, the law-and-order forces, were so eager to support the traditional racial order, southern slavery included, that they were beginning to justify southern secession. They were willing to contemplate another form of Constitution breaking, so appalled were they by the abolitionist redefinition of their region and of the union that they saw as vastly increased by John Brown's supposed martyrdom. Brown and Virginia in tandem had destroyed the remaining middle ground of calm northern tolerance for slavery within the constitutional compromise that had preserved the union until then.

Southern leaders, even those previously moderate, closed ranks in their opposition to Brown, abolitionism, and the still-new Republican Party. Dismissing conservative northern unionists as a hapless and unrepresentative minority, they argued that Brown was but the pointed edge of a northern abolitionist sword being thrust into their peace-loving society.

In a speech to the Virginia legislature three days after he executed Brown, Governor Wise left no doubt about the threat he had just attempted to beat back. He saw a U.S. Senate filling up with Republicans like William A. Seward, who was thundering about the irrepressible conflict over slavery. He warned of preachers from the "anti-Christ pulpit [who have] breathed naught but insurrectionary wrath into servants against their masters, and . . . denounced [the Constitution] as a covenant with death for recognizing . . . slavery." There could be no compromise with such prophets of "mad riot and . . . misrule," Wise insisted. "They must be met and crushed, or they will crush us." Brown's gang were only tools in the hands of a huge, subterranean conspiracy. "Brown himself was not insane," and thus deserving of clemency, but "deliberate, cunning, malignant . . . gangrened by sectional and social hatred to us and ours." Clearly the federal government was incapable of providing security against invasion—the South was "thrown on our self dependence. We must rely on ourselves and fight for peace! . . . To your tents! Organize and Arm!"[54]

Wise expressed the near-unanimous views of southern white leaders. All over the South, amid rumors of insurrection and arson, legislatures committed considerable sums of money to rearm state militias, and they hounded suspected northern spies, as well as people who expressed doubt about southern righteousness, into silence or flight.[55] John Brown had lit the fuse of secessionism. The *Mobile Daily Register* editorialized, "The Harpers Ferry Tragedy is like a meteor disclosing in its lurid flash the width and depth of that abyss which rends asunder two nations, apparently one." Believing that all northerners supported Brown in their hearts, the editors of the *Richmond Enquirer* declared that "the Harpers Ferry invasion has advanced the cause of disunion more than any other event [and] the people of the North sustain the outrage." There could be only one response, the *Savannah Republican* agreed: "Like the neighboring population we go in for summary vengeance. A terrible example should be made."[56] Hunger for retaliation lay at the core of the reactionary impulse in the South.

This wave of hysteria spread among the white community. Women as well as men expressed their fury with Brown and their visceral fear of what was to come, demonstrating that Brown's revolutionary terrorist mission had been accomplished. Amanda Virginia Edmonds, the twenty-year-old daughter of the owner of a large plantation in Fauquier County, Virginia, for example, wrote in her diary after reading of Brown's execution, "I would see the fire kindled and those who did it singed and burned until the last drop of blood was dried within them and every bone smouldered to ashes. Ah! but couldn't I! I don't think my heart would harbour feelings of sympathy for heartless ungrateful wretches." The actual hanging was "an awfully sublime, glorious, charmed scene." In the heart of this young belle, though she was a bit shocked by the bloodthirstiness of her fantasies of vengeance, only fire could repurify the contaminated southern soil.[57]

The enemy was not just at the gate; it had sent in its advanced brigade. J. D. B. De Bow, a renowned New Orleans periodical editor, proclaimed that the North "has sanctioned and applauded theft, murder, treason. . . . There is—there can be no peace." Even though Brown's insurrection had been crushed and he had been brought to Virginian justice swiftly, the northern sympathy for Brown portended worse to come. John Brown was obviously "the first act in the grand tragedy of emancipation, and the subjugation of the South in bloody treason. . . . The vanguard of the great army intended for our subjugation has crossed our borders on Southern soil and shed Southern blood." To "save our wives and daughters," an independent southern nation was the only remaining solution.[58]

As far as leaders like De Bow were concerned, John Brown had exposed the true aim of northerners—they did not mean merely to deny the South new slave territory as the hypocritical Republicans insisted—they intended to invade the South and cause a slave insurrection. Brown had foretold the invasion of slave soil and destruction of everything sacred: peace, community, family, women, the domination of the white race, and the enslavement of the black race. Southern leaders did not believe Republican protestations that they abhorred Brown and his deeds; they picked up rather the Republicans' ambivalence, hearing only the underlying softness on Brown, not the overt condemnation. As a measure of their contempt, they rechristened the Republicans the Black Republicans.

Until John Brown, secessionism had been the position of a hawkish, bellicose subgroup of white Southerners. But Brown and his tiny revolutionary terrorist cell succeeded in producing a general panic that propelled the majority into this extremist camp. It seemed obvious to southerners that Brown was the vanguard of an antislavery conspiracy, that despite its denials the Republican Party meant to conquer the South, and that these aggressors had to be fought even if it meant civil war. In this sense they *embraced* John Brown as the point man of the coming invasion. The Joint Committee of the General Assembly of Virginia made the linkage crystal clear in its January 26, 1860, report on the raid: "The crimes of John Brown were neither more nor less than practical illustrations of the doctrines of the leaders of the Republican Party." On January 12, 1860, Robert Toombs of Georgia, up until then a relatively moderate southerner, urged the U.S. Senate, "Never permit this Federal government to pass into the hands of the black Republican Party. It has already declared war against you and your institutions. . . . It has already compelled you to arm for your defense. . . . Defend yourselves! The enemy is at the door, wait not to meet him at your hearthstone. . . . Drive him from the Temple of Liberty, or pull down the pillars and involve him in a common ruin."[59] Brown's opponents could draw on the Samson analogy, too, when it came to the defense of freedom as they defined it. Theirs was the opposite version of the same American value—that Temple of Liberty—that Brown and other antislavery northerners proclaimed they were serving.

In the fall of 1859, the Florida Committee on Federal Relations linked the "theory and philosophy of the Black Republican party" directly to Brown. "It was this Republican creed, and the mad prophets of its faith, that led to the invasion of Virginia by a band of robbers and murderers, and when, in expiation of their crimes, they were doomed to death by the just penalty of violated law, instead of receiving the merited execrations due the felon, they were hailed by their sympathizing friends in the North as heroes and martyrs in the holy cause of charity and philanthropy." The Florida legislators understood that at his trial Brown had justified his terrorism by redefining the Christian high ground, a task at which he had succeeded for many northern clergymen and their flocks. "Nor does the sin and shame end there. The Christian Church has been desecrated, and the name and mission of the Saviour profaned by assimilating the blood of treason and murder to the redeeming blood of the Lamb of God." Northern churches had become seedbeds of the anti-Christ, John Brown, and his heresy.[60]

Southerners dealt with Brown as a terrorist, and their anger was intensified by the way many northerners subscribed to the martyr's role Brown had created for himself. They believed that his claim to the Christian high ground was scandalously, absolutely wrong and that they were the aggrieved Christian people defending fundamental human values. How infuriating that John Brown, the terrorist devil, had attempted to usurp the Christian faith. They would fight for their moral republic against the false martyr.

Southern sectional fever boiled over the course of 1860. During the unusually hot and dry summer, fires in the countryside and in several towns convinced many that there was a band of abolitionist spies using arson to help stir up the slaves for an imminent rebellion. Some sort of rumored outbreak, spreading through the terrified and vengeful white community, led to the killing of ten whites and approximately sixty blacks in Texas.[61] The election of Abraham Lincoln and an entirely northern antislavery party, however moderate it proclaimed its goals to be, was the final sign that secession was necessary. On December 12, in its message of justification for secession, the South Carolina legislature declared that the North had "encouraged and assisted thousands of our slaves to leave their homes; and those who remain, have been incited by emissaries, books, and pictures, to servile insurrection." The Republicans were eagerly poised to destroy slavery and the white South.

"They have invaded our States and killed our citizens," the *New Orleans Daily Crescent* declared, "and finally they have capped the mighty pyramid of un-fraternal enormities by electing Abraham Lincoln." Mary Boykin Chesnut, whose diary would one day become famous, noted that she had heard some-one insist, "Now that the black radical Republicans have the power I suppose they will Brown us all."[62]

As the sectional chasm opened up, those urging moderation and the status quo were swamped by far angrier and more strident proclamations, north and south. Secession came in anger, but not in misunderstanding, as both sides declared that their version of liberty and Christian truth was the correct one and that the alien others were the forces of evil. John Brown, in dynamic concert with the state of Virginia, had certainly heightened sectional contradictions over slavery and pointed to the path by which they would be resolved. Without the reactions of his captors, Brown's act would have lacked resonance. His ideological assault in the context of the southern counter-attack had an enormously greater impact than had the raid itself—which was precisely the goal of his revolutionary terrorism.

One can imagine alternative, counterfactual scenarios that could have aborted much of the melodramatic interchange between revolutionary and reactionary terrorism, undercutting the meanings and effects of the John Brown cataclysm. If the Marine lieutenant's sword had been sharper and Brown died in the engine house, if there had been no trial, if Brown had uttered no impassioned speeches, written no prison letters, Brown might have outraged the South, but he would not have rallied the North or pushed the retributive reactionary impulse in the South as far as it went. The impact of the raid might well have faded. If, alternatively, Brown had slaughtered his hostages and run for the hills, producing a further bloodbath before his death, the opprobrium attached to him might well have undermined the organized northern antislavery forces through guilt by association, discrediting the Re-publican Party, muting the sectional controversy, and preserving slavery for another generation.

Brown's eloquence, emerging in the context of his hyper-dramatic trial, transformed and broadened the meanings of his raid into what northerners read as a Christian attack on the perpetually violent horrors of slavery. But this Christian sword cut both ways, and southerners grasped it to destroy the prophet of evil and the society that supported him.

Four bloody years after John Brown climbed the gallows steps, on March 4, 1865, in his second inaugural address, Abraham Lincoln, probably without realizing it, replicated much of John Brown's final statement to the court before he was sentenced to be hanged. Seeking to give moral meaning to the appalling bloodshed of a war that Brown had predicted and helped instigate, Lincoln proclaimed, "This terrible war [was] the woe due by those by whom the offense [of slavery] came," by which he meant the northerners who had permitted the institution to flourish as well as the slaveholders themselves. Because all whites had been guilty in their complicity with the slave system, the blood sacrifice of war would have to continue, "until all the wealth piled by the bond-man's two hundred and fifty years of unrequited toil be sunk, and until every drop of blood drawn with the lash, shall be paid with another drawn with the sword."[63]

As John Brown had indicated would be the case by word and deed, only the terror of war extirpated the terror of slavery from the Christian republic.

CHAPTER 2

Terrorism and Civil War

And so the war came.

Viewed from the chaos of combat, war is undiluted terror, and thus using the term *terrorism* to describe events of the American Civil War might appear redundant or even banal. But the framework within which this war was conceptualized—conventional military doctrine accepted by the professional officer corps of the day—sought to separate outlawry and terrorism from the practice of "civilized warfare," ideally constructed as a fair fight among honorable soldiers. These limits of civilized warfare (a term generals and politicians often used for their own actions, at least) included the organization of uniformed troops within a trained, disciplined, and hierarchical set of military structures; the taking of prisoners and their humane treatment (as opposed to shooting them on the spot); and, most especially, the conscious abstention from destroying civilian property, raping civilian women, killing noncombatants, or driving them from their homes. In the words of the essential military law guiding the army, "Justice, honor and humanity [rather than] cruelty [and] military oppression" ought to guide military relations with prisoners and enemy civilians. Thus, judged by the standards of the men conducting the war, actions transgressing such generally accepted boundaries constituted illegal terrorism.[1]

In a war governed by generally accepted conventions of military behavior that both sides sought to observe, "cruelty and military oppression" are modes of fighting defined then as now not as acceptable warfare but as war crimes. Facing this issue we can attempt to construct theoretical boundaries to limit and isolate the definitions of *war crimes* and *terrorism* or we can accept that in the context of actual military action, such boundaries appear artificial. It is my argument that war crimes are forms of terrorism.

As a rule of thumb, one can generalize that the longer the war, the more brutal and sustained the fighting, the more the moral boundaries inhibiting terrorism collapse. And the more one can identify the enemy as a subhuman other, the greater the emotional distance one can place between oneself and that other, the greater will be the license to destroy it, and the fewer the distinctions drawn between civilian and soldier, between fair fight and outright murder. Although the American Civil War did not descend to the chaos of some civil wars, the impulse to commit acts of terrorism often overtook generals and privates, politicians and the public when Americans fought for contradictory versions of Christian civilization and the maintenance of liberty. These behaviors led to horrifying collisions of revolutionary and reactionary terrorism.

Several routes lead into an understanding of Civil War terrorism, from which I have chosen vivid and representative examples: violent psychological propaganda and assaults against civilians as practiced by General William Tecumseh Sherman, the most articulate general engaged on the terrorist side of organized warfare; the shooting of an entire category of prisoners of war, African American Union soldiers; and horrendous assaults on civilians in the widespread guerrilla warfare, unconfined by more traditional forms of military organization, that brutalized much of the contested territory of the upper South. In all these cases, soldiers acted out tribal rituals of us versus other, most often in situations where the others were powerless to respond in kind.

In the fall of 1864, while the great Army of the Potomac was bogged down in trench warfare outside Richmond, Sherman's army captured and destroyed Atlanta after decimating much of the opposing Confederate Army. Letting his subordinate, George Thomas, take charge of blocking the remaining body of Confederate troops who were moving northward, Sherman severed his lines of communication and then, spreading out his soldiers, cut a fiery, sixty-mile-wide swath through the breadbasket of Georgia during his famous march to the sea. After a Christmas break in Savannah, he repeated his only sporadically opposed destructive dragnet by moving north through the Carolinas, destroying civilian property and morale while marching inexorably toward Virginia.

Looking back ten years later on this mode of warfare, Sherman recalled in self-celebration, "My aim then was, to whip the rebels, to humble their pride, to follow them to their inmost recesses, and make them fear and dread us. 'Fear of the Lord is the beginning of wisdom.'"[2] When he searched for language to explain his coolly ruthless pursuit of the enemy's psychic structure, Sherman, a committed agnostic, reached for his King James Bible, quoting from Psalms in a way that he knew would resonate with his Christian countrymen, especially the fallen-from-national-grace Confederates. He also placed himself, whether consciously and ironically or not, in the role of Jehovah, the raging and implacable God of the chosen people, who punished his wayward flock when they worshiped false idols. Sherman's arrogation of the role of the punishing God was a heresy that would have been even greater than that practiced by John Brown had Sherman been sincerely Christian.

Sherman did not just enjoy his own rhetoric; he also attached his often-ferocious sensibility to his actions. After Atlanta had fallen to his army in September 1864, Sherman decided to expel the nearly two thousand remaining civilians through the southern lines. Although not uncommon in the history of warfare, this act of regional "cleansing," the first of its sort in the Civil War, demonstrated how far Sherman was prepared to go to follow a path of terrorism. Anticipating southern reactions with grim relish even before he began his march, Sherman wrote to army headquarters in Washington, "If the people raise a howl against my barbarity and cruelty, I will answer that war is war and not popularity seeking. If they want peace they and their relatives must stop war." When the Confederate military commander John Bell Hood protested, as Sherman had expected he would, about "the unprecedented measure you propose [that] transcends, in studied and ingenious cruelty all acts . . . in the dark history of war," Sherman's response was to keep going, and the Confederate Army was powerless to prevent him. Sherman thus humiliated all Confederates by extension, including Jefferson Davis, through his blunt demonstration of their impotence. He sought to undermine the Confederates' sense of political and individual self-determination by showing them that he was as God, they worthless miscreants meriting eternal damnation—a fate they themselves had chosen. "You might as well appeal against the thunder-storm as against these terrible hardships of war," Sherman told the city fathers of Atlanta when they added their protests to Hood's. "They are inevitable, and the only way the people of Atlanta can hope once more to live in peace and quiet at home is to stop the war, which alone can be done by admitting that it began in error and is perpetuated in pride."[3]

Sherman immersed himself in the terrors of war and used them against the enemy; humiliation, followed by capitulation, was his goal. "You cannot qualify war in harsher terms than will I. War is cruelty and you cannot refine it, and those who brought war into our country deserve all the curses and maledictions a people can pour out."[4]

As he was planning his march through the effectively undefended Deep

South, Sherman was clear in his mind that he wanted to assault the very identity of the people he—and God—despised: "I am going into the very bowels of the Confederacy and propose to leave a trail that will be recognized fifty years hence," he wrote in one letter; in another, "Already the papers in Georgia begin to howl at being abandoned, and will howl still more before [we] are done." Clearly Sherman wanted to destroy the core of southern resistance—the moral selfhood of every citizen, not just the Confederate Army, government, and property. Thus in yet another letter, he declared, "I propose to demonstrate the vulnerability of the South, and make its inhabitants feel that war and individual ruin are synonymous terms." Sherman realized that this form of warfare was unconventional, well outside the bounds of traditional martial doctrine. Persuading his somewhat reluctant commander, Ulysses S. Grant, of the deeper efficacy of ignoring the enemy's army while laying waste to the homeland from which it drew its support, Sherman wrote, "If we can march a well-appointed army right through [Jefferson Davis's] territory, it is a demonstration to the world . . . that we have a power which Davis cannot resist. This might not be war, but rather statesmanship." Justice would come out of the mouths of his guns, Sherman argued, while enacting a public demonstration of primal political logic. "If the North can march an army right through the South it is proof positive that the North can prevail in this contest, leaving only open to question the question of its willingness to use that power." Here Sherman was dissembling a bit; he was unquestionably eager to apply that elemental force.[5]

Sherman's brand of ideological warfare purposely erased any implicit limits on the destructiveness allowed to an avenging army. In theory, Sherman advertised himself as a terrorist—an advertisement calculated to instill profound, disabling fear in the hearts of Confederate civilians even more than their military. This was not conventional warfare but a variation of terrorism aimed at undermining civilian lives, beliefs, and fortitude.

In practice—and this must be emphasized—Sherman and his army were selective destroyers. Unlike terrorist actions employed in other wars against civilian populations, including the protracted American war against the Indians, Sherman's soldiers generally refrained from raping white women or killing masses of civilians (though they were often casual about killing adult men whom they regarded as dangerous to their march). Nevertheless they plundered their enemies, burning what they could not use, including crops, barns, industries, and houses. Sherman later calculated the value of the property destroyed in Georgia at a hundred million dollars, of which 80 percent was sheer waste. This scorched-earth policy went well beyond military practices deployed earlier in the war, and it devastated morale while destroying materiel, particularly as Sherman amplified the meaning of the carnage with rhetorical skill.

Sergeant Rufus Mead of Connecticut captured the festive destructiveness and the deeper psychological purposes of the campaign through Georgia in a letter written home after the army reached Savannah. "We had a glorious tramp right through the heart of the state, rioted & feasted on the country, destroyed all the [railroads]. In short found a rich and overflowing country filled with cattle, hogs sheep & fowls, corn, sweet potatoes & syrup, but left a barren waste for miles on either side of the road, burnt millions of dollars worth of property, wasted & destroyed all the eatables we couldn't carry off & brought the war to the doors of central Georgians so effectually I guess they will long remember the Yankees raid. I enjoyed it all the time." Mead understood and shared Sherman's intent: "The boys wasted as much as they used, in fact I think Genl Sherman didn't intend to leave anything." And it served the South right, Mead believed; given southerners' own "wickedness who can sympathize very much with them." When writing to his wife, Illinois private Ira Van Deusen was a bit more sympathetic about the devastation he and his comrades were visiting on civilians, but not to the point of feeling inhibited about acting out what he also understood to be Sherman's purpose. "You have no idea how the women & children suffer here whear we run there husbands & fathers from there houses & sometimes kill them at their dores & then our men take everything in the house & tair up the gardens & pastures, there wheat fields & burn their fences. . . . Any whear near we pass everything is destroyed."[6]

On Christmas Eve 1864, resting with his army in recently captured Savannah, Sherman wrote to Washington about his next raid, intended to go up through South Carolina, a state reviled for its zealous and haughty secessionist aristocrats, whom many in the North blamed for instigating the rebellion. However, in their treatment of this state, soldiers in his army singled out not just this class for destruction but their ignorant followers as well. Sherman's understanding of the democratic nature of Americans, southerners included, led him to what he believed to be the necessity of terrorizing a whole people in order to kill the secessionist desire to war against the Union: "We are not only fighting hostile armies, but a hostile people, and must make old and young, rich and poor, feel the hard hand of war," he wrote in one letter, and in another: "The truth is the whole army is burning with an insatiable desire to wreak vengeance upon South Carolina. I almost tremble at her fate, but feel that she deserves all that is in store for her." Even some of the senior officers who had been hesitant about the march through Georgia agreed with Sherman about South Carolina. General Henry Slocum coupled religious language with an understanding of American democracy in the same way Sherman did when he wrote to his family, "It would have been a sin to have the war brought to a close without bringing [pain] on the original aggressors."[7]

Giving this religiously fortified avenging mentality, it was no surprise that Columbia, the capital of South Carolina, went up in flames on the night of February 17, 1865, as soon as Sherman's army reached that symbolic core of the Confederacy. On a downtown street the departing Confederate troops cut open cotton bales and set them alight, and a wind blew flaming tufts onto nearby rooftops, starting a series of fires. After the troops left, escaped prisoners and local toughs probably spread the fire while looting. But when members of Sherman's army entered town after Sherman refused to order them confined to camp, they got into the local whiskey distillery and afterward rioted, looted, and burned with real zeal. The next day Union troops restored order and doused the fires. Privately pleased with this result, Sherman nonetheless testified seven years later before a legal hearing that he had never given a direct order to burn Columbia, avoiding the issue of his moral, as opposed to legal, responsibility for spreading the conflagration. Under questioning, he lost his temper, as was his wont, blurting out, "If I made up my mind to burn Columbia I would have burnt it with no more feeling than I would a common prairie dog village." In Sherman's mind, the traitors of the South had dehumanized themselves by deserting the American family, and thus the more he burned out the more salutary the result. He understood the impact of the terror he was spreading and anticipated that unconditional victory would follow his righteous destruction. A bit of exaggeration of what his troops actually did in this case did not bother him in the least.[8]

As almost the entire war was fought in Confederate territory, particularly from 1864 on, southern armies had few opportunities to practice retaliatory anti-civilian warfare. One notable exception came on July 30, 1864, when at the tail end of his raid north that reached the outskirts of Washington, General Jubal A. Early dispatched a cavalry column under General John McCausland against Chambersburg, Pennsylvania, a town of six thousand people twenty miles north of the Virginia border. Early authorized McCausland to demand five hundred thousand dollars in greenbacks or a hundred thousand in gold specie as compensation for federal depredations in the

Shenandoah Valley in Virginia, adjacent to Pennsylvania. If the town authorities refused to pay the ransom immediately, Early ordered McCausland to "lay the town to ashes." After waiting a few hours for the money, McCausland gave the order to burn. Believing it to be uncivilized and illegal, the head of one of the cavalry regiments, Colonel William E. Peters, refused the order and was immediately arrested (he was released the next day), but the rest of the army set to work with much the same ferocity Sherman's men would show during their long raid.

As would be the case in Columbia the following February, many of McCausland's men broke into taverns and got roaring drunk before going on a rampage, pillaging and robbing ordinary citizens and setting fire not only to the downtown business blocks but to at least half the houses, leaving three thousand people homeless and causing $1.6 million in damages. M. T. Norman, one of the raiders, later wrote to his wife about the terror this raid produced, "Nancy the poor wimmen and children and also gray heard men was running in every direction with a little bundle of cloths under there arms crying and screaming." While Norman expressed fellow feeling for his enemies, other Confederates did not, believing that they were attacking an inferior set of aliens meriting destruction. Because many of the residents of this area were Germans—pejoratively called "Dutch" by Anglo-Saxon Americans—the Confederates focused on their origins, damning them with xenophobic energy. There was a "coarseness" and vulgarity in their manners and an alien "twang" in their voices, concluded General Lafayette McLaws, that made such specimens "a very different race from the Southerner." Others agreed that all the women were ugly and the children dirty, clear markers of ethnic inferiority, and Colonel Alexander Pendleton, a Virginia blueblood, concluded that these "Dutch boors [had] heavy brutish lips, and thick drooping eyelids [that] indicate the stupidity of the people."

According General Bradley T. Johnson, one of the brigade commanders at Chambersburg, once the order to burn had been given, his men felt the "license" to strike at northern citizens the way they believed Union soldiers had attacked their families in Virginia. Soon enough, "drunken soldiers paraded the streets in every possible disguise and paraphernalia," acting out a ritual of purgation and purification, a kind of charivari of the sort unleashed on deviants back home. "With all their fierce passions unrestrained," noted a local clergyman, "they seemed to revel, as if intoxicated, in the work of destruction." In this manner the Confederate soldiers, when given the chance, replicated the terrorist attacks on civilians practiced by Union soldiers at places like Columbia: all acted upon their inner destructive urge against a hated enemy in ways that they believed their officers wanted. Knowing this and sharing their men's anger, the commanders effectively authorized them to terrorize enemy civilians while preserving legal deniability by never explicitly ordering the attacks. These officers were aware of the boundary between legal and illegal warfare. In effect they sanctioned war crimes. There was in practice no clear line between civilized warfare and war crimes—in the heat and haze of combat, war merged into terrorism.[9]

Shooting enemy combatants who attempted to surrender and civilian men suspected of aiding the foe was an even more explicit erasure of the wavering line that separated war from terrorism. Executing prisoners clearly was meant to spread fear among the enemy: reciprocal executions bred an escalating atmosphere of terror. Curiously, given the thousands of books on the military history of the Civil War, no scholar has yet written a general study of the shooting of civilians and of soldiers trying to surrender, although many have examined specific incidents and their wider implications.

During the depths of the period of scorched-earth warfare in the Shenandoah Valley in the summer of 1864, the Union cavalry general George Armstrong Custer, encouraged by his commander, Philip A. Sheridan, entered into a vendetta with the Confederate colonel John S. Mosby's Partisan Rangers (a quasi-guerrilla cavalry force that nevertheless was subject to more discipline than other guerrilla units). In October, responding to the killing of Lieutenant John R. Meigs, a member of Sheridan's staff and one of Sheridan's closest friends, by some of Mosby's men while they were in mufti, Custer took seven Partisan Rangers who were his prisoners and hanged them from a tree close to Mosby's camp, pinning a sign to one of the corpses that read, "Such is the Fate of All Mosby's Men." To retaliate, Mosby forced twenty-seven Union prisoners being held at his camp to draw straws and then executed five of them, leaving their bodies near Custer's headquarters, where he was sure they soon would be found.[10]

In several mountainous regions of the upper South and border states far behind Confederate lines, groups of Union sympathizers frequently took to the bush, where they were joined by deserters from the Confederate Army and together formed guerrilla bands. When Confederate soldiers would ferret them out, they would often summarily execute such men on a charge of treason, intending to induce other marauders to flee the region or, in the case of southerners, to rejoin the Confederate Army. In January 1863, in Johnson

County, Kentucky, a hotly contested Union slave state, a rebel contingent captured five suspected Unionists, immediately shooting two of them and stringing up the other three to strangle slowly while the Confederate soldiers beat them with sticks and gun butts. Their corpses were then left dangling from the tree until the flesh rotted off as a demonstration to other Union sympathizers who might pass by. The same month, in the mountains of East Tennessee, a Union stronghold deep in the Confederacy, another Confederate unit executed thirteen civilians suspected of Unionist sympathies without any sort of a trial, tossing some dirt over the bodies and moving on; by the time their families found them the next day wild hogs had feasted on several of the bodies.[11]

In October 1862, in a similar but larger event, later referred to as the Great Hanging, Confederate citizens in Gainesville, north Texas, went from panic to homicidal frenzy when they heard rumors of a Unionist conspiracy in their neighborhood. The local authorities set up a jury trial for the suspects, but when the wider populace grew restive at several acquittals, they replaced the jurors and then lynched many of the accused, killing at least forty-three. Later in the war, in 1864, in the same part of north Texas, Colonel James G. Bourland took to shooting prisoners, gunning down at least seven of those he was ordered to transport to prison. His response to queries from higher military authorities was that he shot the prisoners while they were attempting to escape, the conventional cover story in these situations, but in this instance, particularly as Bourland was hateful to everyone around him, both his own men and his superiors drummed him out of the service for the cold-blooded killing.[12]

Perhaps the largest such extra-military slaughter during the war occurred on August 24, 1863, when a self-constituted guerrilla battalion of approximately 450 men under the command of William C. Quantrill invaded Lawrence, Kansas, burning and looting much of the town and executing about 200 unarmed civilian men and boys. Similar guerrilla bands in Missouri had killed civilians and surrendering Union troops a few at a time, but at Baxter Springs, Kansas, on October 6, 1863, some of Quantrill's raiders slaughtered about 105 fleeing Union soldiers, and the next fall, near Centralia, Missouri, they shot down another 149, including a trainload of unarmed Union recruits, whose bodies they then mutilated. They also beheaded many of the corpses, placing the heads on fence posts, cutting off their penises and sticking them in their mouths, and hanging obscene epitaphs on placards around their necks.[13]

Such viciousness had a political purpose. Guerrillas intended to panic the enemy into flight with their terrorist demonstrations. Their criminal warfare was aimed at purging the land through slaughter. Theirs was perhaps a nihilist fantasy—but they acted on it with fearsome results.

After the Emancipation Proclamation and the federal arming of vast numbers of African American troops beginning in 1863, the previously all-white Civil War also became a race war. At this point prisoner-of-war exchange cartels broke down because the Confederate government insisted on returning captured ex-slaves—the vast majority of such Union troops—to slavery rather than treating them as legitimate enemy captives. In the heat of combat, however, furious at seeing the despised and self-liberated race in arms and thus claiming equality in the martial occupation of "real men," Confederate soldiers more often shot blacks attempting to surrender than took them prisoner. To date, historians have documented at least twelve cases of such slaughters, in two of which as many as six hundred black soldiers were killed, and recent work indicates that killing black prisoners of war was general policy in much of the Confederate Army.[14]

Writing from Poison Spring, Arkansas, on April 18, 1864, a Confederate cavalryman told his loved ones about the massacre of black soldiers from the 1st Kansas Colored Infantry that had just been carried out by his regiment: "If a negro was wounded our men would shoot him dead as they were passed and what negroes that were captured have . . . since been shot." Ordered to remove captured Union wagons from the field, Confederate soldiers competed to see who could crush the most "nigger heads," by rolling the heavy wheels back and forth over them. Choctaw fighting with the Confederates sometimes took the lead in scalping and mutilating black bodies. In all, according to General Edmund Kirby Smith, commander of the Trans-Mississippi Department, who reported to seeing "but two negro prisoners" after the battle, Confederate soldiers slaughtered up to six hundred black soldiers at Poison Spring. And this was not an unintended outcome driven solely by the anger of the moment but terrorism with political goals. Before the battle, Smith himself wrote that he hoped his officers "recognized the propriety of giving no quarter to armed negroes and their officers." And shortly after the battle, the Washington (Arkansas) *Telegraph* editorialized, "We cannot treat negroes taken in arms as prisoners of war without a destruction of the social system for which we contend. In this we must be firm, uncompromising, and unfaltering."[15] For hundreds of years a slave rebellion had been the greatest fear in the white South, and the Confederates refused to admit that slavery had ended. The legal and even moral logic of their own proslavery rebellion meant that it was appropriate to shoot blacks taken in arms rather than dignify them with the humanity accorded to enemy soldiers captured in battle. On the other hand, in so doing Confederate troops ran the danger of retaliation not only from black Union troops but from white Union troops, who might consider that solidarity among soldiers fighting for the Union transcended racial divisions in their own ranks.

Although some Confederates hesitated because of possible reprisals, war crimes against surrendering black soldiers arose spontaneously from the pattern of lethal intimidation that had always characterized slave society. Confederate soldiers wanted to kill "disloyal" runaway slaves who had turned Union soldiers to advertise to all potential runaways just what lay in store for them should they take up arms against their masters and white slave society. Right after Poison Spring, an Arkansas Confederate soldier explained to his family, "Our men is determine not to take negro prisoners, and if all the negroes would have seen what occurred that day, they would stay at home." The shooting of black troops who had surrendered was not random but policy, whether proclaimed overtly or carried out as a tacit understanding between officers and their men. And often officers participated fully, setting the example. On April 25, 1864, a week after Poison Spring, at Mark's Mill, Arkansas, an Arkansas cavalryman reported having watched his commander, General Joseph O. Shelby, club down with his rifle an unarmed black teamster attached to the Union Army and then draw his revolver and casually shoot him.[16]

The propensity to slaughter black would-be prisoners of war characterized Confederate behavior in many places, including under the Army of Northern Virginia, commanded by Robert E. Lee. In Lee's command, the most egregious such attack took place at the Battle of the Crater, on July 30, 1864. With both sides stuck in siege warfare, Union sappers tunneled under the powerful Confederate trenches at Petersburg while a black division drilled to lead the assault planned for after the dynamite planted by the sappers would collapse the Confederate defenses. At the last minute the Union command substituted white troops, most likely in fear that the assault would not work—a failure that would have led to criticism that they had used black troops as cannon fodder—although it may have been done because the commanders doubted the fighting mettle of their black troops. After the explosion, black troops were sent in after the untrained white soldiers, and all ended up milling around at the base of the crater. This confusion gave Confederate soldiers time to regroup and fire down from the rim of the crater with deadly effect. A Georgia sergeant later said, "Negro troops were in the fray, they threw away their guns and attempted to surrender, but our men replied that they had arms and must fight, and continued to shoot them down." Private William A. Day, from a North Carolina regiment, noted that his regiment "fired one volley into the surging mass [of black soldiers], then turned the butts of their guns and jumped in among them. How the negroes skulls cracked under the blows. Some of them ran over on our side and started for the rear, while others made a dash for their own lines. . . . I, boy like, ran up the line to see them. When I got there they had the ground covered with broken headed negroes, and were searching about among the bomb proofs for more. . . . They kept on until they finished up." Several Confederate soldiers recalled the inescapable fate of black troops who threw down their arms and fled toward their presumed captors. Black Federals "had their eyes opened only [to] be butchered like sheep," wrote one, while another added with some regret, "Some few negroes went to the rear as we could not kill them as fast as they past us."

At least some Confederate officers clearly gave orders that these "subhuman" enemies be executed. This was apparent in the description by Major Matthew Love of the actions of his North Carolina regiment during the heat of the battle: "Such slaughter I have not witnessed upon any battle field any where. Their men were principally negroes and we shot them down until we got near enough and then run them through with the Bayonet. . . . We was not very particular whether we captured or killed them the only thing we did not like to be pestered berrying the Heathens." While other officers tried to stop the slaughter, most were either silent or, like Major Love, fully engaged in leading the killing. Brigadier General W. J. Pegram remarked two days after the battle, "It seems cruel to murder them in cold blood, but I think the men who did it had very good cause for doing so." After keeping a certain rhetorical distance from the experience of terrorism he was describing, Pegram added, "I have always said that I wished the enemy would bring some negroes against this army. I am convinced, since Saturday's fight, that it has a splendid effect on the men." For Pegram, the political lessons of reinforcing slavery through massacre were all to the good. For his part, General Lee said nothing that was recorded, then or later, about the actions of his troops. Soldiers in his command had killed about 265 surrendering black soldiers that morning, while only 85 made it to captivity.[17]

Although he later would deny that he had ordered a massacre, on April 12, 1864, troops under the leadership of the renowned cavalry commander Nathan Bedford Forrest (who went on after the war to found the Ku Klux Klan), screaming, "No quarter! No quarter!" and "Kill the damned niggers, shoot them down!" stormed Fort Pillow on the Mississippi River in Tennessee. Forrest's men murdered more than a hundred black soldiers who attempted to surrender and killed several disarmed whites as well. The rebels buried some wounded blacks while they were still alive, and set fire to tents that contained other wounded blacks; they also murdered two black women and four little black boys and threw their bodies into the river. Of all wartime racial massacres, this was the one most investigated at the time, but it formed part of a wider pattern, coming as it did six days before the massacre at Poison Spring.[18]

Eight days after Fort Pillow, on April 20, 1864, a Confederate force assaulted the big Federal post at Plymouth, North Carolina, where a considerable number of white Unionist civilians and escaped slaves had gathered for safety. After the Union commander surrendered, about 800 blacks made a break for it, trying to reach a nearby swamp. Of those who remained behind to be captured, a Confederate later wrote: "They lined up them d——d niggers [and shot] 'em off the dock." Meanwhile many were killed trying to swim across the river, and over the next few days "gunning for niggers" in the swamps near town became a popular sport among the victorious troops. Estimates of the number massacred run from 471 to 600.[19]

So frequently was this form of massacre repeated—always intended as a means of terrorizing black Union troops, not only killing them but warning off potential recruits—that it amounted to a policy of race warfare. Historians have not yet fully examined such slaughters at Saltville and New Market Heights, Virginia; at Mound Fort, Louisiana; and at Fort Wagner, South Carolina, and almost certainly other sites exist that are as yet undisclosed. On June 7, 1863, at Milliken's Bend, a Louisiana fort on the Mississippi, Confederate troops butchered many in the black garrison they overwhelmed—an arriving Union admiral reported that "the dead negroes lined the ditch inside of the parapet, or levee, and were mostly shot on the top of the head." And a Texas private reported that as Confederate foot soldiers escorted black prisoners to camp, "12 or 15" died before they arrived. Similarly, after the rout of black troops at Olustee, Florida, on February 20, 1864, a Georgia soldier wrote that his comrades had "walked over many a wooly head as we drove them back. . . . How our boys did walk into the niggers, they would beg and pray but it did no good." Hearing frequent firing going on all around him after the battle ostensibly had ended confused one Confederate officer, who asked a subordinate what his men were doing. "Shooting niggers sir. I have tried to make the boys desist but I can't control them." Uncontrollable sadistic racism led to a level of slaughter not accorded surrendering white enemy soldiers. Confederate inhibitions of conventional warfare that they applied to white captives starkly contrasted to the criminal warfare that became standard practice when blacks tried to surrender.[20]

As we have seen, not all officers merely observed their men rampage. One wounded white New York soldier who had concealed himself in some bushes by the Olustee battleground later wrote, "I could see the rebels come to our wounded, and take their money, watches, and whatever they found on their persons; while they stripped the dead altogether. The wounded negroes they bayoneted without mercy. Close beside me was a fine-looking negro, who was wounded in the leg. . . . A rebel officer happened to see him, and says, 'Ah, you black rascal, you will not remain here long!' and, dismounting from his horse, placed his revolver close to the negro's head, and blew his brains out." In all, Confederates executed up to fifty blacks who had been wounded or attempted to surrender that February day.[21]

Certain Confederate outfits took pride in their reputation for systematically killing surrendering black troops. One such unit was the infantry brigade commanded by Brigadier General Matt W. Ransom of North Carolina. On March 9, 1864, six weeks before the Plymouth massacre in which it also played a major role, Ransom's brigade overran a black unit at Suffolk, Virginia. "We did not take any prisoners," an unidentified member of the brigade wrote, an outcome several of his comrades corroborated. "Officers and men were perfectly enthusiastic in *killing* the d——d rascals, as I heard many call them." This trooper recalled setting fire to a house holding ten black soldiers, bayoneting those who attempted to escape, and watching the others "burned to cinders. . . . Ransom's brigade never takes any negro prisoners. Our soldiers would not even bury the negroes." Moreover, knowing full well what was their policy, local citizens supported the brigade. Major John H. Graham wrote to his father that the "ladies [of Suffolk] were standing at their doors, some waving handkerchiefs, some crying, some praying, and others calling to us to 'kill the negroes.' Our brigade did not need this to make them give 'no quarter,' as it is understood among us that we take no negro prisoners." One of the brigade did note, however, that race-based terrorism might go both ways: "If any of us should be captured by them, our fate would be hard," he wrote. In a similar fashion, R. P. Marshall of Shelby's brigade celebrated the brutal reputation of his unit when he wrote in his diary, "People call us rough and Savages we had to be we had to lay aside the Golden Rule with the [black] Federals and treat them just like they treat us. And as old David Haram said do it First."[22]

It is not surprising that African American troops were often overrun. Rather than being stationed with the front-line units, most were relegated to fatigue duties and to manning remote outposts along lines of communication, forts that would be most vulnerable to fast-moving Confederate cavalry units. Then too they were more poorly armed than their comrades, and they received less pay, shabbier uniforms, and worse nutrition and health care than the white troops—black soldiers' rate of death from disease was 18 percent, two and a half times greater than that for whites. Black soldiers were far more likely to be shot for desertion—an astounding 80 percent of Union soldiers executed for mutiny were black, although they composed only 12 percent of the army. Being treated like second-class soldiers undercut the morale of the black troops.

Neither could embattled black troops be reassured that their fellow Union soldiers supported them, and this social distance increased their level of isolation and fear. Many, perhaps most, white Union soldiers shared the endemic racism of their countrymen and did not want to have anything to do with black troops, whom they considered inferior and undependable. Seeing them in battle changed the opinions of some, but on the whole blacks were kept out of combat—one marker of this form of discrimination is that while 6 percent of white Union soldiers died in combat, among blacks the figure was around 1.5 percent. This discrepancy was used in turn by white soldiers to fuel their resentment against blacks for being pampered, in one of the many profound ironies for African Americans of the Civil War.[23]

Many commanders of the major Union armies doubted the combat potential of black soldiers, as was demonstrated by Grant and George G. Meade's refusal to use specially trained black units at the Battle of the Crater. Out West, Sherman, a strident racist, managed to keep all black units out of his army, resisting their inclusion to the point of refusing direct orders from Washington on the subject. Under pressure to admit black regiments, on September 4, 1864, he wrote to army headquarters—in a letter that he intended for circulation—"I have had the question put to me often: 'Is not a negro as good as a white man to stop a bullet?' Yes, and a sand-bag is better; but can a negro do our skirmishing and picket duty? Can they improvise roads, bridges, sorties, flank movements, &c., like the white man? I say no. Soldiers must and do many things without orders from their own sense, as in sentinels. Negroes are not equal to this. I have gone steadily, firmly, and confidently along, and I could not have done it with black troops, but with my old troops I have never felt a waver of doubt, and that very confidence begets success." Writing privately to an old friend later that month, Sherman was more overt in his contempt for those pushing black troops into his army. "I like niggers well enough as niggers, but when fools & idiots try & make niggers better than ourselves, I have an opinion."[24]

Sherman's officers and men picked up on their commander's opinions, which most of them already shared in any event. When a black infantry regiment was finally attached to Sherman's army at Savannah, it was stripped of its guns; some of the men were handed picks and axes while others were sent to guard hospitals and drive wagons, well out of the line of white combat units. When Sherman's men later ran into well-organized black units in Beaufort during their march through South Carolina, they rioted against them, killing two or three and leaving many more wounded. In this way were such presumptuous black soldiers "taught to know their places & behave civilly," an Ohio soldier reported.[25]

Despite their enormous likelihood of being killed if captured, despite their resentment over the discrimination they suffered at the hands of Union authorities, despite the contempt and abuse they experienced from their white comrades in arms, African American soldiers remained eager to engage the enemy in combat. Indeed, Union policies that were intended to marginalize them and Confederate attempts to terrorize them into defeat through a no-prisoners policy only served to make blacks determined to retaliate. And unlike their experience of slavery, from which most of these men had so recently escaped and in which whites held all the power, in the army African Americans had guns, uniforms, and organizations that enabled them to confront their oppressors with the most extreme violence they could muster. Indeed, a day after the slaughter of the 1st Kansas Colored Infantry at Poison Spring, the white officers and black enlisted men of the 2nd Kansas Colored Infantry swore that "in future the regiment would take no prisoners so long as the Rebels continued to murder our men." On April 30, 1864, less than two weeks later, at Jenkin's Ferry, Arkansas, the 2nd Kansas isolated a Confederate artillery battery, killed most of the artillery horses with one volley, dispersed supporting infantry with another, and then assaulted the enemy troops with fixed bayonets; screaming, "Poison Spring!" as they charged. They killed every man in the battery, including at least three who sought to surrender. Later they set to killing all the wounded Confederates they could find after the larger engagement had resulted in Union victory, though the white Iowa

Union regiment fighting alongside them tried to stop the slaughter. The Confederate surgeon David S. Williams reported, "Many of our wounded had been mutilated in many ways. Some with ears cut off, throats cut, knife stabs, etc. My brother . . . was shot through the body, had his throat cut through the windpipe and lived several days. I saw several who were treated in the same way. One officer wrote on a bit of paper that his lower jaw and tongue were shot off after the battle was over."[26]

To date, historians have examined fewer examples of black counterterrorism than of Confederate terrorism against blacks, yet it is clear that black troops retaliated ruthlessly when they could. Confederates were terrified of surrendering to black units, and with good reason, as their chances of being shot along the march back to a prison camp were considerable. In one large-scale operation late in the war, on April 9, 1865, shouting, "Remember Fort Pillow," a black infantry division led the charge against Fort Blakely, outside Mobile, Alabama. Black units threw the Confederates into a panic when they poured into their earthworks. Many Confederates jumped into the water and drowned or were shot while they tried to swim to safety. Others threw down their arms and ran toward white Union units, "to save themselves being butchered by our niggers," in the words of a white Union infantryman. A white lieutenant in one of the black regiments later wrote home, "The niggers did not take a prisoner, they killed all they took to a man."[27] By this point in the war, at least in the more organized battles, white soldiers still tended to take other whites prisoners while they cut black throats in a pattern of terrorism that continued the essential inhumanity of slavery, a pattern that would be extended into the postwar world for decades to come. During wartime itself, black men gained the power to cut throats in return, but that opportunity was the exception to the rule of racial ordering before and (as I shall discuss in the next chapter) after the Civil War.

White southerners fighting a race war within the Civil War acted not out of momentary hatred but in order to obtain exclusive possession of lethal force to subordinate another, "inferior" race. Killing disarmed black prisoners of war was a political action, an expression of a policy of racial ordering that would have to be construed and enforced through systematically violent means.

This experience vividly demonstrates the ways in which white reactionary terrorism merged with war crimes, creating long-term contexts in which earlier forms of brutal domination were reworked when the need to dominate was most at risk, when whites faced organized and armed black Union troops. Confederate soldiers perpetrated war crimes for politically reactionary ends.

As we shall see, former Confederates went underground after the war, using similar terrorist means to overturn Reconstruction rule. The war crimes the southern troops perpetrated on surrendering black soldiers were an earlier modality of the reactionary and counterrevolutionary terrorist movement they developed to seize state power in the former Confederacy in the 1870s.

Across great expanses of the border states and the Union-conquered upper South, where there were insufficient numbers of regular troops to police the region, guerrilla warfare duplicated much of the savagery characteristic of the race war between Union black soldiers and Confederates. In most of these regions, poorly trained and often self-organized soldiers on both sides shot enemy captives and executed considerable numbers of civilian men, as they did at Gainesville and Lawrence. Guerrillas and counterinsurgents looted, burned, assaulted, and destroyed with little reference to the supposed line demarcating soldier from civilian. Indeed, many of the soldiers operated in unofficial and self-constituted bands; such guerrillas needed the protection of the civilian population, who aided them and spied for them. In turn, coming to consider all civilians potential enemies, regular troops sloughed off most of the discipline that soldiers usually observed in areas dominated by official armies, devolving into goon squads fighting goon squads. The conventions of civilized warfare more typical of the large standing armies simply evaporated. War became a series of criminal activities, approaching a war of all against all.

The purpose of the guerrilla war was to terrorize enemy soldiers and civilians alike. Even apparently random violence inflicted on isolated individuals reflected a wider intentional pattern—concerted political violence—for Confederate guerrillas and their counterinsurgent Union counterparts recognized that news of any brutal actions would spread throughout the neighborhood, promoting physical and psychic desolation, panic, and flight. Although at times it was denied by a command structure that in fact urged it on, the no-prisoners policy was widespread. And on their side, guerrillas did not just shoot defenseless captives, they often mutilated the bodies of dead enemies, the better to spread terror among the foe and reinforce their own solidarity. In perverse fashion, fighters in this ugliest of wars adapted their Christian inheritance and their belief in American liberty and justice to explain how their terrorist system could be conducted in defense of their primary values. Only scourging the land of its enemies could rescue and purify it for its sanctified people. Only blood purges would suffice to free the oppressed and secure their freedom.

An attack could come at any farmyard on any night. On November 17, 1864, in rural Missouri a band of nightriders galloped up to Pauline Stratton's door. "Two men dressed in Federal uniforms came and knocked at our door and said they wanted to warm," she recorded in her diary. "[My son] Tom told them to go round to the other door and then without thinking let them in. They jumped on Tom with their pistols and demanded his revolver. He told them he had none. They said there was one here and they would have it. Tom had to get Mat's which John had. I was very scared and sorry Tom had got up and let them in. They shot Mr. Jones through his door. But at Mr. Harmon they would not let them in and they went away." Stratton could not have identified the men from their uniforms—she would have known that Confederate guerrillas frequently dressed in Federal uniforms, and Federal soldiers often freelanced as terrorists outside their shaky command structure, so there might have been a big cavalry unit out in the yard, or the two men might have gone off on their own with a few pals. As Pauline Stratton had learned from similar experiences visited on her neighbors, the consequences of such raids were uncertain: maybe the invaders would be satisfied with a pistol, but maybe they would ransack the house and burn it, and certainly they might shoot men they accused of aiding the enemy, as these soldiers shot Mr. Jones that night while refraining from shooting Tom Stratton. No outcome was predictable; no response was appropriate. Writ large and repeated endlessly, Strattons' experience was the deadly paradigm of thousands of moments of terror during the guerrilla war, when roving bands of terrorists raided and killed unpredictably.[28]

A year earlier, in Gentry County, in northwest Missouri, two men pounding on her door awakened Pauline Ellison, a widowed mother of five daughters. She asked who was there and they replied "that it was none of my business—I must open the door or they would open it dam roughly." When she let the men in they pushed past her looking for arms, and then they spied a trunk where "they guessed was a thousand dollars" but found only a lead pencil for the taking. Going to the kitchen "they put a candle to the ceiling and remarked that they wondered if the house would burn good, saying suppose we try." But as suddenly as they had come they left, warning Ellison that if she did not leave the county in seven days they would return. The next morning Ellison went to the Union provost marshal in Albany, the nearby county seat, to swear out a deposition on the incident, in part out of anger and in part from a fear that she might be reported as a collaborator if she did not. Ellison knew that the soldiers in the Federal garrison in town were afraid of the lurking guerrilla foes who controlled the countryside at night while they holed up in their stockade. Therefore it took Union authorities a full month to persuade Ellison to identify her two attackers, neighbors whom she had known for nearly a decade. Without armed men in her family to protect her, without real security even from nearby Union troops, Ellison was terrified, though her material loss had been only a small lead pencil.[29]

Military disorganization increased the terror. Even large guerrilla bands, lacking coherent hierarchies and disciplined battle plans, often acted capriciously. At Lawrence, the largest and bloodiest guerrilla action of the war, the guerrillas passed various places by and refrained from killing some men while slaughtering others. At the Fitch residence on the edge of town several guerrillas demanded to see "the man of the house," whom they shot dead in front of his wife and three young children, after which they set fire to the house, refusing to allow Mrs. Fitch to take her husband's body from the burning structure. The neighboring Bissell family, seeing and hearing the destruction in town—"the people running, black and white, young and old and the *Fiends* dashing after them, firing as fast as they possibly could"—buried their money and their valuables in the yard, "and waited for them to come," Sophia Bissell wrote to a friend two weeks after the massacre. Two guerrillas arrived and demanded to see Henry Bissell, the man of the house. When he came out, the guerrillas asked him whether he had ever served in the Union army. He denied it. "If you had told me you did I would have shot you dead," one of the guerrillas said. Henry Bissell gave the two men ten dollars, and they rode off, warning the family that they were going to come back later to burn them out of their home. Soon a different guerrilla rode up and politely asked for a drink of water, "and said we were not agoing to be burned," Sophia Bissell recalled. "We took a little courage" at this point, Bissell said, though looking toward town she could see "the houses of our friends . . . all ablaze." When, after what seemed an infinitely long wait, five mounted men rushed toward the Bissell house, torches in hand, "we knew our time had come." They rode right up on the porch, ransacked the house, and set it on fire. Then they began to beat Henry with their gun butts, but perhaps because Sophia was very attractive and pleaded with tears in her eyes for her brother's life, they let him run for the safety of the cornfield instead of killing him. "They then tipped their hats [to the ladies] and bid us good morning. We returned the salutation."[30]

This weirdly twisted moment of chivalry amid the burning and slaughter of civilian homes and men hardly diminished the terror for the civilians in

Lawrence and elsewhere. But it did serve as a marker of one of the few limits of this dreadful warfare. Guerrillas generally maintained an element of respect for the women of the other side even as they terrorized them, refraining from raping or killing them. This was due in part to their clear knowledge that their own women were in effect hostages to enemy soldiers who could easily retaliate but also to the guerrillas' belief that they were fighting for independence and social decency against barbarian invaders, which meant above all preserving their families and all families, particularly the women who animated civilized living. Such forbearance did not apply to Indian or black women, who were frequently raped and murdered; it pertained only to white women, whom the guerrillas recognized as essentially human, like their own womenfolk. This attitude did not prevent the guerrillas from massacring innocent men in front of their families at Lawrence—that was the norm, and Henry Bissell's escape the exception. But even these ruthless terrorists sought to preserve elements of what they considered their humanity—their "character"—as they demonstrated in their actions toward Sophia Bissell and her brother. They chose not to shoot Henry, momentarily proving to themselves that they did not kill indiscriminately, even while they murdered many other civilian men and boys without compunction that same day. Like John Brown, these terrorists sought to maintain moral deniability that they were really terrorists, only terrorists.

Yet how did Sophia or Henry Bissell cope after the massacre with the burning of their house and the killing of their best friends? What became of their sense of family and self when terrorists turned their world to ashes? When the invaders destroyed those everyday bulwarks, their victims were overwhelmed. Nothing made the sense it had all their lives. By utterly destroying the security of its victims, illegal and unconventional warfare merged into criminal terrorism as the cultural norm, overturning the fundamental social expectations that define us all. Emptied of any affirmation of inner value and the social continuity of everyday life, civilian victims lost their peacetime identities, their normal senses of self, and reassembled themselves in harsh new ways. I call this process "character doubling" and "psychic numbing." For the attacked—but for the attackers as well—it was the "not-me," the victim or the warrior, who had enacted terrorism or been assaulted by it, and the "real-me," the peaceful person within, who remained detached, outside the almost instantaneous disintegration terrorism brought, even when observing the embattled not-me from an eerie and surreal distance.

Such doubling was always accompanied by numbing, an almost matter-of-fact surface acceptance of terrorist violence as the new norm. During the terrorist seasons in Civil War Missouri, many letter writers reported with seeming sangfroid that death was all around them but that they were still all right. J. W. Woods, a schoolteacher, wrote to his favorite aunt, "Things are in such a commotion here & if no one is killed we think it is not of much interest & we hear of some outrage almost every day. [Civilians] are the prey of both armies. . . . Now and then [guerrillas] kill a man. There have been two or three such characters brought in and shot—informally of course." At about the same time, another Missourian wrote a friend, reporting on the death of one acquaintance and the rumored killing of another: "Times are about as usual in this county. Occasionally we hear of a man being shot or a horse stolen. No houses have been burnt recently. Recently we have begun to think times tolerably quiet. Old Man Staley was shot a few days ago, since has died. I have enquired in regard to Hy Litton but hear nothing of his being killed. He is reported in the neighborhood of home." And from the Kansas side of the border, the politician Samuel Ayres wrote a friend about the "depredations" committed by passing Confederate guerrillas and pro-Union Redlegs (Kansas units that behaved in Missouri much as Confederate guerrillas acted in Kansas): "They pay us a visit occasionally and levy a tax to the amount of one or more horses—Sometimes plunder houses—run off cattle—kill a few men and burn some houses."[31] Underneath the coldness of expression each of these reports reveals considerable repression of compassion, a loss of the internality of peacetime humanness. Systematic criminal assaults produced zombies, the sort of psychic result terrorists of all sorts intend for those they attack, to weaken them for final elimination.

Often accompanying psychic numbing, and running parallel with it, was greed. Whenever they had the chance, usually in a well-fortified Union center where commerce could continue or in a distant place where refugees had moved, those who had been assaulted by wartime terrorism often developed an insatiable lust for food, clothes, ornaments, and especially money. From Paris, Texas, one Missourian reported, "I have gotten to believe that there is a kind of madness taken possession of or giving [my fellow Missourians down here], a great propensity for lying. . . . Everybody is run mad after money. Money is all they care or think about." In Rolla, Missouri, a railhead and major Union garrison town, Timothy Phillips, an infantryman from Iowa, reported that life in that safe haven contrasted vividly and terribly with the human misery he had seen in most of the surrounding countryside. "[The] streets are thronged with people each seemingly bent on his own thoughts or schemes of gain. . . . The business portion of the place is a crowded mart with throngs of eager purchasers or those wishing to dispose of their merchandise." Phillips was observing, as he almost certainly understood, a massive fencing operation, in which plunder taken from across the state was illegally disposed of, and such greed angered him as a materialist assault on elemental Christian decency. Greedy trading was one of the corruptions of terrorist guerrilla warfare—it was a set of criminal exchanges grounded in massive theft and destruction, a bizarre wartime adaptation of mercantile capitalism.[32]

It had become almost impermissible to continue to feel authentic emotions under these circumstances—terror coarsened the surviving victims while it hardened the terrorists. Before the war most of these same people would have believed in and striven to practice the Golden Rule, but now, because such values were useless to protect them, the victims adopted an interim survival strategy, withdrawing from others and becoming indifferent to them when not overtly hostile. At least this was the immediate response while the terrorism continued. What was going on underneath the numbness or what would happen to emotional and community life after the terrorism ended were different matters. But terrorism seemed likely to be the dominant mode for as long as anyone could foresee, and normal self-conception and social interaction were suspended while a culture of terrorism bloomed.

While guerrillas on both sides warred among them, there usually came a moment when almost all the civilians in a town or rural area suddenly panicked and fled—the central goal of all terrorists. Analyzing a typical frenzy occurring in much of their state during the summer of 1864, three leading civilians of Huntsville, Missouri, wrote to the military commander of the Department of the Missouri, "There is a perfect panic here. People are leaving their homes and have lost all hope. . . . All parties share the panic alike. The people are without organization and cannot resist such large bands." And then, realizing that broadcasting news of this panic would only induce similar stampedes elsewhere, the three men begged the authorities, "Please do not publish in the papers."[33]

Those fleeing left a deeply alienating desolation in their wake. Many Union soldiers on the march through the ravaged Missouri countryside reported to the folks living in comfort back home about the horrors they found where once there had been cultivation and civilization. Philip Welsheimer wrote to his family in Illinois that northeast Missouri was naturally "a fine country but now forsaken. The Rebels first drove off the Union men and since [our] troops have got in a great many rebels have left." In several towns, "but two or three families" remained, and everywhere he marched he found "fine brick houses & fine frame houses standing empty and some with the furniture in and one with diner standing on the table," a tribute to the suddenness of the onset of the panic. Another Union soldier described Clay County, along the burned-over Kansas border in 1864: "This once beautiful and peaceable land is forsaken and desolated, ruined and only fit to bats, owls & cockralls to inhabit." Another soldier, John A. Martin, from a Kansas regiment reported about the same region that everywhere he traveled he saw "crops ungathered, houses deserted barns & stables falling to peaces, fences torn down and stock running loose." All these observers understood that the desolation they saw was the opposite of what good people produce—cultivation, hard labor, Christian worship and good works. As Martin concluded, this vast destruction represented the central meaning of a terrorist war "terribly portrayed."[34]

Desolation of the countryside was matched inwardly by the desperate and often broken sprits of the fleeing refugees. In the summer of 1863, the Reverend Francis Springer, chaplain of the 10th Illinois Cavalry, reported on the condition of civilians fleeing the guerrilla warfare despoiling northern Arkansas for the Union stronghold at Cassville, Missouri. Looking over the refugees flooding his regiment's camp, Springer saw "unwashed, half-clad & shoeless boys and girls . . . in pitiable abundance." For housing, the refugees "either live in their wagons or in tents made by spreading a few quilts over a pole resting at each end on forked sticks planted in the ground." All the women seemed exhausted. Springer noted several driving their crude ox carts into camp, loaded with cakes and pies to sell to the soldiers, and he implied that sometimes they were driven to sell their bodies as well. Just outside the fortified town, "thievish brigands and secesh [secessionist] spies are hovering," and Springer feared that some of the women in the Union camp were spying for the enemy. From another refugee camp, this one near Saint Louis, a Union military officer reported, "The worst feature . . . is the cowed and dispirited state of the people. All manhood appears to have gone out of them. Alike in fear of the soldier and the bushwhacker, all they ask is military protection of provost-marshals and the privilege of neutrality." Terror had produced individual and collective dehumanization. And it could destroy reason altogether. Reverend Springer wrote that one day, "a wild man . . . was seen descending the adjacent hill densely covered with trees. He seems an apparition suddenly revealed. He is barefoot, hatless, scratched with briars & with no covering for his nakedness but a coarse dark gray homespun blanket over his shoulders and reaching halfway down his thighs . . . His countenance is expressive of extreme dejection. He refuses conversation, takes but little food, & seems alike careless of the attention of friends & the threats of foes. His constant posture from morning until night is sitting or crouched on the floor of the guardhouse."[35]

Ravaged land, broken spirits, populations in panic and flight: all these were proof of the success of a war fought not against soldiers but against all. This was a separate piece of the general war, illegal by the standards of both armies when they fought as more disciplined entities. This was war where the lines between warfare, war crimes, and terrorism had been erased.

Between them, while they ravaged the countryside and drove civilians to despair, panic, and flight, the guerrillas and counterinsurgents created a martial ethos that included as standard operating procedure killing captives rather than taking them prisoner. While this occurred sporadically among soldiers in the official war of organized forces, and, as we have seen, as a general practice when the Civil War became a race war, in the guerrilla war mutual slaughter among white fighters became the norm rather than the exception. Describing Salem in south-central Missouri after panic had done its cleansing work, Union soldier J. Martin wrote that what was a "once pleasant country village" had turned into a nightmare. "Around us we see the ruins of buildings, despoiled of doors, sashes, and everything movable. Others, among them the Court House—pierced with loopholes, evince former apprehensions of attack. Bands of guerrillas prowl about the neighborhood, committing occasional depredations. They are, however, kept in *wholesome terror* by Co. Q 3rd Mo. Cav. Stationed here, who make it a point to take as few prisoners as possible." Martin's language was chilling in its matter-of-fact reporting that shooting prisoners was standard procedure: under the circumstances, Martin thought this practice was a healthy form of terror—a pragmatic assessment that demonstrated just how far terrorism had gone toward redefining combat and morality in general.[36]

Both in the field and on the national level, the command structure clearly sanctioned shooting enemy guerrillas—fighters dressed in civilian clothes and operating outside of regularly defined military units—rather than taking them prisoner. Early in 1862 the district commander in Jefferson City, Missouri, issued an order that "all those . . . who are known familiarly as guerrillas, jayhawkers, murderers, marauders and horse-thieves, will be shot down by the military upon the spot when found perpetrating their foul acts." This order soon was made official for the whole state, and on April 23, 1863, the military authorities in Washington issued General Orders No. 100, which expanded the no-prisoners policy for guerrillas to the entire nation.

This policy reflected and rendered official the reactions by field officers to the clandestine murders of their soldiers, officers who would then push their men to retaliate by executing enemies when they discovered them. General Samuel Curtis, an experienced and intelligent West Pointer, wrote to a state official in Kansas that the "butchery" of guerrilla warfare demanded and justified "horrors" in putting it down. Recently, one of his men bathing in the Little Red River had been "shot and beaten to death with clubs. I have ordered such villains not to be taken prisoner." Private George Wolz, a German American from Saint Louis stationed in Springfield, noted similar orders given to his unit when he wrote to his parents, "There are strict orders against taking any more prisoners that is found in arms or as bushwhackers but to leave them on the ground we found them on." Ordinary soldiers like Wolz hardly required official commands to respond to the terrifying killing of their comrades by direct retaliation. But officers could be impatient with their men if they could not bring themselves to execute captives without some kind of hearing. Reacting to the capture of the guerrilla leader Bradaway and his band, Colonel Bazel F. Lazear wrote to his headquarters, "I am sorry they are prisoners on my hands, as they should have been shot on the spot." After all, everyone knew the code for reporting the shooting of guerrilla prisoners. Thus, for example, Union captain Thomas Thomas reported from the Ozarks in 1864 about the fate of two "notorious" bushwhackers, John Rustin and John Inman: "On the march to camp the prisoners attempted to make their escape by running, and were both instantly killed."[37]

The execution of guerrilla captives, while it reflected a radically different threshold of violence from the one that pertained in most places during the war, was not unprecedented historically, either in the American experience or more generally. Union officers educated in military history were well aware that Napoleon had treated guerrillas with extreme ruthlessness, particularly in Spain, where local men took to the hills in support of the English forces who were fighting the French invasion. When he justified countering butchery with butchery, thereby going contrary to the rules of civilized warfare he had been taught at West Point, General Curtis noted, "Brigands have no rights, and Napoleon had them shot down by regiments." If communities sheltered guerrillas, he insisted, they should be sacked and burned. "It is time that communities in this country understood that such breaches of public confidence are to be followed by such terrible consequences as to deter the people from their repetition. We must end the war as we go, either by parole or devastation; and where paroles are rendered useless the alternative is a terrible military necessity."

Francis Lieber, the German American scholar who was responsible for creating General Orders No. 100, intended it as an anti-guerrilla policy that would set ethical and legal limits to the unbridled slaughter of enemy guerrillas, lest the Union soldiers become terrorists themselves. General Orders No. 100 noted that Napoleon "frequently substituted the harshest violence for martial usages." While adapting Napoleon's policy, arguing that captured guerrillas were "brigands" who merited execution, Lieber remained disturbed that such a draconian policy lay outside the controlling spirit of any legal framework for delimiting military behavior. He believed that Napoleon "frequently substituted the harshest violence for [legitimate] martial usage." It was as if Lieber knew that executing guerrillas without due process amounted to the state sponsorship of retaliatory terrorism—war crimes. He realized, as Curtis did in a very different way, that executing guerrillas almost certainly would include killing their male civilian supporters. Though he wanted to discipline the Union Army to execute only the guilty, only actual fighters, the problem with General Orders No. 100 was that there was no clear line between guilty and innocent enemies, as all looked exactly alike.[38] Official appeals to constraint proved to be of limited application in the killing fields where guerrillas operated.

Such moral queasiness as Lieber expressed (and that Curtis denied) had not characterized the homegrown guerrillas who had been part of the American army that had fought the Indians ever since colonial times, hit-and-run warriors of the first order. Neither side in that protracted if episodic struggle took prisoners, and neither distinguished very regularly between fighter and civilian, even between men and women and children.

This martial tradition was at hand to help instruct Union officers in how to fight another stealthy enemy. General George Crook, a noted Indian fighter before and after the war, clearly made this connection when he published his autobiography twenty years after the Civil War. An 1852 West Point graduate, he had commanded troops in the late 1850s during the Rogue River and Yakima wars in the Pacific Northwest. In the fall of 1861 he took over command of the anti-guerrilla struggle in central West Virginia. "The question was how to get rid of [the bushwhackers]," Crook later recalled. "Being fresh from the Indian country, where I had more or less experience with that kind of warfare, I set to work organizing for the task. I selected some of the most apt officers, and scattered them through the country to learn it and all the people in it, and particularly the bushwhackers, their haunts, etc." Then the hunt began in earnest. "When an officer returned from a scout he would report that they had caught so-and-so, but in bringing him in he slipped off a log while crossing a stream, or that he was killed by an accidental discharge of one of the men's guns, and many like reports. But they never brought back any more prisoners," Crook concluded approvingly. That was the way it had been when fighting the Yakima, and the system was readily adaptable to fighting thugs in the mountains of West Virginia. Of course, this stance assumed that because guerrillas were the same as "savages" in Crook's conceptualization, there was no moral problem in fighting terror with terror.[39] Crook's ethical system led him to veto General Orders No. 100 in practice. He had no problem with fighting a different war by standards that would have been illegal in conventional warfare, a distinction he understood clearly.

Guerrillas were furtive warriors lurking within a civilian population. They fought outside any regular command structure in temporary and self-constituted bands and then melted back into the general civilian population. Therefore, anti-guerrilla fighters had no ready means to distinguish civilians from guerrillas, and they knew that many of those so-called civilians supported the guerrillas in ways that put their own lives at risk. Only Solomon could have told an active guerrilla from a civilian, and when the atmosphere reeked of lethality it was plausible—and easiest—to conclude that all civilians were at least potential enemies deserving to be killed. Many acted on that premise, but others held back, not wanting to turn their war against the innocent, a separation they needed to maintain lest they see the whole world (perhaps including themselves) as evil. And at least among the organized military, it would be impossible to license the killing of every suspect—after all, the Union was fighting in the name of maintaining and extending liberty, not destroying it, even when extirpating enemy devils.

Thus in General Orders No. 100, when the Union authorities sanctioned the summary execution of guerrillas, they also made it clear that there were legal (and moral) limits to attacking civilians. "Military oppression is not martial law," the orders philosophized; "it is the abuse of the power which that law confers." Sheer tyranny was impermissible. "For the very reason that [the soldier] possesses the power of arms against the unarmed," he had to remain "strictly guided by the principles of justice, honor and humanity," rather than by "cruelty." For "peace is [the] normal condition; war is the exception. The ultimate object of all modern war is a renewed state of peace." The writers of these orders wanted to believe that "civilization had advanced" beyond the lex talionis to warfare that demanded just treatment of civilians, even enemy noncombatants.[40]

But how, to repeat, could one distinguish innocent civilian from guilty guerrilla in a conflict built on the intentional blurring of just those identities? Frightened and furious men in the field had to act as clearheadedly as they could, but their instincts told them to shoot first and cover up afterward. They knew the formula about shooting the enemy while he was attempting to escape, and they usually believed that they could get away with reporting any dead male as a guerrilla as guerrillas wore no uniforms. And of course dead men could tell no tales. Given the dynamics of confronting such enemies, guerrilla warfare always tended toward escalating terror.

One counterexample to this rule of reportage, an exception that also demonstrated that officers in organized armies could not appear to license simply killing everyone, came in the experience of Captain John D. Meredith, who was hunting guerrillas along the Missouri River in March 1865. Meredith sent out a five-man party disguised as guerrillas, and they asked a local farmer named Graves which side he was on. Graves said he had "always been a Southern man, and that he had had no cause to change his principles." Asked whether he would report guerrillas to Union authorities, Graves answered, "I would not report on anyone." Although this answer was ambiguous, implying that Graves also would not report on Union activities to guerrillas, when Meredith arrived with his platoon, after listening to the report of his spies, he concluded that Graves was a "quiet, determined, and dangerous man; a man of some influence and one who could and would do more harm by his acquiescence and aid (unarmed though he was) than if he were in the bush with his revolvers belted around him." Meredith executed Graves on the spot. Then he made the singularly obtuse mistake of telling the truth about the incident in his report. His commander, General Clinton B. Fisk, told him not to report on the incident to him, "and he therefore he does not know what I did," Meredith wrote when his report was passed up the chain of command. Meredith did not fully realize the implications of reporting—without using the appropriate lies to disguise his action—that he had executed an unarmed civilian on suspicion alone. Therefore he fell into the camp of tyrants, by the definition of General Orders No. 100. Fisk passed Meredith's report to his superior, General Grenville M. Dodge, agreeing that Graves was "the devil himself," while insisting, "No order for the . . . killing of an unarmed citizen ever emanated from my headquarters." Meredith was lightly reprimanded, but his honesty under the circumstances and the response to it indicated that the Union command wanted to maintain a fictive distinction between innocent civilian and guilty guerrilla, at least when it came time to rationalize and publicize what its soldiers had done. Fisk had told Meredith to fight with gloves off, and there was almost certainly considerable merit in Meredith's analysis of this enemy civilian, but Meredith lacked the finesse to know how to pretend that the gloves of civilization had remained on even when he was fighting a dirty war. Of course, such circumlocutions made no difference to Graves or, for that matter, to all the other men reported shot while attempting to escape. But the highly convenient lies reinforced the abstract ideology of guerrilla warfare and placed it within legal and moral limits, helping to cleanse the records and the consciences of the military commanders. They knew the distinctions between legal and illegal war, vigorous action and criminal behavior, war and terrorism.[41]

Yet, as Samuel Curtis insisted they must, whatever their understanding of conventional military constraints, anti-guerrilla units had to return "horrors" to the enemy's "butchery," and this made all of them terrorists in Curtis's estimation. This problem sometimes led soldiers to have moral reservations, often more intuitive than explicitly stated, which provided some curb to the endless slaughter, a standing back that could characterize the guerrillas, too, even in Lawrence, as we have seen. Nevertheless, fighters on both sides most often ignored such doubts in the heat of direct and lethal action. Indeed, given the reciprocal nature of guerrilla warfare, each action grew from a desire to avenge previous actions by the enemy against one's brother fighter. In the case of Joe Hart, an eighteen-year-old guerrilla chieftain in northwest Missouri until he was killed in July 1863, slaughter offered vengeance for the killing of his brother John. He proudly wrote to his mother (in a letter found in his pocket after he was shot) that he had avenged John's death by executing three Yankees, and he was now embarked on a career of vengeance that would make him infamous. "I am going to . . . kill off Andrew County—every last devil and they know it. You bet they fly where they hear of me up here—they say I am a damned sight worse than Quantrill."[42]

Fighters on both sides not only sought to avenge the execution of their comrades and the burning out of their civilian supporters, they also wanted to get even for the mutilation of the bodies of their fallen comrades, a desecration performed with the intention of driving them mad. Thus, Sergeant John Thomas Booth, from Ohio, wrote of an atrocity in West Virginia, news of which had spread throughout his regiment. His unit had come across a murdered Federal soldier, "his abdomen . . . ripped open, his bowels extricated, his head severed from his body and placed all gashed and bleeding in the cavity." At Centralia, Missouri, on September 29, 1864, "Bloody Bill"

Anderson's guerrilla squadron hauled twenty-four men off a train and executed them at trackside. Of these, Colonel Daniel Draper reported, most "were beaten over the head, seventeen were scalped, and one had his privates cut off and placed in his mouth. Every man was shot in the head. One man had his nose cut off." Anderson and other guerrillas made it a practice to weave the scalps of their slain enemies into their horses' bridles; the Union troops discovered this when they shot the raiders in return. In certain areas at least, mutilation of executed enemies became the norm, a demonstration that what was most forbidden for conventional soldiers had become standard practice for these warrior-criminals. As the Union won the war and kept the records, less is known of atrocities on the Federal side, but it is likely that this form of vengeance recurred on both sides in a circle of terror.[43]

Vengeance could lead to public exaltation. In 1863, when Alfred Bolan, a guerrilla chieftain in southeastern Missouri who bragged that he had shot forty Union men, was killed in turn, his body was brought to the city hall of the nearest town and put on display. Timothy Phillips, an Iowa private, wrote in his diary about seeing the body: "I went to see the murdered murderer. His hair was all matted with blood and clotted over his face, rendering him an object of disgust and horror. Yet there were hundreds who were acquainted with him and had many reasons to rejoice at his death. There had perished a monster, a man of blood, of every crime, who had no mercy for others and had died a death of violence, and today hundreds gaze upon his unnatural carcass and exult that his prowess is at an end."[44] In peacetime, as Phillips and all those present knew, a dead body would be washed and laid out with dignity: this odious wartime display was the opposite of such respect.

Submerged in the terrors of guerrilla war, combatants sought release in the annihilation of the very face of the other, the obliteration of the temple of his body, which carried his soul. This was a spontaneous form of religious worship, service to the God of Good by enacting total vengeance against the countenance of the Evil One. In a sense, such worship amounted to Manichaeism—a dualistic heresy implicit in Christianity in which the devil is the other God and the world is divided between equal forces of light and dark. Slaying the servant of the devil and rejoicing over his mutilated carcass could serve to bind the threatened servants of the true God together.[45]

This religiously tinctured thirst for vengeance colored every action and every justification fighters made. And yet these reprisals were political, not just personal retaliation. Pro-Confederate guerrillas believed they were fighting for their new nation. Many of them came from slaveholding families and were defending the peculiar institution, although few made that ideological point explicitly. One who did was S. Cockerill, who wrote to the Union commander pursuing him that he was fighting to protest the burning out, exiling, and killing of "defenseless men . . . for no other cause than being opposed to the negro-thieving policy of the Administration." But more were like Bloody Bill Anderson, who wrote to the citizens of Lexington, Missouri, that he had led his ruthless band in a policy of terror because Unionists had killed his father and his sister. "I have fully glutted my vengeance. . . . I have tried to war with the Federals honorably, but for retaliation I have done [fearful] things [to] let the Federals know that Missouri's sons will not be trampled on." Of course, Missouri's particular right that ought not be trampled on was the right to own slaves, and Anderson encoded that politics in his message, but his animating passion in fighting was to gain revenge against enemies who held antislavery views and were out to kill him. He intentionally crossed into what he knew were war crimes for political reasons.[46]

Facing a firing squad on May 20, 1864, William Francis Hadly laid out the most common reason for southern guerrilla military and political behavior explicitly: "I went into the war to be a terror to the Feds. No man in this country has done more than I have. I went in to rob and steal without regard to law. I thought the South had her rights trampled upon. I am now sentenced to be shot. But I feel I have been fully revenged."[47] Vengeance justified war crimes, the face of terrorism in the guerrilla war.

When confronting their enemies in hostile territory, Union troops believed they were dealing with an alien and degraded race. They contrasted the values of those they called the Butternuts from the upper South—poor whites who stained their homespun clothing with dye made from butternut bark—to the far more "evolved" and superior culture of the North. Sergeant Webster Moses from Minnesota wrote in his diary about the citizens of Clinton, Missouri, a town his unit had just destroyed: "The inhabitants here are most all very ignorant and consequently Secesh. . . . The curse of slavery is visible. Business has been neglected and houses are going to decay. They need a little Yankee enterprise here. Many of the male inhabitants spend their time either in card playing or loafing around the public well." Slavery was felt to deepen the degradation of the inferior culture, for it was tied to sloth—using slaves demeaned the value of labor. Private Stanley E. Lathrop from the 1st Wisconsin Cavalry drew the same conclusion about the way slavery ruined white people. "The people live almost exclusively on 'corn dodgers' and 'bacon' or smoked hog. They are as a class rather under the common standard of intelligence, while the slaves seem to be quite intelligent. As one of the boys said the other day—'I was in favor of abolishing slavery before I came here, but now I am more so than ever, when I see that the niggers know more than their masters.'" This was a backhanded form of abolitionism, expressing more contempt for the master class and poor whites than compassion for the slaves. There but for a free society goes all white labor, including mine, they seemed to be saying.[48]

At times, cultural contempt could lead to reformist impulses. When the 1st Wisconsin Cavalry spent the Fourth of July 1862, relatively early in the war, in a (to them) dreadful Missouri town, Colonel Edward Daniels threw a huge picnic and gave a rousing patriotic speech, arguing that "the great reason for their being so many [Secesh] in Missouri—and indeed the great reason of the whole rebellion is—IGNORANCE. . . . Very few of [you] think for [your]-selves, and demagogues and secession leaders befooled [you] with such talk as an educated class of people would never believe. . . . *Educate your children.*" After this speech, one of Daniels's admiring men reported, twelve hundred civilian men took the oath of allegiance. In this manner Union soldiers applied their beliefs about American liberty and independence to the degraded southern enemy. Obviously a well-educated citizenry of free and equal men working for their own advancement was the key to progress. Southerners threatened every element of that ideology—they might pull down the entire nation with them, and therefore they had to be not only beaten in war but also fundamentally reeducated.[49]

Yet living under the reign of terror, most Union soldiers dropped any reformist impulses they may have felt and concentrated on the obliteration of the alien others. In 1863, Iowa lieutenant Richard J. Mohr wrote to his sweetheart about anti-guerrilla warfare in southeastern Missouri. "If I had my way I would devastate the whole region and shoot every man I caught running from the flames of the burning homes. Do you think I am cruel? If you would do picket duty by standing for twenty-four hours in a cold rain[,] . . . stand by the bunk of a dear comrade and listen to his dying groans as his shattered bones pain him for the last time[,] . . . and then reflect on the fact that these villains are the cause of it all, I think that you would feel just as I do now." Although Lieutenant Mohr did not appear to have acted on his impulses at that juncture in the conflict, he may have done so at another time, and other Union troops certainly acted on theirs. The thirst for revenge was clear in the reactions of Union soldiers to prisoners whom their comrades had not, for whatever reason, shot on the spot. A Kansas cavalryman wrote in his diary one day that when "five bushwhackers were . . . captured and executed in front of the Court House, the youngest boys of our company volunteered for the job of execution and burial." This seemed to have been a rite of blood initiation into anti-guerrilla fighting. Similarly, a Kansas sergeant reported in 1864 from Lexington, Missouri, about "capturing a few Rebs in blue uniforms [who] were next morning hung and shot both at the same time." This overkill was reflected in orders given by General Clinton B. Fisk, also in 1864: "Try the bushwhacker by drumhead count-martial tonight, and let every soldier in Macon shoot him if he is guilty, as he doubtless is." Such vengeance was a form of collective mutilation, encouraging every soldier in the unit to gain his measure of pleasure from destroying the enemy. Because guerrillas still in the bush would hear about them, brutal executions were intended to have a chilling general effect as well as giving Union soldiers a release through destruction. This escalating brutality demonstrated that war crimes of a kind rarely practiced, much less celebrated, on the conventional Civil War battlegrounds had become what before the war all the combatants would have considered be un-American, unchristian, immoral acts—except when practiced against enemies of other races.[50]

Far from criticizing such terrorist acts or even being shocked by them, Union noncombatants supported the troops who thus acted out retribution for the suffering of civilians like themselves. Even at the beginning of the war, Union supporters in affected areas underwent a rapid resocialization from compassion to destructiveness. Along the Kansas border, Henry Miles Moore, a Leavenworth lawyer of New York origins, wrote concerning marauding Missouri guerrillas: "Fiends in human shape who would be guilty of such cowardly & blatant acts should be *burned at the stake,* hanging is too good for them." On January 2, 1862, visiting the most notoriously terrorist Kansas regiment, led by Colonel Charles R. Jennison, the Kansas politician John J. Ingalls wrote to his brother, "If there ever was a band of destroying angels in one congregation I saw them here. They take no prisoners and are not troubled with red tape sentimentalism in any form."[51]

Governor Ingalls reformulated his Judeo-Christian values to sanction terrorism against the terrorist enemy. Or perhaps more accurately, he deployed that version of those values in service to a God of War—if peacefulness and the Golden Rule formed the benevolent side of his ethical framework during peacetime, obliterating the subhuman enemy population during war constituted the equally available dark side. In the Crusader-like regime of terrorist Christianity, Christ was best worshiped by avenging angels. The diary of the devout Connecticut Congregationalist Sergeant Sherman Bodwell of the 11th Kansas Cavalry demonstrates just how clearly the most violent terrorist ends could be constructed as service to God's good.

Bodwell felt a deep obligation to witness his faith by serving the good Union people his unit encountered deep within Missouri guerrilla country, and he entered such thoughts and the emotions that accompanied his actions into a diary he kept during the war. Stationed in Jackson, near the Kansas border, in the summer of 1862, Bodwell ran a Sunday school to teach literacy and the Bible to black children. On July 4 his regiment attended a banquet, the offering "of the kindly colored friends of Independence. . . . The colored people seemed very intelligent, and glad to be able to do such a kindness." If in somewhat paternalistic fashion, Bodwell was one of the few racial liberals in that Kansas regiment. The banquet "will have I think a good effect upon our few 'negro haters' who by the way were not slow to enjoy it." Bodwell wanted to further the abolitionist ends of the Union effort, and, unlike most Union troops, he was even concerned about racial justice for African Americans.

But when it came to the Confederate enemy, civilian and guerrilla alike, Bodwell took his task to be purifying destructiveness. When, for example, three Union families that had been burned out by guerrillas in the middle of the night, "not giving the women and children time to dress even," appealed to his regiment for help, "we made arrangements to outfit them at the expense of the secesh about [in the area]," Bodwell wrote, not mentioning the means they used to do so. On another occasion on July 13, 1863, Bodwell's unit heard that the Widow Holly had spied on his regiment for the guerrillas. "That amiable lady," had gone off to a nearby town "on a sympathizing expedition," Bodwell recorded in his diary. "We put fire to her house. . . . She probably knew better how to sympathize on her return and having no home will be able to devote more time to carrying the news." Just down the way from the Holly house, Bodwell's men found "strong indications" of a guerrilla encampment at the Alderman farm. "Alderman taken to one side to *examine* as to bushwhackers whereabouts, he attempted to escape, and was killed by R. Heard. Capt. Harry tells the wife of his death. She showing no feeling but a little more anger, and the children none at all." Rather than responding to Mrs. Alderman and her children as human beings who had been shocked into numbness by the execution of their husband and father, Bodwell took their apparent absence of emotion as an indicator that the Aldermans belonged to an inferior race completely lacking in Christian compassion, for whom any punishment was fitting in service to higher ends. Bodwell entirely erased the line between punishment due soldiers and that due civilians in his mode of warfare: all previously forbidden acts of destructiveness now were licensed. He burned and killed on uncorroborated suspicion and celebrated himself as an avenging angel: righteous slaughter had displaced Christian forbearance and love of one's fellow man.

In Bodwell's eyes, when they took to the bush, enemy men became furtive and terrorizing animals. On October 4, 1863, Bodwell's regiment came upon a recently deserted guerrilla camp along a wooded ravine. There they saw a Union corpse swinging by a rope fastened to a tree branch, a note pinned on it that read, "This man was hung last evening, in revenge for the death of Ab Haller. He says that his name is Thomas and that he belongs to the Kansas 7th." The camp seemed to be the creation of hellish creatures, Bodwell felt: "There seems to be something of the deathlike brooding over these camps. Always hidden where hardly more than a horse track points the way, in heavy timber and creek bottoms, offal lying about, cooking utensils, cast off clothing. . . . The very air seems thick with the clime with which so lately they seethed."

Enraged when he saw such evidence littered by fiends who were locked in lethal combat with his own noble Union forces, Bodwell took satisfaction from hunting down and executing every guerrilla his unit uncovered. On September 26, a week before coming upon the fetid encampment decorated by the executed comrade in arms, Bodwell reported that his outfit had gone on a guerrilla hunt. They had flushed out a small enemy band, shot their horses, and then taken off after them on foot. "The race lasted for about $\frac{3}{4}$ of a mile, the boys firing after them as they ran, Lt. R[eese] finally bringing down that last. I came up, just as the Lt. finished him with a shot through the head. Took supper and moved on." If there was something matter-of-fact about this report, five days later Bodwell took the trouble to record in great detail his participation in such killings. This time the regiment's major "brought him down" from his horse with a pistol shot. Lieutenant Reese then asked, "Are you through with him & Major nodded assent." As the others mounted and rode off, Bodwell lingered while Reese "aimed and fired, a revolver ball striking just back of the eye & he was with his judge with all his imperfections on his head." Clearly believing that this nameless and faceless enemy was headed to hell, Bodwell was sorry that he had not been able to look at him at the moment of his execution, but Reese was standing in the way as he shot. Fascinated by the mortal moment, Bodwell asked Reese to describe it. "Lt. says he intentionally raised his hand to protect himself and an ashy paleness overspread his face, as when a cloud passes over the sun." Clearly, Bodwell inferred that this had portended the downward flight of a condemned soul. Presumably if he had been heaven bound, the man on the ground would have glowed with his imminent deliverance, but that he and all his kind were damned was evidenced by that ashy paleness.

This was the same hyper-militant abolitionist ideological terrain John Brown had plowed before the Civil War. As had Brown, Bodwell separated terrorist means from holy goals, the better to practice his atrocities with the conviction that he was divinely sanctioned, that his terrorism destroyed human evil and served Christian truth. So convinced was Bodwell of his Christian mission to obliterate the devil that he evidently felt no more guilt or moral reservation about his murderous deeds than had Brown. Blood-soaked purging of the land of evil others was both a political and a moral goal. Not only could he successfully separate his avenging self from his loving one, he could find inner means to gain conviction that the one served the other as an acting out of God's will through his human agent. Terror was the portion of God's enemies, the children of Satan. In his last diary entry, on September 20, 1865 (the day he was mustered out of the army), Bodwell wrote that although he himself might have faltered, the God of Love had never deserted him. "So ends my service, in all three and a half years filled with tokens of loving kindness of Him who granted me the privilege of standing in my lot . . . on every march and in every engagement. [For] the loving, comforting, strengthening of the Holy Spirit, even when I have been most unfaithful and forgetful of my Christian obligation, I can never, I feel, be grateful enough."[52]

Under the stresses of guerrilla war, Christianity could be re-envisioned as a (self-) righteous system for engaging in acts of terrorism without losing one's humanity. By making of the enemy a deeply threatening species of subhuman who deserved obliteration, one could feel oneself to be a child of God even as one committed atrocities.

Although Bodwell provided himself with comforting religious justifications for any wrongs he might have committed, others developed doubts about the righteousness of their ways, though sometimes only later, when they sorted through their memories of war. Speaking in his native Minneapolis in 1886, twenty-one years after he left his command in the southwest corner of Missouri, General John B. Sanborn tried to analyze the debacle he had contributed to when he had fought terrorism with terrorism. By 1864, in the five counties under his jurisdiction the population had dropped from an average of 6,500 per county to about 300. It was clear to Sanborn what had brought about the depopulation: "During one week a Confederate force would pass through the country for a hundred miles or more and burn the houses and destroy the property of every loyal man, and before my arrival [on January 1, 1865] the Federal forces would soon go over the same section of the country and destroy the houses and property of all the disloyal." Calling off further Federal search-and-destroy operations when he took charge, Sanborn nevertheless accelerated the depopulation by banishing 150 suspected Confederate families. In 1886, speaking in retrospect, Sanborn tried to figure out what had gone wrong, and he did not flinch from self-criticism. Thinking back, he no longer considered the Missouri Confederates vulgar low-down no-accounts who deserved death. Rather, he now believed they had been typical American Christians who had turned ruthlessly destructive when their society had been visited with prolonged terror. "If there is anything of value to a future age to be learned" from such terrorist warfare in the American heartland, Sanborn now believed, "it is that there exists in the breasts of people of educated and Christian communities wild and ferocious passions, which in a day of peace are dormant and slumbering, but which may be aroused and kindled by . . . war and injustice, and become more cruel and destructive than any that live in the breasts of savage and barbarous nations."

It was the core American principle of liberty and justice for all that had been violated by both opposing armies, along with Christian forbearance and fellow-feeling, Sanborn reasoned: with these deeply cherished values suddenly overturned, the thirst for vengeance against fundamental social wrongs was no longer bounded by their restraints. Previously civilized men had fought to the death when the "elements of justice implanted in [their] bosoms" were violated, most especially by "the putting to death of innocent men for the offense of another man." It did not matter whether it was the disorganized guerrillas or an army "authorized by . . . government" that had done the killing. By falling in love with force, warriors had become false gods in themselves. Both sides had shared in hateful and sustained guerrilla terrorism, pushing their land into an endless and cycle of mutual retaliation. Under the duress of such attacks, "human nature itself [had burst into] open opposition to such an exercise of Tyranny, [and against] the introduction of the reign of chaos." Both republican and Christian values had collapsed, Sanborn concluded, because the destroyers on both sides had refused to heed the words of King David: "He that ruleth over men must be just, ruling in the fear of God."[53]

On April 14, 1865, just five days after Robert E. Lee signed the surrender for the Army of Northern Virginia, John Wilkes Booth assassinated Abraham

Lincoln, committing the first counterrevolutionary terrorist act in the long southern white-supremacist war against Reconstruction and racial equality. Even as the Confederacy lay in smoking ruins under the military rule of the triumphant Union, southern whites began resisting that conquest and any suggestion that race relations should fundamentally alter. Slavery was abolished—the Civil War established that fact—but Booth's act betokened alternative modes of racial domination that were to triumph for nearly a century.

Motivated by virulent racism and hatred for the conquering government that planned to obliterate white southern self-rule, Booth, a Shakespearean actor from a famous family of thespians, was also driven by a compulsion to perform grandly as a romantic hero, obliterating tyranny in the name of a higher freedom. As he was himself aware, his desire to enact an anarchy of the deed in order to change the course of American history made Booth the direct descendent of John Brown.

After the Harpers Ferry raid, not wanting to miss the grand show of Brown's execution, Booth had managed to don a uniform and infiltrate the Virginia Grays, who stood guard while Brown was hanged. At first, he wrote, "I looked at the traitor and terrorizer with unlimited, undeniable contempt." And yet he had to admit that he also pitied Brown, standing alone on the scaffold. "He was a brave old man," he wrote to his sister; "his heart must have broken when he felt himself deserted."

Remaining in the North during the war, Booth, a white supremacist who openly detested the Union war effort, served as the leader of a circle of Confederate spies. When Lincoln was nearing reelection in the fall of 1864, Booth's contempt for the man and everything the triumphant Union would impose on southern whites led him to begin planning the assassination: in this frame of mind, John Brown, whose abolitionist principles he despised, nevertheless served as a great inspiration. Lincoln was just a "sectional candidate," Booth wrote his sister, a "low" and "vulgar" man of ill breeding who, if reelected, would be transformed into a "king" tyrannizing over the supine South. "He is made the tool of the North, to crush out, or try to crush out slavery, by robbery, rapine, slaughter and bought armies. He is walking in the footprints of old John Brown, but no more fit to stand with that great hero—Great God! No. John Brown was a man inspired, the grandest man of this century." If he still hated Brown's goals, Booth admired and emulated Brown as a man of violent and highly politicized action, a model terrorist he could emulate in performing a grand terrorist act that would set off resistance to Union rule. By contrast, Lincoln "is Bonaparte in one great move, that is, by overturning this blind Republic and making himself a king."

After Lincoln's reelection, Booth believed he was ordained to destroy the Republican monster for his treason against natural justice. "The South can make no choice. It is either extermination or slavery for *themselves* (worse than death), to draw from. I would know my choice." Right before he killed Lincoln, Booth declared that Union victory had left him "supremely unhappy with history itself." He had to do something "great and decisive," to strike at tyranny by killing its leader.[54]

Although some southerners regretted the killing of an enemy leader they believed might prove magnanimous, many others, particularly women of the planter class, rejoiced in Booth's act, coming as it did hard on the heels of Lee's humiliation at Appomattox. Several wrote that they found the news "cheering." "Hurrah!" the South Carolinian Emma LeConte responded. "Old Abe Lincoln has been assassinated! It may be abstractly wrong to be so jubilant but I just can't help it—After all the heaviness and gloom of yesterday this blow to our enemies comes like a gleam of light. [I now have] thought with exultation of the howl it had . . . sent through the North and how it would cast a damper on their rejoicings over the fall of our noble Lee." LeConte regarded Booth's act as a sign of better days to come and the enactment of God's truth. Our "hated enemy has met the just reward of his life. . . . Could there have been a fitter death for such a man!" Loula Kendall Rogers believed that "the tyrant Lincoln's death" was "retribution from the hand of an all powerful God." Booth had performed "the boldest [act] I ever heard of in fact or fiction."[55]

This last terrorist act of the Civil War, the first act of terrorist resistance to Reconstruction, demonstrated the continuity of systematic political violence used to enforce white domination of African Americans during two hundred years of slavery in the past and a hundred years of segregation to come. White hegemony would once again demand terrorist means.

CHAPTER 3

Blood Redemption
The Counterrevolutionary White-Terrorist Destruction of Reconstruction

3:oo A.M., September 6, 1875, Clinton, Mississippi. Alzina Haffa and her husband, William, a white Republican activist, were startled from sleep by a mob of about seventy-five men on horseback who had surrounded their house. Several men then broke down their door and burst in. When Alzina screamed, "Murder! Murder!" so loudly she could be heard two miles away, one of the mob leaders, Mr. Mosley, who was the local sales agent of the Singer Sewing Machine Company, held a pistol to her head and then choked her, though not to death. Then the Haffas' landlord, Sid Whitehead, and his son Jimmy shot William Haffa. After that the mob departed. Alzina and her daughter Florence helped William to his bed. As the day dawned, William said, "Mama, I want water," and some black friends, the Stevenses, came over to help. Sid Whitehead returned to the Haffa home and told Alzina she could not fetch a physician, saying contemptuously that her husband would die anyway. William then said, " 'Mama, I am going to die,' and he asked God to have mercy on his soul, and he laid his head on my shoulder and expired," Alzina later recalled.

That night, the Whiteheads and many of the men returned, "looking like hungry wolves," according to Alzina Haffa. Chasing away the Stevenses, they sat down to drink and curse their enemies. "They said that they were fully armed now and would show the niggers and the northern people who helped them that they would rule and do what they pleased with them." They refused to allow Alzina Haffa to buy a coffin in which to bury her husband, compelling Alzina and Florence to wrap him in a sheet, cram him into a rude box, and dig his grave. The marauders also denied William a Christian burial with a congregation of the Haffas' black friends, the only friends they had, and desecrated his corpse. At the same time several of the men went over to the Stevens house, took the father and son down the road, stood them on a tree stump, and shot them. Over the following few days the mob disarmed all the black people in the area, forced them to disband their Republican club, pinned red ribbons on them, and compelled them to march in a Democratic club parade. (For decades after the Civil War the Republicans were the more progressive, interracial party, the Democrats the bastion of traditional white supremacists.)

Five years earlier the Haffas had come down from Philadelphia to farm. William soon became involved in local politics, teaching school to black children and running successfully for local magistrate. For these activities the Haffas were ostracized by the local white community, a number of whom frequently threatened them. One Saturday afternoon in 1873, several of the local white leaders led by one Frank Bush had come by the Haffa house, seized William, and lashed him bloody with a rawhide whip as well as violently throwing Alzina against the doorframe of her house. "You have got no business to be down here among such an illiterate class of people," they said as they were whipping William. "We will show you what southern blood is." Two years later they finished their demonstration.[1]

At the same time that the Mosley-Whitehead crew was killing William Haffa, carpetbagger Republican and friend to black people, other armed men were searching for his friend, State Senator Charles Caldwell, a leading figure in the black community of Mississippi. When Caldwell's wife, Margaret Ann, told Mr. Tinney, a local white Democratic leader she knew well, that her husband was gone—fled to the relative safety of nearby Jackson, the state capital, where the government was in Republican hands—Tinney told her, "Tell him when you see him that we are going to kill him anyhow. We have orders to kill him, and we are going to do it. . . . Any man that sticks by the republican party and is a leader, he has got to die."

Four months later, after he had returned home for Christmas, Caldwell was walking to town when a friendly old white acquaintance, Buck Cabell, stopped him and insisted that they share a drink. Caldwell declined, saying he did not want to celebrate Christmas in that way, but Cabell insisted, "You must take a drink with me." He took Caldwell by the arm and led him down the stairs into the basement of a local store. Just as they tapped glasses in a Christmas toast, the prearranged signal, someone shot through a window, knocking Caldwell to the ground. Caldwell's professed white friends, the storekeeper Chilton, Judge Cabinis, and Preacher Nelson, three pillars of the white community, gathered outside the store along with a considerable crowd. "Take me out of the cellar, I don't want to die like a dog," Caldwell pleaded, begging to be taken home to see his wife before he died, but the mob refused. Caldwell said, "Remember when you kill me you kill a gentleman and a brave man. Never say you killed a coward." Preacher Nelson carried him up from the cellar and dropped him in the middle of the street, and then all the men shouted, "We will save him while we got him; dead men tell no tales," while they riddled him with thirty or forty bullets. At about the same time someone killed Mrs. Caldwell's brother Sam on a nearby street, shooting him off his horse with a bullet through the head.

That afternoon, a newly arrived trainload of white paramilitarists from Vicksburg marched into the Caldwell house, where Charles Caldwell's body and that of his brother-in-law had been brought, and barged into the parlor where several of their African American friends had gathered. Making as public a tumult as possible, the widow later recalled, "they cursed them, those dead bodies, there, and they danced and threw open the window and sung all their songs and they carried on like a parcel of wild Indians over those dead bodies. Some even struck [the bodies] and challenged them to get up and fight. . . . Then they said they could not stay any longer."

The next day, Judge Cabinis came by and with great paternalistic warmth asked the widow whether there was anything he could do for her family, claiming that he had done everything he could for her husband but that those wild men could not be stopped and he was now "crazy" with grief over the killing. Margaret Ann Caldwell replied to the judge that she had seen him standing in the crowd that killed her husband. She told him, "Judge, you have already done too much for me"; "I don't want any part of your friendship."[2]

The leaders of the white South called themselves Redeemers when they organized as white-supremacist state parties, dedicated to the abolishment of Reconstruction, the Republican attempt to reform the South by guaranteeing civil and political rights for African Americans. They succeeded. They saw their activities as more than just a political strategy. The redemption they intended was a moral and religious revival of the southern white "nation" as well as a political conquest: they intended to preside over the rebirth of a sacred white community with a blood ritual—the spilling of as much blood as it would take to seize control of their states by destroying the political viability of their hated opponents. In most places, the Redeemers used terrorist campaigns to seize state power, similar in many ways to the recent Bosnian Serbian paramilitary campaigns that the rest of the world has defined as terrorism and war crimes.

When seizing power, Redeemers acted as preemptive reactionary counterrevolutionaries. Although Reconstruction was a halting and partial experiment in biracial government rather than a reversal from white power to black power, the Redeemers loathed it as an immoral revolutionary movement designed to crush the white race, the natural rulers of the South. They feared all forms of black political participation, seeing it as a precursor of black domination, and they anticipated with intense anxiety a race war initiated by armed and organized blacks. This was the perceived black revolution from which they intended to save their race.

The dreaded black uprising was in fact a self-serving fantasy, as anti-Reconstruction whites retained a near-monopoly of organized force. But as had been the case with anticipated slave revolts before the war, reinforced by recent memories of escaped slaves, armed and in Union uniforms, repeated rumors of black insurrection helped the Redeemers mobilize overwhelming white power. In the Deep South, counterrevolutionary and reactionary white terrorism crushed a revolutionary black terrorism that existed only in the minds of the white community. And the apartheid system the Redeemers created out of this terrorist movement lasted for generations—a racial tribalization that was frequently reinforced by political violence, a long-lasting social ordering that still casts deep shadows on American society.

Redeemers took different paths in each of the southern states, and the timing of their victories varied, although the process was completed everywhere by 1877. Rather than survey this broad regional history, I shall focus on one subgroup, the White Line, which operated in Mississippi in 1875, examining to a lesser extent the Red Shirt revival in South Carolina that triumphed the following year. In these two Deep South states, each of which had a black majority population—in several counties in Mississippi blacks outnumbered whites by as much as nine to one (see map)—the Redeemers were particularly well-organized, deploying violence in a programmatic and explicitly political fashion: the terrorism endemic in all Redeemer member organizations was especially virulent and effective in the blackest parts of the South.

The fates of William Haffa and Charles Caldwell were typical results of the forces that lay at the core of the Redeemer movement in White Line Mississippi. Although such classic terrorist violence did not occur everywhere or at all times, it was consciously used as often and as powerfully as necessary to inspire a level of fear among blacks and their white allies that would make them submit to the resurgent white-supremacist party. Political violence always underlay the more legitimate forms of gaining political power used by

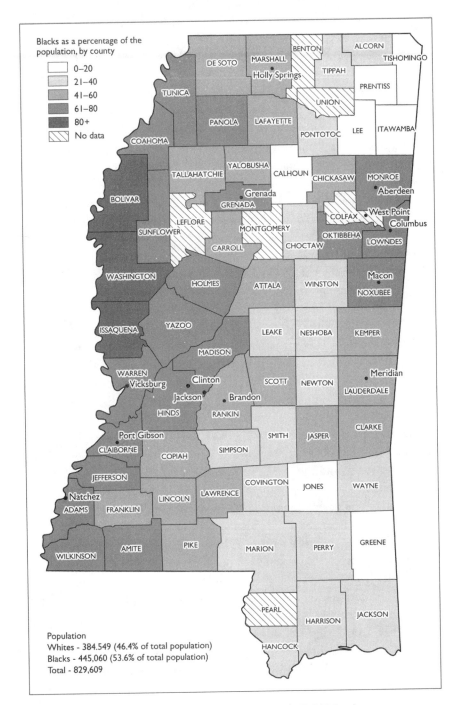

Blacks as a percentage of the population, by county

- ☐ 0–20
- ☐ 21–40
- ☐ 41–60
- ☐ 61–80
- ☐ 80+
- ☐ No data

Population
Whites - 384.549 (46.4% of total population)
Blacks - 445,060 (53.6% of total population)
Total - 829,609

Black and White Population, Mississippi, 1870 (Drawn by Bill Nelson) the Redeemers. Indeed, the motto of the Mississippi movement, "Peaceably if possible; forcibly if necessary," made the threat of political violence perpetually clear to the racial enemy. Violence was not loosed chaotically, nor was it the work of a few lowborn malcontents running wild. To the contrary, its use was strategic, intended as a means to regain unchallenged political domination. Once back in power the Redeemers planned to rule blacks with an iron rod and promote a strong economy in well-ordered work camps—"plantations"—with submissive and apparently content workers kept firmly in their places, much as in the slavery days for which the White Liners yearned.

The Redeemers could be said to have midwifed the rebirth of tried-and-true ideological and paramilitary methods. During the secession crisis of 1859 and 1860, southern whites had rallied their communities behind the race banner. As John Townsend, a previously moderate South Carolina planter and politician had put it, "This Union was formed for the white race, for white men and their posterity." Racial solidarity trumped union as white men rushed into militias. In South Carolina, where white men placed blue cockades in their hats, whites who failed to don the racial badge or to vote for secession were ostracized, and any whites who had the temerity to defend free blacks from attack were banished from the community as subversives. Militias also drove off "vile intruders," as Townsend called them, often innocuous people like Yankee peddlers and schoolteachers—now labeled "foreign . . . enemies [whose] true purpose is to murder, to burn, to ruin"—frequently after beating or tarring and feathering them. There was to be no debate about secession or racial solidarity. As Townsend put it, free white men with families and property and the "sensitive institution" of slavery to defend would not allow themselves to be "tampered with by the crude experiments of a crazy and impracticable [abolitionist] fanaticism." These militias became founding elements of the Confederate Army, and after the war their networks, values, and martial energy remained in ready reserve for future paramilitary and ideological resistance to those who attempted to change the social order. These proto-counterrevolutionary terrorist cells were in their own eyes revolutionaries, but in the political context of their era they were reactionary terrorists.[3]

As they had during the secession crisis, Deep South Redeemers saw themselves as a white-liberation movement, a moral revitalization rather than a political reaction. The red shirts worn as the uniform of the South Carolina Redeemers (replacing the blue cockades) were almost certainly copied from the uniforms of Garibaldi's militia, which had just completed the reunification of Italy through military means. And the slogan of the Mississippi White Liners was apparently first used in 1839 by the most militant, so-called "physical force" faction of the English Chartists, a democratic, populist reform movement. The Hungarian revolutionary Louis Kossuth also used the slogan during his celebrated tour of the United States in 1854, when he attacked European tyrants. Others had used the phrase—including Abraham Lincoln in a discussion about provisioning Fort Sumter in 1861, although the Redeemers probably were not thinking of him when they rallied to secure white supremacy through well-organized political violence.

Liberation meant overthrowing all southern Republican state governments and all significant attempts to construct biracial political organizations at whatever level, including the most local. Although the verbal attacks often focused on such issues as taxation and corruption, those criticisms of southern Republican rule were but surface expressions of hatred for assertive blacks, a people most whites believed were intended by nature to stay subservient to them, and for their white allies, whom the vast majority of whites considered race traitors. That blacks seemed to have escaped their "place" and gained a public, political voice during Reconstruction ran against the deepest beliefs of most southern whites. For them, this elevation implied a terrible reversal of power, in which the natural leaders inevitably would be ruled and ruined by the unfit. The Redeemers would restore the appropriate hierarchy to the social structure, after which the whites would take care of the downtrodden black race once more. But paternalism could be offered only as a free grant from above—whites had a Christian moral obligation to treat blacks well, but blacks had no innate rights. "Redemption" meant a guarantee of the principle of absolute and unquestioned white power, the only political formula from which the group believed peaceful government could flow.

White Line leaders were unapologetic about both their racial beliefs and their terrorist methods. In fact several members shared their ideology quite openly with the subcommittee of U.S. senators sent in 1876 to investigate the events of the previous year. The Senators attended to the political thought, among others, of Reuben Davis of Monroe County in northeastern Mississippi, hard by the Alabama line. Davis, born in 1832, was the leading Democrat in his part of the state and a congressman in Washington before the Civil War, and then had served in the Confederate Congress. Considering himself a conservative rather than a radical, he nevertheless shared a worldview with the most radical White Liners and worked with them as a matter of white solidarity, living comfortably enough with the terrorism his allies enacted.

Asked whether he believed that blacks were a "well-disposed race of people," Davis replied in a biologically determinist mode that harked back to the great chain of being: "I think the world is made of various grades of life. I think the negro is about two degrees below the white man. I think that God put the white man as the last link in the chain." Davis then described his beliefs about the essential black racial character. "I think the negro is by nature dishonest; I think the negro by nature is destitute of all ideas of virtue, and I think the negro is capable of being induced to commit any crime whatsoever, especially if he is encouraged by bad white men." The black man was never the "equal of the white man intellectually or morally. . . . I don't think he can ever be civilized." Asked to define a scalawag (a southern-bred white Republican ally of blacks), Davis responded, "It is a mean, dirty, low white man, who is capable of selling himself and his honor for the sake of having an opportunity to plunder honest men." Carpetbaggers—white men who came south to help blacks—were just as bad; neither were fit members of the white community.

Still, blacks had been "put" in the South, and God must have had some purpose in creating them, Davis believed. It was the white men's "duty to God and to themselves . . . being of a higher order of human nature, to do for the negro all that can be done to elevate him as high in the scale of morals, or civilization and Christianity, as he can be elevated." Davis did not note the contradiction of seeking to elevate a race that was in his opinion incapable of being elevated—it was if he were discussing a race of perpetual moral children. Nevertheless, Davis did all he could to practice what he preached, he insisted to the senators. For example, one time he gave two dollars to a hog thief he had successfully defended in court after the black clerk and black sheriff had turned his loan request down; the black thief had taken the money and gone off without expressing gratitude and, of course, without ever offering to repay his debt. Still and all, Davis concluded with the patience of an exasperated father, "I will defend them today without price and loan them money." As well as being ungrateful, blacks who gained power were "cunning," a much less childlike quality, but Davis still believed it was his Christian duty to help support the black race, whom nature had debased.

Given these beliefs, Davis had joined in the White Line campaign of 1875 and made many speeches around Monroe County. "I said that the colored peoples are banded together in hoops of steel pretty much against the whites [and that] I would see no other remedy only for the whites to band together for their protection . . . but I said the color-line does not mean hostility between the races, but that . . . the white men, having the intellect and the information and the honesty, ought to . . . govern the State for the good of all, and that we desired that the colored people would unite with us."

When it came to allowing black participation even in the most subordinate possible way within the Democratic Party, Davis explained that "my party . . . did not indorse me" but instead overwhelmingly passed a harsh resolution against it at a countywide meeting to which he had submitted and "upon which we made the [electoral] fight." Davis was now behind the times. He was a New Departurist, or "soft-shell," Democrat who hoped to win black voters over his party by forceful persuasion. But the White Liners, who had taken over the Democratic Party by 1874, had moved past the New Departurists to a stance of radical exclusionism. Their resolution stated in part that the Republican Party of Monroe County, "composed . . . of negroes and a few white political adventurers," had refused since 1869 to have friendly relations with "responsible" white leaders. Instead the Republicans had maintained their organization "upon the principles of the black line" and had ruled in an "utterly destructive manner." The race line, first adopted by the black enemy and its scurrilous white allies, had been "forced" upon whites, who therefore were compelled to fight a political race war—they were the victims and black people the victimizers; they were morally obliged to fight for their freedom in self-defense.[4]

Reuben Davis remained actively engaged in the party that drew the race line, with which he agreed, but without any paternalistic softening of the sort that he preferred. And in the heat of the election campaign of 1875, the Democratic press, while reporting white political violence in a highly subdued manner, preached virulent race hatred as the key to the election. On its masthead, the Forest (Miss.) *Register* proclaimed, "A white man in a white man's place. A black man in a black man's place. Each according to the eternal fitness of things." The Yazoo City *Banner* linked white rule not just to the natural biological order but also to divine authority: "Mississippi is a white man's country, and by the Eternal God we'll rule it." In their editorials these and other Democratic papers defined black nature as subhuman and threatening, and terrorism its inevitable concomitant. As the Forest *Register* proclaimed on September 15, 1875, "God Almighty, in farming out his privileges to mankind, drew a line as to qualifications. He never exacted from a nation or tribe impossibility. . . . Does any sane man believe the negro capable of comprehending the ten commandments? The miraculous conception and birth of our Savior? The high moral precepts taught from the temple on the mount?" This editorial writer constructed a subhuman, unchristian other to rationalize a campaign by terror. In his formulation, protecting blacks would be as misguided as allowing black political participation. "Every effort to inculcate these great truths but tends to bestialize [the black man's] nature, and by obfuscating his little brain unfits him for the duties assigned him as a hewer of wood and drawer of water. The effort makes him a demon of wild fanatical destruction, and consigns him to the fatal shot of the white man." This was the logic of reactionary terrorism rather than reconciliation: black demons deserved to be destroyed by whites purging civilization through cleansing retributive terrorism. In times of counterrevolution, kindly or even grudging paternalism had to be dispensed with; domination by any means necessary was the goal.[5]

As I have discussed, white-nationalist ideology reinforced by whip and noose was anything but new; it was consistent with proslavery beliefs before the Civil War, particularly during the secession crisis, and with resistance, often armed, to the entire course of Reconstruction. By 1875, political contexts had shifted sufficiently to enable the White Line party to sweep away all opposition in a conclusive armed struggle. Some of the changes were local, but national political currents were also moving toward abandonment of African Americans by the Republicans in power and even by many of the reform activists pushing for their enhanced civil rights. The major depression of 1873 had undermined both state and national tax bases, throwing hundreds of thousands of workers in the new industrial cities out of work. In many states like Mississippi, property taxes were relatively high, often to support public education for blacks as well as whites (paying for black education out of public funds particularly infuriated white property holders) and to under- write railroad bonds. Bad times led to defaults on bonds and a great uproar about even higher taxes. And in 1874 major floods along the Mississippi River destroyed the best cotton crops in the state. Depression and desolation pro- vided fertile ground for the rise of violence and terrorism.

Nationally, labor unrest increasingly disconcerted business leaders and their representatives in Washington—the leadership of the Republican Party —who thus were distracted from continuing reform efforts in the South. Implacable opposition to Reconstruction on the part of hostile anti-black Democrats in the North as well as the South—especially after the dramatic congressional elections of 1874, in which the Democrats gained control of many state houses as well as the House of Representatives—undermined much of the power base of the pro-black Republicans. Growing scandal in the Grant regime led many reformers to break away from their party in the name of fiscal reform and government honesty—and when they considered the question of the South these reformers increasingly listened to white Democrats who were making the same criticisms of Republican rule in Dixie. In this context, continual unrest in the South seemed more and more a no-win political problem for the Grant administration. The Republicans came to believe that they could not maintain power in the South solely by means of a black base supported by a shrinking number of white voters and an insufficient federal military presence. They understood the powerful potential of the profoundly racialized politics of the Democrats and came to believe that they had only weak weapons with which to combat the regrouping of the white community around the sort of men that even many Republicans considered the "natural leaders" of southern society and government.

Many politicians and journalists traditionally friendly to black rights began to lose interest in black political participation in the South. Senator Charles Sumner of Massachusetts, the radical par excellence of the Reconstruction period, declared in 1872, in language that indicated that he was willing to appease anti-black white southerners, that it was time for the "two sections and the two races [to be] lifted from the ruts and grooves in which they are now fastened, and instead of *irritating antagonism* without end, there shall be *sympathetic cooperation.* . . . I am against the policy of hate. Pile up the ashes; extinguish the flames; abolish the hate." The desire for national reconciliation trumped the drive for racial justice, and leading figures seemed ready to make a historical bargain with white southern Democrats, a bargain that amounted to capitulation. An editorial writer in the Springfield (Mass.) *Republican* captured the flavor of this shift when he wrote, "We must get rid of the Southern question. There is no chance or hope of healthy politics until we do get rid of it. . . . So long as the 'war issues' are capable of being warmed over from year to year and election to election; so long as a large section of the country is disturbed by violence and paralyzed by misgovernment; so long as white is arrayed against black . . . so long will our politics be feverish with disease." Looking south, James Redpath, who had been a major abolitionist supporter of John Brown, wrote in the formerly radical *New York Independent* that the defense of black rights was an agenda whose time had passed: "Sentimental abolitionism was well enough in its day; but Mississippi owes its present sad condition as much to sentimental abolitionists as to fiendish Negro-haters. The blacks were ruined as good citizens by the chronic prattle about their rights, and they were never roused to a noble manhood by instructions about their duties. . . . Let us empty our minds of cant and sentimental philanthropy, and learn that our black ward is in very truth a barbarian and needs our best efforts to uplift him in the scale of civilization." Former Confederate congressman Reuben Davis would have been gratified to read such a message from a northern reformist pen. The North's abandonment of Reconstruction, which was well under way in 1875, prepared much of the ground for the white southern terrorists by helping to delegitimize biracial Republican governance in the South. The concept of black barbarism was a core white-supremacist justification for the use of political violence to put blacks "back in their place," at the bottom rung of the social ladder.[6] The ground was clearing for an onslaught of counterrevolutionary terrorism against the biracial political advances of the previous few years.

Back in 1869, following the passage of the Fifteenth Amendment and the massive voting registration of blacks, the Republican Party had come to power with a considerable activist white membership in Mississippi, as elsewhere in the Deep South. According to the closest student of Mississippi politics of this period, the black base of the party consisted of ninety thousand black men (of a hundred thousand registered to vote). But while fifty to sixty thousand white men voted Democratic, a sizable minority of fifteen to twenty thousand whites—18 to 28 percent of those casting ballots—voted Republican. Approximately five thousand of these voters were carpetbaggers. But the majority of the white votes in Mississippi came from native sons—scalawags, as the Democrats slurred them. Some of these voters, mainly poor farmers from the hill country in the north of the state, had remained Unionist throughout the war, while others, including the leadership cadre of the party, were merchants and plantation owners, most of whom had been Whigs before the war and reluctant Confederates during it. As Republicans, these former Whigs maintained their long-standing antipathy to the Democratic Party, which many of them considered captive to demagogues and small farmers. This was the beginning of the racial coalition that radical Republicans in Congress hoped to foster.[7]

Under the leadership of the former Whig and scalawag Governor James L Alcorn, who had been elected with a Republican majority in the legislature in 1869, Republican rule gained a foothold in Mississippi. At first Alcorn maintained his popularity among black voters by supporting legislation that would strengthen their economic and legal interests, while he consolidated his base among fellow scalawag voters by bringing them into a wide variety of offices, thus solidifying a southern white–dominated version of Republicanism. By keeping officeholding essentially white and southern, Alcorn also gained some legitimacy in the eyes of a variety of white Mississippians as the man who could hold the more radical Republicans at bay. This stance held out enough hope for continued white dominance that the New Departurists in the Democratic Party began to echo the Republicans in thinking that their party ought to include black voters.[8]

But the New Departurists were a distinct minority; the majority of whites loathed any concessions that allowed any sort of revised racial order in society or government, and they set out to eradicate Reconstruction as expeditiously and completely as possible. By 1870, and climaxing in the spring of 1871, the hooded nightriders of the Ku Klux Klan were terrorizing considerable reaches of Mississippi. In Monroe County the head of the Negro Republican Club was seized one night, severely beaten, and then disemboweled in one of several dozen Klan murders that targeted white as well as black Republican leaders. Several blacks were murdered in a nightrider "riot" in Meridian, a town to which dozens of terrified black Alabamians had fled after brutal intimidation in their home state.

At this stage of Reconstruction, the federal government was still willing to use army detachments already stationed in the South as well as the federal courts to re-enforce Republican state governments. The Klan thus had to remain a clandestine organization, for it faced an armed federal opposition, however scattered. Indeed, in late 1871 and early 1872, 525 indictments were handed up in federal courts in Mississippi, and 465 convictions obtained during trials against Klan members. All the accused pleaded guilty, but they received suspended sentences, perhaps to placate angry Democrats. Federal action, though limited, served to break up the Klan in Mississippi, and the experience in South Carolina was similar, though on a larger scale.[9] The most peaceful elections in Reconstruction history took place in 1872. Fearing exposure and punishment, organized counterrevolutionary terrorists receded into relative silence.

By that year, the more radical elements in the Mississippi Republican Party had grown restive under Alcorn's brand of moderate southern white domination. Blacks had become more confident of their growing and increasingly disciplined political organizations—they frequently marched behind flags and drums to sizable political rallies, where they proclaimed that as the vast majority of the governing party they ought to have their fair share of offices as well as greater financing for their schools and other interests. Supporting them were most of the white Republican carpetbaggers, led by former Union general Adelbert Ames of Massachusetts. In their campaign to obtain the Republican nomination for governor in 1873, Ames and his partisans split the Republican Party. They argued that southern whites like Alcorn were acting out of personal interest rather than "vital principle," and that all Southern whites, even those who had migrated to the Republican Party, had been "blighted" by slavery. True reform had to be imported into the South from the culturally superior North. "The carpetbagger represents northern civilization, northern liberty, and has a hold on the hearts of the colored people that nothing can destroy," Ames argued. "He is the positive element of the party and if the South is to be redeemed from the way of slavery if must be done by him."[10] Ames's linking of biracial politics to northern abolitionism discredited Mississippi Republicanism for many racist northerners, and it was a red flag to southern Democrats.

As might have been expected, Ames's version of imported enlightenment, coupled with the promise of a significant increase in black officeholding (which, indeed, occurred after his election), alienated almost all previously sympathetic southern whites—in this context it is surprising that approximately six thousand scalawags voted for Ames in 1873.[11] But by dividing the whites in the Republican Party, Ames had narrowed his party's already tenuous political base. And his timing could not have been unluckier, given the economic cycle over which he had no control. The depression of 1873 hammered the southern economy. Cotton prices dropped by 50 percent in the five years after 1872, as did the prices for other commodities. Farmers, nearly 90 percent of the population, were plunged into increasing debt while their sources of credit evaporated. Commerce slowed dramatically, affecting artisans, merchants, and manufacturers alike and pushing the unskilled laboring people of both races further into poverty.[12] Had prosperity returned at this point, perhaps some sort of biracial governance might have survived in the South. But it did not, and the White Line movement gained greater urgency and credibility during hard times. White supremacists broadened their base by insisting that immediate—and violent—attacks on their Republican enemies were the swiftest road back to prosperity as well as to white domination. They linked pocketbooks to guns in a stridently racist analysis of politics and economics.

The Redeemer movement was not simply political; it was a social-evangelical counterrevolution. Grounded in hyper-violent political terrorism against blacks and their white supporters, the White Line also orchestrated a broad-based, well-organized, quasi-religious rally of the white race. Building white solidarity meant eliminating any notion of black political legitimacy and individual leadership, and it meant bringing all whites into one tent, regardless of social class, as well as extirpating any persisting white support of blacks. Control of the streets and the town squares was a literal project— whites paraded, held picnics, and flocked to mass orations while denying blacks their own processions and assemblies. White political meetings, like white political violence, amounted to rituals of racial rebirth, the dramatically staged intensification of the story of white purity and the white right to rule. Once back in their rightful place, the leadership of the White Line promised there would be renewed protection for blacks, but it would be granted only to politically neutered blacks. If this was paternalism, it was paternalism at gunpoint: Redeemers used as much implied force and outright political terrorism as they deemed necessary to destroy forever any surviving remnant of a biracial social alliance that might regain power in a future election. They sought to construct a white-dominated society of such permanence and solidity that they could consider themselves ever afterward the party of conservatism and peace, the only political party qualified to govern.

Rumors of an imminent organized black attack on the white race preceded every major instance of white violence and served to justify it. As has been noted, such rumors recalled the fears of an impending slave insurrection that had intermittently swept the white South in the relatively recent past and the shock Confederates had experienced when they found themselves fighting armed black Union soldiers during the Civil War. Demographics also fanned the flames of rumor. In Mississippi as a whole, in 1870 blacks outnumbered whites 54 percent to 46 percent, and in many counties blacks outnumbered whites by ratios ranging from three to one to nine to one. These blacks were no longer slaves but voters, often organized into Loyal Leagues, people who had built their own churches and were freed from the bonds of mastership. Blacks had gained latitude for a self- and communal construction that had never been possible in the slave South. Beyond that, Republican power in many county courthouses and in the statehouse was a perpetual confirmation of white fears of an imminent cataclysm. In particular, whites worried that Governor Ames would raise a powerful black militia to enforce Reconstruction in cases where the federal government was unwilling to interfere. And, in fact, at one point Ames did plan the creation of two black regiments, although he quickly abandoned this project in the face of massive white opposition. Even more threatening than a black state military force was the hint of black militias arising in the towns and the countryside, and whites tended to construe every black political organization as a nascent militia. After all, large numbers of blacks, many of them Union veterans, were already marching to their rallies behind fifes and drums. Any such evidence of black organization infuriated white southerners, who remembered their horror when black Union forces first marched through their states during the Civil War, at times answering atrocity with atrocity rather than taking prisoners of the other race, and then were stationed among them during Reconstruction.

It must be emphasized that in the 1870s fears of an imminent and well-organized armed black revolution were only panic-inducing fantasies, but they galvanized white counterrevolutionaries. To prepare for this nightmarish black uprising, white leaders began to use the telegraph and the railroads to concentrate a considerable, well-armed private militia that could be called upon whenever the need might come. Along the borders of Alabama and Louisiana, Mississippians also could depend on white fighters to cross the state line rapidly when summoned.

Whites' anger at the reversal of power they believed might soon doom them intensified every incident of their relations with blacks. E. D. Vetner, the Democratic candidate for sheriff of Claiborne County, where blacks outnumbered whites 9,996 to 3,390, had been infuriated when Ellen Smith, a young white girl, had eloped with Haskins Smith, a well-educated mulatto member of the state legislature. When Haskins Smith was then protected by the local police, who kept him out of the vengeful hands of Ellen Smith's relatives, Vetner admitted in his later testimony before the Senate investigating committee, "I told the sheriff . . . by the eternal gods, if ever again such a thing were repeated, blood was thicker than water, and we would kill the last son of a bitch; that if ever such insults were heaped on us again we would not stand it." Vetner believed that he could discern an evolving pattern of insults. One Sunday, according to him, an African American band stopped to play loudly in front of a white Methodist church in the middle of services, blasting away in a manner "that created an intense excitement among the gentlemen present," who, however, refrained from attacking the band. Vetner also believed stories that black domestic workers were telling their mistresses "that they had better behave themselves; that the white women were in their power; that they were in the ascendancy." However minor the provocations might have been in fact, rumors of incipient general insurrection mushroomed: "The whole community was in a very feverish state of excitement," Vetner recalled.

Then came election day in Port Gibson. Vetner organized about eighty armed white men to stand by the poll, where blacks had outvoted whites 1,000 to 200 in previous elections. About noon, two columns of black men came marching up "quite military-like," according to Vetner. An "uproarious" young black man then drew a gun, which a young white Democrat grabbed from him. Several of the white men then drew and fired, killing one man and wounding six others, causing the black would-be voters to scatter. Vetner then telegraphed for fifty men each from three surrounding towns. By the end of the day 250 whites armed with rifles and a cannon had surrounded the polling station. Mr. Briscoe, the Democratic candidate for attorney general, shouted out to the crowd just before firing recommenced: "These damned niggers shall not vote for these God-damned scoundrels; we have stood this thing long enough and ain't going to stand it any longer." Asked whether the black organization would have continued voting in a peaceful fashion if he had not intervened, Vetner replied, "No sir, I conscientiously, and with the fear of God and my solemn oath, tell you I do not think it, that I was instrumental in getting up the force to come to that town for no other purpose than self-protection."[13]

For Vetner, the evidence all added up: a black revolution was under way, and only organized political violence could put an end to it. This was actual reactionary terrorism carried out in self-defense against revolutionary black terrorism that never occurred. Of course, Vetner believed that his forces had nipped the enemy terrorism in the bud—the one-sided violence proved only that the whites had been appropriately aggressive. Similarly, E. L. Webber testified to the investigating senators about the emotional climate among whites in Wilkinson County in the Mississippi Delta, where blacks outnumbered whites by more than three to one. Webber claimed that the black people were organizing into a club to "exterminate the white people. This is the actual state of affairs in our section of the State. I cannot picture it to you, gentlemen; it is a matter of impossibility almost for any one to do so."[14]

The frightful rumor—constructed from very little evidence by white supremacists—of an imminent, well-organized, and massive black assault—sanctioned, in the minds of whites, any and all actions in response to protect everything that was holy and just, that is, the white race. In their minority report, congressional Democrats, mainly northerners, agreed with the sense of gross insult that they believed southern whites were suffering. "A condition of affairs which would be incredible and utterly intolerable in any of the Northern States exists in many of the black counties of Mississippi, where the property, intelligence, and character of the community is trodden to the earth, insulted, and ignored by the most ignorant and sometimes vicious members of the community." In such circumstances "forbearance" was exceptional, the congressional Democrats believed; aggressive self-protection on the part of their fellow Democrats in the South was both legal and moral.[15]

And so where every black organization and political action was seen as an element of an imminent revolt, a conspiracy along a racial black line, organized political violence was often the first recourse to rumored threats. Typical were the sentiments of T. M. Miller, a lawyer in Mayerville, Issaquena County, Mississippi (a black-belt county where blacks outnumbered whites 6,146 to 741). Although he characterized his own relations with blacks as "very pleasant. . . . They are naturally a very good-natured and clever people, but very easily inflamed," in the run-up to the election of 1875, Miller credited reports that "they had nightly drillings and were thoroughly armed. . . . They were very threatening and the white people were completely at their mercy," and in the "general apprehension" he joined in the violent response of the White Liners. Later he did not argue that only lowborn toughs had been involved in the ensuing violence but to the contrary affirmed that "law-abiding, high-toned citizens" like himself had acted for the "preservation of peace and good order in their neighborhood." He was certain that white gentlemen never engaged in "wanton cruelty and revenge" but that "if they did kill the negroes in the manner described by a good many it was, as they regarded it, in self-defense and in defense of their homes and families."[16] Unlike others, Miller did not deny what the White Liners had done. Indeed, by accepting a rumor of black revolution as a fact this normally calm and mature local leader, a self-professed friend to the blacks, had joined in the violent attack and justified it as legitimate self-defense of home and Christian values.

Miller's associate in Issaquena County, W. D. Brown, who also characterized himself as a "conservative, prudent man . . . one that sets a high value upon the life of a colored man," somewhat more forthrightly argued on his oath before the "Supreme Power" that "if life had not been taken . . . if these turbulent characters had not been stopped in their career . . . they would, in less than a week, have precipitated a conflict that would have resulted in the killing of a number of white people and the slaughter of a large number of colored people."[17] In the run-up to the election of 1875, White Liners killed at least thirteen black men in Issaquena County. According to Brown, this preemptive killing in the name of conservatism had headed off a larger race war. That such actions might in themselves *be* a race war fought on White Line terms, Brown did not venture to consider. For him the need for counterrevolutionary terrorism was obvious and compelling.

Far from sporadic, even if the intimidation and killing were prompted by panic, the violence that ensued was well-organized and politically targeted, and it was coordinated to produce an overall effect: terrorizing blacks into political capitulation. In many places Republican leaders, both white and black, were targeted, and at times political violence produced what whites characterized as "riots," meaning overwhelming collective force used against blacks who were, in the opinion of White Liners, gathered together in large numbers for nefarious political reasons.

The White Line movement developed a serious intelligence operation aimed at discovering the leaders of the Republican Party: the White Liners knew that by decapitating the party they would demoralize blacks opposing their political ascendancy. Take, for example, threats offered to two literate, mature black leaders in Madison County, in the center of the state. On polling day, W. G. Johnson, the leading figure in the Madisonville Democratic Club, approached P. C. Powell and told him, "I will give you ten minutes to get off this ground. . . . The whole of the white people have got their eyes on you; they have you spotted, and if you ain't away from here in that time you will be killed. . . . Tonight, if we can find you, we will hang you." At about the same time, elsewhere in the county, Johnny Neal and several other Democrats led by a Captain Baskin approached the local black Republican leader, Eli Hunt, while he was out in his field picking cotton. Neal walked up to Hunt, put his hand on his shoulder and said, "You are the very buck I am looking for. You are the Captain Devil of all the niggers in Madison County. They would all vote the democratic ticket if they didn't fear you." After debating whether to hang Hunt or shoot him, the rest of the gang agreed to let Neal shoot him, as he was eager to do. When Hunt ran off, Neal shot him in the back, but Hunt managed to survive by sprinting through a nearby orchard.[18]

Back in Issaquena County, a Colonel Givens of Vicksburg approached Derry Brown, a leading black Republican whom Givens had long known, and told him that he had heard Brown was intending to kill an elderly white couple named Watson. Brown replied that he was hurt that Givens would assume such a thing. "I have always tried to live a peaceable and harmony life. . . . I tries to live respectable and treat every man respectful." The Watsons later denied any such threat in a letter to Givens, a copy of which they sent to Brown. When he saw Brown later, Givens warned him to leave home, even after admitting, "You have not done anything particular; but they think you have got a little courage in you, and they will turn out and kill you."

Derry Brown fled the county, ending his days as a black activist. Exile was the only alternative to death that White Liners would accept.[19]

Many other Republican leaders, white and black, did not get away, and therefore were not able to tell their stories later. They were not simply killed; many were tortured to death, and the White Liners then mutilated their bodies. This was a demonstration of contempt, of course, but defiled corpses also were intended to serve as clear signs to remaining Republicans of what lay in store for them. Torture and mutilation were central to White Line "justice" and the reestablishment of white power. These acts were gruesome representations of the core meaning of the reactionary terrorism in the Deep South, demonstrations of the absolute nullification of the other. Killing was insufficient; dismemberment destroyed every element of humanity. Several dozen examples were given in testimony in 1876 to the Senate committee.

In Vicksburg, Weldon W. Edwards, a black member of the Mississippi legislature, testified that he had been walking the streets early one morning, "and saw this man, Ben. Johnson, lying dead, with coal-oil or something poured on him and set on fire, and his face and his abdomen all burned in a gristle." In the same city, a group of white men under the leadership of Samuel Elmo pistol-whipped Ben Allen, a black Republican, in front of other Republicans of both races. "While old Ben Allen was lying there," the African American Republican M. G. Bennett later related, "a whole lot of white boys took spittoons . . . and mashed him about the head when he was senseless." While Allen was dying, Bennett and the other black people fled.[20]

To terrorize every element of the hated enemy organization White Line members applied their treatment to leading white Republicans as well. A. H. Silvey of Raymond reported on the fate of his cousin Martin Silvey, the young son of a distinguished Whig planter and prominent scalawag in Clinton. The day after Silvey was seized during a "riot," his cousin reported, "We found his body in a cotton-field . . . with all the top of his head mashed in, with several wounds from pistol-shots . . . his abdomen ripped open with a knife, and his intestines protruding. There were also several other bruises, made by blows from clubs or some heavy instrument, about his body and face. A considerable piece of flesh was torn from his finger where his ring had been pulled off. His shoes were gone and his clothing torn all to pieces, he being nearly stripped naked."[21]

As well as gaining revenge over the demons who had, as they perceived it, threatened and insulted them, thereby finding collective relief in the destruction and mutilation of their enemies, White Liners intended with such acts to let everyone who opposed them politically know the cost of resisting the new order. Mutilated carcasses hanging from trees, lying in the middle of city streets, or dotting country roads served as emblems and warnings of the fundamental meaning of white power. Terrorism was not just a means to an end; it was intrinsic to the end, the most powerful manifestation of the reactionary counterrevolution.

Although some people might be swept up and killed as collateral damage in the heat of the White Line campaign, the leadership of the movement targeted specific enemies for elimination—their terrorist acts were premeditated and systematic. In South Carolina in 1876, urging the assassination of leading Republicans, former Confederate Major General Martin W. Gary wrote in his "plan of campaign" for the Red Shirt rifle clubs, "Never threaten a man individually if he deserves to be threatened. The necessities of the time require that he should die." William Tolbert, another leading Democrat, later testified unabashedly to a congressional committee that his group's plan was "to find out where the negroes were holding Union Leagues . . . fire into them and kill the leaders." Before election day the plan was to seize ballots from Republican campaign officials and if anyone resisted, "shoot them and take them by force." As for Republican speakers—"shoot them, kill them, stop them."[22]

At times in Mississippi, White Line units subdued any potential misgivings they might have by turning their enemies into subhuman others, making dehumanizing jokes as they shot the men they considered to be their main enemies. They did this in earshot of other blacks and Republican whites, the better to let them all know the joy they took in killing their enemies. Thus, in Wilkinson County, in the southwest corner of the state, White Liners burst into a cabin where, as a black witness later testified, "one was in a bed and said he was sick, and they said to him to turn over and take a pill, and they shot him right in the mouth." In Yazoo County a black witness heard two white men brag, after their rifle unit had driven a group of black men into the Yazoo River, "that from the number of cries and groans they must have got a bushel of them. . . . They were all driven into the river and jumped in like frogs."[23]

Because the white-owned press refused to report most Redeemer terrorist attacks unless they were so massive that they gained national attention—thus acting as the propaganda arm of the white counterrevolution they supported by their silence—it is impossible to assess, even with the aid of the congressional testimony, how widespread the killing was. But it is certain that political murder was common, and other forms of intimidation even more so, and that murder underlined the potential outcome of other forms of threat. In Mississippi as in South Carolina and the other Deep South states, Redeemers launched a sufficient number of large-scale murderous campaigns to plant profound fear in the hearts of all Republican activists and their followers. This was counterrevolutionary terrorism at its most fundamental level—aimed at seizing state power by concerted and focused political violence. The attacks were not random or sporadic actions but a conscious strategy.

The tone of large-scale violence was set in December 1874 in Vicksburg. Racial tensions had mounted earlier in the year, but when Peter Crosby, the embattled black sheriff, had attempted to obtain military assistance, federal authorities in nearby Jackson refused. After a long hot summer during which both white and black militia units were said to be training, as an act of desperation Crosby called for armed black men to come to the city to aid him, but he soon was pleading with them to disband in the face of several hundred armed white men who had quickly gathered in the city. No black revolutionary paramilitary force was organized because Crosby and his supporters understood that banding together would only result in their own destruction. Successful in meeting their chief objective of destroying any idea of black organization, the White Liners had constructed a counterrevolutionary template that they would apply across the state in their upcoming campaign.

Disbanding, however, provided no protection from White Line terrorists for Vicksburg's black activists. As the black men dispersed outside town, the whites chased them down on horseback and opened fire, killing about thirty-five. The White Line military squads then swept the nearby countryside, hunting down and killing as many as three hundred blacks whom they considered insurgents, or who were just in the wrong place when the raiders came. Two whites were killed during the massacre. This systematic terrorism, aimed not at a genuine but a suspected threat, grew into an assault on the whole black race from which the anticipated insurrection might arise, then or at some time in the future. Caught up in the throes of widespread terrorism, White Liners did not need an armed enemy to justify their blood purges.[24]

Several months later, as the election campaign heated up, whites killed large numbers of blacks and their white supporters in several similar "riots" triggered by rumors of black uprisings. The lesson of December 1874 was not lost. The mainstream press fanned the flames with terrorist propaganda, instigating still more political violence. As the Vicksburg *Monitor* announced, *"The same tactics that saved Vicksburg will surely save the State, and no other will."* Major outbreaks occurred in Water Valley, Woodville, Louisville, Macon, Aberdeen, and Yazoo City (where several white Republican leaders were lynched). Unknown numbers of blacks and their white Republican allies were killed during this campaign, as many as ten or fifteen in each incident. Then in early September 1875 in Clinton, near Vicksburg, after an altercation between a black policeman and a drunken white man, a group of armed and mounted whites ran down local black men, killing between ten and thirty of them. In response to an urgent telegram, heavily armed White Line units soon poured into Clinton by train. Over the next few days they stormed through the nearby plantations, killing as many as fifty more leading white and black Republicans, including William Haffa, the white school teacher, and Charles Caldwell, the black State Senator.[25] The white leadership was eager to eliminate a hated political group while at the same time anxious to suppress reports of the numbers killed, in order to prevent federal intervention and perhaps out of concern that the violence might frighten off their entire black labor force. But to terrorize their enemies they also had to advertise how willing they were to use force and how well organized they were. This need to spread the news while maintaining an element of deniability meant that the level of actual killing was never established, though it clearly was part of a pattern rather than a disparate group of incidents. And the uncertain nature of the attacks emphasized the unpredictability of future attacks, another central mass-psychological purpose of terrorist campaigning.

Another major component of the White Line strategy was the elimination of white Republicanism not just through the killing of its leaders but also through social ostracism and violent threats against all white Republican voters, particularly scalawags, who could be both attacked and appealed to as fellow southerners who had fallen from grace. White Liners often permitted these white voters reentry into the white Democratic fold if they repented or, in some cases, fell silent and voted the right way on election day.

One clear measure of the white supremacists' level of organization and the growing strength of their strategy was the number of newspapers that went over to the White Line policy of attacking white Republicans from a previous editorial policy that was more sympathetic to black voters and their supporters—or at least more sarcastic than overtly angry. Hard-line racist newspapers now were joined by previously more conciliatory Democratic journals and even by Republican press. On July 1, 1875, for example, the Brandon *Republican* insisted that blacks were demanding social equality from their "white-skinned allies," and that some were being taken into white homes "fully and freely." It was certain that "the man who invites one of these social equality pimps to his table offers an insult to his family." Two weeks later, the Brandon paper made perfectly clear how the rest of the white community responded to such social contamination in its headline: "Social Intercourse Denied to Straight-Haired Niggers." And the Canton *Mail* published lists of names of white Republicans to be shunned, particularly by "every true woman." Active support of Republicanism turned a white man black, into a polluted race traitor to be ostracized. It sparked political targeting—an implicit threat of future violence if lesser attacks proved insufficient. In this sense implied violence was part of a wider terrorist strategy to dominate every element of society by any means necessary.[26]

Shunning was a powerful psychological weapon to use on fellow southern whites, a tactic that always carried the threat of future murder. In Noxubee County, the scalawag J. W. Robbins explained to the investigating senators how White Liners had used the power of ostracism to politically neuter all but the most committed white Republicans. He was certain that he knew all twelve actively engaged white Republicans in his county. "There are more white men in that county . . . who have expressed themselves to me that they were republicans, and would vote with the party if they could do so without the sacrifice of their business interests and social standing." It also followed, as Robbins indicated, that economic boycott was directly connected to social ostracism. Dr. John T. Harrington, a South Carolinian by birth, explained to the Senate committee precisely how such boycotts worked. He had engaged to buy ten bushels of corn on the first day of each month from a neighbor named Robinson. But when Harrington's son went to collect the first delivery, Robinson sent him back empty-handed with word that "I have taken an oath not to aid any leading radical for love or money and I cannot let you have any more corn." In his medical occupation as well, "where once I had a good practice before, they have universally went into some kind of understanding that they would not patronize me after that as a physician." Harrington believed, "I was ostracized because I am a radical." Many of his previous southern white allies told Harrington that they would no longer vote Republican, though they wanted to. "Our families would be ostracized," one old friend told him privately. "They have got lists . . . of every man how he is going to vote, and if they don't say that he is going to vote with our side they put him down on the negro side. I could bear it for myself but not for my family."[27]

Neutrality was insufficient: scalawags had to commit themselves as Democrats to escape ostracism and the real possibility of death by gun or rope. In 1875, the White Line movement stepped up the pressure with the aim of shrinking the white vanguard to a tiny, isolated, and ineffective squad that could then, if necessary, be killed more easily and with fewer repercussions.

Beyond ostracism and economic boycott aimed at destroying livelihoods and reputations—terrible weapons in themselves—lay even more explicit death threats, which, as we have seen, were often carried out, thereby making them all the more frightening, as their victims could never know whether the act would follow the word. After the election, in which he supported a black candidate for sheriff of Clay County, Dr. Harrington recalled that a former Republican officeholder had come up to him following a speech and said, "That was the damndest radical speech [I have] ever heard." The man then told him that the county Democratic convention had created a quorum of ten men "that has agreed to hang you if you ever make another such a speech. . . . He then said that they had no ill-will against me individually. . . . They thought you was the managing talent of the party . . . and we were determined to beat this election." There was nothing hot-blooded about such a threat; what was planned was a political assassination rather than mere homicide: thus was a pattern of counterrevolutionary terrorism repeated and amplified.[28]

At times, threats were made anonymously, which added to the terror, as the victim could not discern their source. Judge W. B. Cunningham, who had heard of general threats from nearby Yazoo County, where a "riot" had wiped out organized local Republicanism, was certain that such a method would work as well in neighboring Madison County, where he resided. Colonel O. R. Singleton, who would be elected to the legislature in 1876 as a Democrat, told Cunningham one day that "the election was bound to be carried at all hazards." A few days later, Cunningham received a package in the mail that included the Jobs Available section of the New York *Herald,* "and marked [with] some very appropriate ones," rolled around a four-foot length of rope with a hangman's noose at the end, tied "in a very nice style." Cunningham said that he ignored the threat, passing it off as a sick joke.[29]

Faced with permanent ostracism and death threats, the majority of Republicans backed away from their political activism. Henry Kerneghan, an Irishman by birth brought up in Louisiana, was running as a Republican for state senator from Brandon, just south of where Cunningham lived. He received a visit from Colonel A. J. Myers, a leading Democrat, who later would be elected circuit court judge. Myers asked Kerneghan to step outside his office, where he told him calmly, "I have come to tell you that you are . . . looked upon as a republican leader, and you will be the first man that will be killed if we have any disturbance here." Later, in the dead of night, someone put up a cartoon transparency across the street from Kerneghan's office that read, "H. K. BeJabers for the senate," an insult intended to remind Kerneghan that he was a doubly unwelcome alien. From time to time, Kerneghan heard voices outside his office threatening that their owners would break down his door and hang him. When Myers approached him again, Kerneghan took him back inside his office and dared him to repeat his threat in front of a black member of the legislature named Hicks. Myers then said, "I just came to warn you as a friend," to which Kerneghan replied, "I don't care for such friendship as that." Then he said, "If you will give me a white man's chance [and] come at me one at a time . . . I won't fear you. I will tell you right now that I will not come down [step back from my political activism]; I will run the race through."

After courageously confronting Myers, Kerneghan did in fact back down, feeling the constant terror just outside his office door. On election day he did not go out of doors, much less to the polls, "and simply let the whole thing go by default. . . . I was afraid of being assassinated; that was just the whole truth of the matter." And many other Republican candidates and voters behaved in a similar fashion. As the Democrats had intended it, Kerneghan had to agree that "it was extremely quiet on the day on the election." This sequence was yet another variation of enacting the slogan "Peaceably if possible, forcibly if necessary," another terrorist threat to achieve political conquest in reaction to a suspected threat.[30]

To reclaim their membership in the politically unitary white community, many scalawag Republicans publicly recanted their political sins and returned to the embrace of the Democratic Party. With considerable satisfaction, George Glenn of Madison told the visiting senators about Captain Priestly, a Republican justice of the peace who came over to the Democrats gathered outside a Republican rally, "and said that his people was down on him because he had been a republican; that his wife was not a republican and hence he was not going to be any longer. . . . He cried like a child and took my hand . . . and said he had been the prodigal son," and then rejoined the Democrats. Glenn was contemptuous of such a weak man, who had foolishly joined the republicans and then allowed pressure from his wife to turn him around. On the other hand, this was a perfect political equivalent of an evangelical conversion scene, where a fallen sinner repented and entered the party of God and his own race.[31]

Some prodigal sons even joined in making terror. Although he did not literally become a Democrat at this point, no less a figure than James L.

Alcorn, former scalawag governor, who denied ever having been a "Black Republican," cobbled together an anti-Ames ticket in his home county, Coahoma, and led a white invasion of an African American Republican meeting, killing several fleeing blacks, to make examples of them and discourage other black men from organizing politically.[32]

Other southern white Republicans also abandoned their political beliefs and their friends after staring into the face of ostracism and death, but only with deep anguish. Henry Kerneghan put the choice of survival versus principle eloquently when he described the immense and brutal pressure White Liners placed on southern white Republicans. He realized what it had meant to drop his campaign in 1875 and remain indoors, denied the American privilege of voting freely. And he captured vividly the profound impact of terrorism on the terrorized. "It is absolutely true that [we] didn't dare exercise [our] rights that day. There was a horror, and the atmosphere was loaded with it. I can not describe it, nor no other man in the world can describe the feeling of the few white people of Mississippi [who still considered themselves Republicans] on that day." Threats and political murder were ruthlessly applied and effective core components of the White Line counterrevolutionary strategy to retake power from the Black Republicans.[33]

Also central to the White Line campaign was the violent and concerted destruction of all claims blacks might make to the right to use public spaces for political demonstrations and thus the white monopolization of all meaningful political participation. In an era when political partisans, in Mississippi as elsewhere, marched behind flags and brass or fife-and-drum bands to picnics and rallies where leaders filled the air with ringing speeches denouncing the enemies and praising the friends of freedom, the elimination of Republican rallies was a central means of preventing blacks from retaining any share of power, sending them back into public silence, isolation, and submission. By driving their enemies from the public sphere, White Liners destroyed their ability to express their opinions collectively—the basic civil liberty of political freedom in a democracy. Redeemers used the language of outraged republicanism to denounce what they often called the "carnival" and "depravity" of black political participation—blacks engaged in collective political action were by definition nothing but "lawless mobs" that needed to be violently silenced and dispersed. Only whites acting through the same public forums could be the conservators of peace and lawfulness, even as they were breaking up black rallies with intimidation and violence.[34]

In many parts of the state large, heavily armed, well-organized Democratic paramilitary outfits broke up Republican rallies. E. H. Stiles, the Republican district attorney in Port Gibson, recorded one such attack, which took place on October 30, 1875. As the Republican procession marched through town, it was "subjected to numerous insults; pistols and guns drawn on it, and some of the persons in it even subjected to blows." At the picnic grounds, about five hundred well-armed Democrats on horseback "dashed up, dismounted, formed a line and dared the republicans to come on." Stiles believed that these men were "crazy for a fight." They proclaimed, "We will carry [this election] or kill every damn nigger in the county." At this point Stiles advised the Republicans to disperse, and they did so. A week earlier, in Aberdeen, the scalawag mayor reported on a meeting where the Democrats invading a similar rally "cut the heads out of drums and beat colored men over the heads with pistols," driving the Republicans off the ground.[35]

In rural Madison County, a Republican club with about 260 members presided over by the African American justice of the peace, Green Foster, had been in the habit of holding political meetings every Saturday night. On one evening in November, right before the election, a band of white horsemen under the leadership of a Dr. Holland rode up to the rally and sought out Green, asking whether he was a peace officer: "Well in place of your keeping the peace you are president of the club here, keeping the colored people beating drums around here." Green replied that his group was keeping the peace by acting out their democratic right to assembly: "We don't go by anybody's house and make any noise; we has our particular place to meet, and never interferes with anybody." Holland then declared, "By God! I want you to quit that, and if you meet here again . . . we will kill every last one of you." Holland's men then opened fire and scattered the African American Republicans, although it is not clear whether anyone was killed. But the following Wednesday, several white men from the same group broke into the house of a member of the Republican club and cut up their drums, then put five members in jail, fining them ten dollars each for trying to prevent the Democrats from destroying the drums. The white men then marched over to Foster's house and told him he had twenty-four hours to leave the county, that they would hang "these damned radical niggers" if they didn't leave. On election day, Dr. Holland approached Foster near the polls. When Holland threatened him again, Foster said that he had not come "prepared for a fuss." Holland replied, "By God! We came prepared. . . . I have got two hundred [pistol] balls in my pocket, and I haven't killed two hundred niggers yet today." Given what the White Liners had done elsewhere, Foster was unlikely to assume that Holland was bluffing: there had been enough terrorist massacres to give credibility to such threats. Only 50 of the 260 black Republicans voted that day. Most of the men had been sleeping out in the fields every night, Foster knew, so they would not be shot in the dead of the night. "They were Scared to death."[36]

These were the standard White Line tactics in the run-up to the election —sometimes resulting in more actual bloodshed, sometimes not. Forbidding blacks to beat drums and cutting the drums up were especially common events—drums were obviously symbols of political engagement, a means of accenting participation with a martial cadence. On election day in Aberdeen, J. W. Lee, the scalawag mayor, was speaking at a political rally. When a black man began to beat his drum in applause, a white Democrat pulled out his revolver and pointed it at the drummer, saying, "Stop that; you cannot beat that drum here. This is a white man's country, and we don't allow that." When the white men then began beating blacks with sticks and pistols, Lee stopped speaking, and the crowd fled. As they ran off, several whites overtook the drummers, "and just took a knife and cut the head out of the drum, and then they stamped on the kettle drum and burst it all to pieces." On election day, when White Liners dragged a twenty-four-pounder to the polling place and then began beating potential black voters, the blacks "fled in wild disorder and confusion," Lee testified. The Republican vote in that district fell from 1,400 in 1873 to 90 in 1875.[37]

White paramilitary units frequently brought cannons with them, firing them off for maximum psychological impact. One White Liner, the lawyer Lex Brame, later admitted that his group had brought a cannon along to a Republican barbecue in western Clay County and fired it. But it was only "a little piece of artillery—a little short gun." Also confirming that his comrades had been armed (though he carried only a tiny Derringer), Brame insisted that none of his group had intimidated anyone during the campaign and that in fact the election was "very quiet, much more quiet than any election I have ever seen."[38]

Another common White Line tactic was to insist that Republicans and Democrats hold joint campaign rallies, and then cow the Republicans into silence by standing among the black voters with hands on pistols while the Democratic orators dominated the meeting. White Liners also "invited" Republicans to their own rallies, sometimes compelling them to speak on Democrats' behalf. Henry Kerneghan, the scalawag candidate for state senator in Brandon, was involved in one joint rally at which James Hill, the Republican candidate, was not allowed to give a speech but was permitted only to announce his presence and compliment the Democratic candidate sitting with him on the platform. This was public speech without "freedom," and Hill responded without his usual "vim," Kerneghan recalled. In Clay County, J. W. Caradine, a black member of the legislature, was told that because he had "risen up a great element . . . of feeling in the colored man" with his speeches, if he wanted to live and to "demand some respect" among white Democrats, he would have to "go around and make some speeches" on their behalf. Caradine went along and made three tepid speeches that he knew the Democrats "did not really appreciate." But having humiliated him publicly in front of mocking white Democrats while alienating him from his Republican friends and his black community, the White Liners let him alone.[39]

As in the case of "joint rallies" that included blacks but were actually demonstrations of white power, threats were often combined with false hospitality in order to show black assemblies who was in charge and what democracy would mean in a future white state. For example, blacks had traditionally made use of Sykes Chapel near West Point for Saturday night political meetings. One Saturday about two hundred armed White Liners appeared, dragging their cannon. Dr. Harrington, the scalawag physician, noted that "they took out their cannon, and a lot of whiskey and tobacco, and told the negroes to come and eat, chew tobacco, and drink whiskey. And they took out their cannon and fired it again and again. . . . They told the negroes to come and drink their whiskey; but the negroes said they wanted to drink first; and [the White Liners] had to drink first, and then the negroes drank." Having restored what they considered to be proper racial protocol at that meeting, the White Liners roamed the county throughout the campaign, "booming away" with their cannon, to restore the traditional political structure of white men on the top, black men, stripped of political liberty, on the bottom.[40]

Even when subjected to intense intimidation in an atmosphere charged with the knowledge that political assassination was spreading throughout the state, some blacks resisted the White Line terrorists. When P. C. Powell, head of a Republican organization in Madison County, went to the railroad station to pick up Republican voting tickets, W. G. Johnson, leader of the local Democratic organization, came up to him and told him he had ten minutes to disappear. "The whole of the white people have got their eyes on you; they have got you spotted and if you ain't away from here in that time you will be killed." This threat followed months of armed white violence. "They rode around and shot eternally," Powell recalled, "they was always doing so." After Johnson's threat, Powell spent the night in the woods, but the next day he went to the polls and voted, as did "a good many other colored men." Powell and these others were willing to court death to retain their political freedom. As he told senatorial investigators the next year, "They tried to keep me from voting, but I had such a pluck as a republican for the rights that Congress had given us for many years past that I went there and voted; I could not have helped it if I had got killed."[41]

Defiance in a terrible situation also characterized the behavior of M. G. Bennett of rural Warren County, near Vicksburg. On election day, Bennett had been leader of about a hundred blacks who were forced away from the polls by four armed Democrats. Later, aware that he was risking his life, Bennett testified against the men before a grand jury in federal court in Oxford. When Bennett was walking to the train station to return home, the four men, who clearly had been lying in wait for him, came up to him, and their leader, a Mr. Hawsley, said to him, "Go on, you God damned, lying lousy son of a bitch, I will fix you when I get you to Warren County." Bennett replied, "I would just as soon die as live a slave," and "I might as well die as not to have my liberty as a citizen." In similar fashion, threatened with hanging if he did not leave Wilkinson County, the preacher Alfred Black told the men who threatened him, "I am not going to leave; I am not one of those scared chickens."[42]

To encourage blacks to stand up to the White Line intimidation and vote, leading African American Republicans in the state, led by Senator Blanche K. Bruce and State Senator Charles Caldwell, issued an address in early October 1875 warning what the impact on blacks would be of the terrorist campaign: a complete White Line victory that would destroy Republicanism in Mississippi. "The success of the Democratic party . . . frenzied as it is with hate and rancor, will, to all intents and purposes, sound the death knell of all the hopes that the colored man has indulged of education, elevating and improving his race in this State. Once under the iron heel of Democracy, the colored man will at once sink back to the status he held in 1865—free in name, but not in fact—poor, ignorant and helpless, hedged in by unfriendly laws, which he will have no power to circumvent, a 'hewer of wood and a drawer of water' forever." It was clear to these men that "practical disenfranchisement" would follow a White Line victory, and all they could do was urge every black man to approach the polls with a firm resolve to vote.[43] African Americans clearly understood the stakes involved in the White Line assault on their liberty, and they fought as strongly as they could for a republic that included them as political equals to whites.

Yet defiance came at such a fearful price that many if not most Republicans withdrew from active participation in the election—including Bruce, Caldwell, and other statewide leaders—and large numbers of blacks stayed away from the polls. It was clear that Republicans exercising basic democratic rights—speaking freely, conducting political meetings, testifying before juries, and voting—were all targets of the terrorist branch of the White Line movement. In Columbus, Lowndes County, in central Mississippi along the Alabama line, Robert Gleed, a prosperous African American shopkeeper, had been declared candidate for sheriff. As was true elsewhere in the state, in Lowndes County the Democrats campaigned in arms, including cannon, threatened blacks with economic boycotts, and generally established a pattern of intimidation. In this atmosphere, Gleed and several other leading Republicans agreed to a meeting with the Democratic leadership in the county courthouse to see, in Gleed's words, whether they could devise a plan to "avoid any collision" on election day. Gleed told the Democrats that as he knew he was the target of so much white animus, he would "forbear to hold office, or forbear to run for office or even vote as an individual." The white leaders, Dr. Lipscomb and Judge Sims, replied that these concessions would be inadequate; the whole black community would have to agree to abstain from voting. Gleed said he could not speak for others, then went on, "We used to ask for life and liberty, but now, if we could just be spared our lives, so as we could go peacefully along, and be permitted to enjoy our lives as men and as human beings, we would be satisfied with that." Dr. Lipscomb took offense at this statement and said that "there was no danger to our liberties" and that of course blacks were entitled to life, liberty, and the pursuit of happiness, as enshrined in the Declaration of Independence. The night before the election, however, a white mob invaded the black neighborhood and burned down four houses, shooting up several more, including Gleed's, driving the black families onto the streets, and beating the men, killing four of them. It had been insufficient for Gleed to concede, with great regret, the loss of his voting privilege; even his explicit withdrawal of any future claim to equal rights had not prevented whites from killing black Republicans. The terrorists exercised power completely as they willed it. Power was an all-or-nothing proposition, residing entirely in white-supremacist hands.[44]

Under the tidal wave of the White Line counterrevolutionary campaign, most blacks lost heart in political participation. In Brandon the carpetbagger H. R. Ware noted that during the campaign Republican political organizations "simply disbanded when this intense excitement existed in the county. . . . They were abandoned entirely . . . and I advised them to abandon them for one." After they began abstaining from holding rallies—the public arena designed for affirming political engagement—black people "seemed very much crest-fallen; perfectly cowed," Ware concluded.[45]

Across the state, in Issaquena County—where the pattern of violence was equally intense—Derry Brown was compelled to make a macabre "compromise" with the White Line leadership, agreeing to help compile a list of eight leading black men, including himself, who would be killed in exchange for general peace at election time. In the previous months, four black men had been killed during one outbreak of white violence in that county, and three during another nearby. While this was going on, Brown had responded to a white carpenter named Tom Groom who had threatened him in nearby Vicksburg, "I endeavors to keep inside of the law and to abide by it, and I almost as soon would be dead and buried as to have a man oversee me something like my old master used to do; that goes pretty hard." He intended to return home "like a man, and not go back like a dog, a runaway." He knew he would be hunted and that he would be without the protection of the law, "but I don't care about going back up there as a runaway." The others on the death list fled the county, but Brown stayed and was seized and strung up, although someone among the group of white men attacking him cut him down before he died.[46]

Everyone understood the connection between the control of public places and the control of public power. Depriving blacks of the right of assembly— making music, parading, holding picnics, giving speeches to large gatherings, showing up at the polling places to vote peacefully—the White Line at the same time exercised all those rights at the top of their lungs, their power growing out of the barrels of their rifles and cannon. Destroying black rights and celebrating white dominance were one and the same thing. And by holding their own loud, assertive public events, the White Liners rallied a whole race to their banner. They gave whites gloriously powerful pageants in which to celebrate their collective rebirth as the dominant race. Theirs was a civil evangelical revival, intensely attractive to their partisans not only for the humiliation inflicted on their Republican enemies but also for the exultation that participation in their movement provided.[47]

The Saturday before election day, reacting to posters announcing that the Republicans of Macon intended to hold a mass rally, a thousand armed White Line men rode into town. According to J. W. Robbins, a scalawag newspaper editor, "There was a cannon that the Democrats had planted in the street . . . and [they] were firing it off. They had a brass band at their head and marched all over town; marched by my office . . . pointed their pistols at me . . . and insulted me. They filled the town with music and shooting that day; but when the attempt was made by the colored men to make a little music on their drums, the democrats seized and destroyed them, and after that we could have no music of our own."[48] Decades later, a leading White Liner in Panola County in northwestern Mississippi proudly recalled the glory of the White Line seizure of power through terrorist means: "Our purpose was to overawe the negroes and exhibit to them the ocular proofs of our power . . . by magnificent torchlight processions at night and in the day by special trains of cars . . . loaded down with white people with flags flying, drums beating, and bands playing, the trains being chartered and free for everybody."[49]

The omnipresent dark half of the Janus face of the White Line movement —the destruction of black political legitimacy by force—coexisted with the light half: celebration of the reemerging white republic. White Liners gathered their coracial brothers and sisters to them with jubilant pageantry designed to solidify the white hold on all public spaces. Rallies lasted all day. They started with marches conducted by the Democratic clubs—mounted, armed, and often in uniform, and frequently accompanied by marching bands and drums of the sort forbidden to blacks. At the meeting place, the heads of the Democratic apparatus gave a round of long, impassioned speeches, and a grand barbecue followed, provided by the men with the greatest wealth and authority in the community. After nightfall, torchlight processions illuminated the main streets, with householders also lighting lanterns in their windows along the way. Drums, cheers, booming cannons, and fireworks heightened the powerful emotions aroused by these intense displays of white power. Later, the Democratic press would spread the news of the glorious day. We can scarcely imagine the terror these celebrations must have caused in the black community.

One of the largest such events took place in Holly Springs late in October. "Thousands of men, organized in clubs of fifties and hundreds, marched into town that morning with bands playing, banners waving, and raising such shouts of patriotic enthusiasm as were never heard in this part of the world," the Natchez *Democrat* reported. "After parading the streets, the immense crowd of men dismounted and were addressed [with] the most telling and eloquent speeches. At night the torchlight procession and pyrotechnic display took place. Two thousand illuminated cartoons and three thousand torchlights were being carried, besides the illuminated wagons, carriages, etc., counted by the hundreds. Seven thousand men were in the procession."[50]

Although the leaders of the movement were the well-heeled men of property and standing in the community, the rallies were intended to solidify racial solidarity across class lines while terrorizing blacks. As the Jackson *Clarion* reported of a rally in Beauregard, the "white people of this country [acted as] a band of brothers." Egalitarian white supremacy through the suppression of black power by terror was the goal across the Deep South, as in South Carolina, where one leading Democrat called the process a "touching of elbows" by all white men, regardless of class. With the mission accomplished in the smashing electoral victory, the Oxford *Falcon* celebrated the white democracy of the victory: "No man can arrogate to himself that he has done more in redeeming our state than has anybody else. The redemption of Mississippi is due to the fact that every man did his duty. It was not the work of political leaders but of the people."[51]

After the crushing defeat of the Civil War, the humiliation of emancipation, and black political participation in Reconstruction, rising up again as a state and a region to seize control restored traditional racial domination and white pride. The endemic violence of counterrevolutionary terrorism was communally cathartic—the expression and the fulfillment of raw, effective power.

White Line pageantry incorporated the language and symbols of the long American tradition of republican liberty. In Brandon the most conspicuous of the many placards plastered around the town before the election read, "Trust in God, and keep your powder dry," a reference to the Minutemen's slogan in the American Revolution. And newspaper editorials also referred to the tradition of the War God of the Old Testament. The Yazoo *Democrat* proclaimed, "Send forth . . . the soul-stirring announcement that Mississippians shall rule Mississippi though the heavens fall. Then will woe, irretrievable woe, betide the radical tatterdemalions. Hit them hip and thigh, everywhere and at all times."[52] A King James–style prophecy of blood revenge was the natural language in which to express the political purgation of the evil others from the Promised Land.

But of course the deepest religious equivalent to the fervor of the White Line movement was the evangelical revival so central to the experiences of these white warriors. The all-day rallies themselves were civic versions of evangelical meetings, designed to overwhelm the senses and fill previously passive citizens with a sense of racial mission and elevating spiritual equality. The White Line campaign was aimed at a great triumph at the polls that would overturn the minions of the devil: this was the righteous conclusion of an apocalyptic struggle. The Oxford *Falcon* urged its white readers a few weeks before the election, "Give yourself wholly and undivided to the great work, and with God's blessings we will achieve a triumph that will mark that day as the most memorable of our lives."[53]

Singing hymns and praying together were always components of the mass meetings conducted by the Redeemers. In South Carolina, Red Shirt Democrats began their rallies with prayers—one county organization passed a resolution that they would sing "joyful hosannas" when victory was theirs. When scalawags joined their cause, Democrats called their conversion "crossing Jordan." These new white allies had "come over to the Lord's side." Several key clergymen in South Carolina pledged themselves to the redemption of their state, and with similar evangelical sentiment, the Central Committee of the Democratic Party called for a day of prayer and fasting to purify themselves before doing battle for the Lord at the gates of Armageddon.[54]

The drama of the Redeemers' white revival was played out especially vividly in South Carolina, where the well-bred and wealthy Wade Hampton, a former Confederate cavalry general, marched triumphantly through the state in September and October 1876 during his gubernatorial campaign. The Red Shirts had organized themselves into gun clubs, generally with fifty to sixty members each, perhaps thirty thousand in all, often commanded by former senior officers in the Confederate Army. Units of this self-constituted extralegal militia greeted Hampton at each stop, and others accompanied him along the way. Hampton's march concluded in Charleston a few days before the election with an enormous procession and a banquet that included the most prominent citizens of that aristocratic state.[55]

On October 7, 1876, Hampton and his Red Shirt militia rode into Sumter. In the town square the local Democrats had constructed a speaker's platform on which the crowd, as they surged toward the square, beheld a human figure robed in deathly black and bound in chains. As Hampton strode to the platform, the enslaved and dehumanized figure threw off its chains and black robe, revealing, as a journalist noted, "a radiant young woman in pure white." She wore a tiara boldly lettered with the words "South Carolina" on her head, as she stood "tall and stately, head uplifted and eyes shining like the stars." The rebirth of this vestal virgin from slavery into freedom caused a huge wave of emotion in the crowd, and they reacted with Rebel yells, loud whooping, and oaths of dedication to the cause of redeeming the state from Reconstruction. Late into the night Red Shirt horsemen rode the streets shouting, "Hampton or Hell!" Not for the first or last time in southern history, evangelical metaphors mixed with rather more pagan terms in a purification cere-

mony designed to cement the emotional solidarity of the captivated crowd
and deepen their commitment to bringing about the reborn white Christian
republic.[56]

Coupled as they were with the recent memory of violent terrorist campaigning and the promise of more if needed, these rallies not only celebrated
white solidarity, they intimidated and degraded the Republican enemy. In
Granada, Mississippi, W. E. Kelley and State Senator William Price were
the most important white leaders of the Republican Party. Both men were
subjected to such intense intimidation that they desisted from campaigning,
and in the election their earlier majority of 700 turned into a Democratic
majority of 250. The night before the election Democrats held a torchlight
procession in Granada; one wagon carried two coffins marked "Kelley" and
"Price." On a second wagon, as Kelley later described it, "They had a large
platform built up, and on that they had a fire built, with a large cauldron . . .
filled with tar . . . and around it men representing devils, stirring up this kettle,
and going around it. I saw an old colored man lying on top there, and
inscribed around him was 'Here lies old Price.' They paraded the streets, and
came round in front of our building, shouting and hurrahing, some of them
calling for a rope to hang Price and Kelley with." At the end of the parade, the
marchers placed the coffins in the center of the town square to serve as a
warning to all.[57]

This grotesque procession amounted to a charivari, an often violent folk
drama of communal solidarity, akin to other White Line methods of achiev-
ing political ends that were all designed to isolate, punish, and ultimately
destroy people who deviated from agreed-upon moral standards. Kelley and
Price had, by this definition, contaminated themselves by their association
with the under race, and they could either recant and rejoin the white community or be destroyed. During events such as the funeral procession in
Granada, the White Line celebrated its reclaimed moral and social hegemony. The redeemed community purified itself racially by casting out the
blackened others while worshiping the white virgin. Once again, and for the
century to come, there was only one parade in town.

As the White Line marched violently to power in the summer of 1875, Republicans all over the state flooded Governor Ames's office with pleas for
support. Certain that only the federal army could provide the necessary security, Ames wrote to President Grant in September requesting troops. Grant,
who was resting at his summer house in Long Branch on the Jersey shore,

instructed his conservative attorney general to respond, and Edwards Pierre-pont telegraphed to Ames quoting Grant as saying, "The whole public are tired out with these annual autumnal outbreaks in the South, and a great majority are now ready to condemn any interference on the part of the government." Pierrepont advised Ames that his only recourse was to fend for himself and enlist his own state militia, presumably from among his overwhelmingly black base of support. "I suggest that you take all lawful means and all needed measures," Pierrepont admonished Ames. "Why cannot you 'strengthen yourself,'" by calling the legislature together, "and obtain from them whatever power, and money, and arms you need . . . to preserve the peace by the forces of your own state, and let the country see that the citizens of Miss[issippi] who are largely favorable to good order, and are largely Republican, have the courage and manhood to fight for their rights and to destroy the bloody ruffians who murder the innocent and unoffending freedmen." Grant's actual wishes may have included greater supportiveness for Ames, but Pierrepont's letter was clear, uninformed, unrealistic, and unhelpful.[58]

Some historians have argued that the upcoming election in Ohio tipped Grant toward dropping Ames and the Mississippi Republicans, given that such partisan uses of federal troops in the South had grown increasingly unpopular in the North. But more generally, the depression that had begun in 1873, the election of a Democratic congress in 1874, the general shift in north-ern interests away from justice for blacks and toward issues of business and labor, and the growing belief that the Reconstruction governments were hopelessly corrupt, taken together, were accurately reflected in Pierrepont's message that public opinion had tired of what the northern press referred to as the Southern Question.

Although the Mississippi legislature had, in fact, authorized two regi-ments of ten companies each several months earlier, the use of black soldiers was certain to create antagonism, and there were few other men to fill the ranks. Finally Ames managed to scrape together two companies of black troops, but the white Republican sheriff of Yazoo County declined to use these militiamen when Ames offered them. On the other hand, Ames's efforts provided great impetus to the White Line in their recruiting drive, for they seemed to substantiate the terrorists' rationalization that they were orga-nizing in self-defense against a black Republican militia. It was at this junc-ture, on October 12, that Ames confessed to his wife that he thought he had lost the struggle for Mississippi: "Through the terror caused by murders and threats, the colored people are thoroughly intimidated. Yes, a revolution has taken place—by force of arms—and a race are disfranchised—they are to be returned to a condition of serfdom—an era of second slavery." Ames momentarily blamed black people for refusing to arm when they had a chance, but he placed more onus on the Grant administration. "The political death of the Negro will forever release the nation from the weariness from such 'political outbreaks,'" he concluded bitterly. In the absence of federal intervention, counterrevolutionary terrorism had swept all before it; this was the eve of the destruction of the brief biracial Republican experiment in governance.[59]

Some White Line leaders were only too willing to help ignite an all-out race war they were certain they would win, but the political leadership of the movement acted more shrewdly. In part encouraged by an emissary Pierrepont sent to arrange a truce, on October 13, Ames agreed to a "peace conference" with James Z. George, a lawyer from Jackson who was spearheading the Democratic campaign, and several other leading White Liners.[60]

In this "compromise," which was actually a capitulation covered by the most transparent of fig leaves, Ames offered to disarm and disband the two companies of militia that had only been half-formed. In return, George and the others assured the governor in writing that "there was no other desire among the whites than that the peace should be preserved, the laws enforced, and a fair election be had," and that "they would do all in their power to preserve peace and good order and secure a fair election." So eager was Ames to obtain some kind of face-saving formula that he extracted no promise from the Democrats to disband and disarm *their* entirely extralegal militia. He conceded the essential point that the terrorist White Liners had created de facto legitimacy through overwhelming organized violence, power at the end of a thousand guns. Although Ames might well have wanted to believe the word of these men, the political violence they sponsored soon picked up with even greater intensity, including the terrible outbursts in Clinton and Yazoo City and dozens of other acts of political terror, both before voting day and at the polls.[61]

The Redeemers claimed to be conservatives—men like George and Congressman, later Senator, Lucius Q. C. Lamar—solid citizens who reassured anyone who would listen that they sought peace and a fair, paternalistic relationship with black people. Despite *using* the language of conservatism on occasions such as their meeting with Ames, however, they were really rationalizing their campaign of politically reactionary counterrevolutionary terrorism, a campaign they continued to lead even while they were making what appeared to be peace treaties. In 1875 they donned no Klan disguise: the same men who openly guided the terror talked with the governor, offering nothing more concrete than a promise that their well-armed and organized militia was designed to ignore. When analyzing the South Carolina Red Shirts, the historian Stephen Kantrowitz has referred to this linguistic cover-up as a "spurious and complicated protection racket." Men like George and Lamar promised peace, suggesting that Republicans ought to submit to well-bred leaders such as they, lest the savage white mob be let loose among blacks. But these mobs were their own shock troops acting out planned political assaults. White Line leaders maintained a public, consistent line of revolutionary rhetoric, employing it as openly as they did their alternative conservative language. Which language they used depended on changing tactical necessities. Of course they insisted their counterrevolution would usher in a new era of peace; of course they rallied the white citizens of their state with violent language stirring violent actions. Violent means were not the last resort but often the first because terrorism was such an efficient means of destroying their opposition. The subsequent peace continued to be based on terrorism— withheld, threatened, acted out, and always renewable. Ames had it right the day before the "peace conference." The withdrawal of the Grant administration from intervention in Mississippi meant capitulation to a counterrevolution that would return black people to the near-slavery of serfdom.[62]

Election day itself was eerily peaceful in many places—the successful effect of the long terrorist campaign. As one witness described the atmosphere, "It was a very quiet day in Jackson—fearfully quiet." In several places blacks voted the Democratic ticket, showing the white men surrounding the polls their open ballots. In other places they stayed in the woods or swamps rather than approach the polls. But in many other locales the White Line reinforced their monopoly at the ballot box though violence. In several counties armed men fired on would-be black voters "by accident," and in several towns, including Forest, Okolona, Port Gibson, and Aberdeen (where the local White Line leader imported mounted troops from Alabama), white militiamen cut off and surrounded groups of potential black voters, then charged into the crowds, sticks and pistol butts flailing, stampeding the terrified blacks into flight. In Granada, where W. E. Kelley and William Price had been the targets of the election eve charivari, a White Liner began beating a potential black voter with an ax handle. At that moment, as if on cue, the Democratic poll captain rolled out a cannon while his supporters dashed for the rifles they had stored nearby; blacks fled the scene, ballots uncast. This was the archetypal moment of triumph. The victory of the White Line terrorists was complete, there and across the state.[63]

The election resulted in a sweeping Democratic victory. In the only state-wide contest, for state treasurer, the Republican majority of 22,976 in 1873 turned into a Democratic majority of 31,544. Democrats swept five of the six congressional elections, including the victory of a turncoat republican, G. Wiley Wells. And in the state senate, where half the members were up for reelection, Democrats now outnumbered Republicans (including six hold-over blacks), 26 to 10, while in the lower house the Democratic majority was 95 to 20. This result was produced both by a reduced Republican vote and by what appears to have been a much-increased white vote—90 percent of white voters turned out, a tribute to the effectiveness of the White Line campaign to rally the race while scaring off black voters. This figure also included considerable ballot-box stuffing. In many locales of greatest violence the results were extraordinarily one-sided. In Aberdeen, where the Republican sheriff locked himself in the jail for safekeeping on election day and black voters fled the polls, the Republican majority vote of 648 in 1871 converted into a Democratic majority of 1,175. In Yazoo County, site of sustained political violence including one major "riot," the vote for state treasurer reversed from a Republican margin of 2,427 to 411 in 1873 to a Democratic victory of 4,044 to 7.[64]

Continued political violence rather than peace greeted this victory. In the aftermath of the election many remaining Republican officeholders fled the state in fear of what was to come. In Issaquena County, scene of so much political violence, the Republican vote actually increased in November 1875 because of the tiny white population (741 whites to 6,146 blacks), but the next month White Liners drove black officeholders out of the county with death threats and arms. A federal grand jury, called in Oxford to examine possible charges stemming from the political violence of the election campaign, returned no indictments, many of the jurors having been threatened with their lives. This weak attempt at justice marked the end of federal intervention in Mississippi for eighty years, during which the white-supremacist regime would remain unchallenged.[65]

In January 1876, Governor Adelbert Ames faced the revolutionary new White Line legislature in Jackson in an atmosphere of fear, punctuated by the nightly shooting of guns in the streets, sometimes aimed at the Governor's Mansion itself. Ames repudiated the validity of the new legislature, calling it an illegal body produced by a pattern of violence and fraud. For their part, the victors immediately impeached the superintendent of schools and the lieutenant governor, and began drawing up impeachment charges against Ames. At this juncture, Ames wrote to a friend in New York that he was not charged with corruption, the usual base for impeachment. "Nothing is charged beyond political sins. . . . Of course, with them that is a sin which to Republicans is of the highest virtue. Their object is to restore the Confederacy and reduce the colored people to a state of serfdom. I am in their way; consequently they impeach me." Ames's wife, Blanche, engineered an honorable departure with the legislators that would allow her husband to resign in exchange for their dropping all charges against him. After the resignation, they published the charges anyway. Not only did they want to destroy their enemy, the legislators wanted to be seen in public destroying him; honorable settlements did not apply to a carpetbagging race traitor such as Ames.[66]

Reactionary terror for political ends continued into the next election year, 1876, as a sort of mopping-up operation. Lynching spread, augmenting the by now tried-and-true methods—Democratic invasions of Republican meetings with cannons firing, economic intimidation, destruction of African American parades, and so on, in a pattern that had come to be called bulldozing. In May, 150 black men were rumored to be arming themselves in Wilkinson County in response to a lynching. Sheriff William Noble, a former scalawag turned Democrat, called in forces from Louisiana and, with the aid of some local whites, trapped the black men against the river, where they killed at least 50 of them, suffering no fatalities in return. The results of the 1876 election solidified the revolution of the previous year. All six congressmen were now Democrats, and Samuel J. Tilden, the Democratic candidate for president, carried Mississippi by a majority of 55,853 more votes than the Republican Rutherford B. Hayes.[67]

Although white domination was never again challenged in nineteenth-century Mississippi, black political participation of a clearly subordinate and ineffectual kind continued in several regions of the state. In part this was due to the fears of plantation owners in cotton country that their entirely black labor force would emigrate if conditions became too horrendous. Under what white leaders called the "fusion principle," blacks would continue to vote, would be allocated minor county offices—never the sheriff's job, however—and might be permitted one member in the legislature in a heavily black area. These officeholders could even call themselves Republicans, though they were always vetted: approved or disapproved by the local Democratic leadership. Between 1876 and 1890 the number of black legislators varied from eleven to seven, and there were still six sitting as late as 1890. But for all intents and purposes, the Democratic counterrevolutionaries had eradicated meaningful black participation and restored white rule through extreme and constant violence.[68]

Thus some tattered remnants of Reconstruction remained even after the successful White Line revolution of 1875. Across the South, the incomplete system of informal segregation and highly circumscribed black political participation left the white Democratic parties uneasy, particularly when the Populist movement threatened to split the white electorate and gain power with the help of black voters. And in the late 1880s, a widespread panic began sweeping the Deep South that black men were careening out of control—in particular, that they had begun a campaign of raping white women. This was another poisonous rumor, descendent of the rumor-mongering that had infected the white South during slavery days and Reconstruction. This panic, which led to a significant spike in the number of lynchings, reinforced the belief that it was time to fully institutionalize a segregation system and thoroughly disenfranchise blacks once and for all. Consequently, a series of constitutional conventions implemented a system of apartheid. All public places were legally segregated through the posting of signs and the enforcement of the courts, and more informally by the police, who often acted in concert with vigilante groups of white men outside of and unchecked by the law. Indeed "legal" enforcement was often intentionally linked to extralegal communal violence. There was a continuously reinforcing aspect to the reactionary terrorism that had seized state power.

Like their fellow white supremacists across the South, the writers of the Mississippi constitution of 1890 conceived of themselves as reformers. On the road to stripping blacks of the vote and other civil rights, these constitutional fathers could even admit that they had seized power in 1875 and had maintained their rule afterward through dishonesty and political violence. As Judge Chrisman told the Mississippi convention, "Sir, it is no secret that there has not been a full vote and a fair count in Mississippi since 1875, that we have been preserving the ascendancy of the white people by revolutionary methods. In other words we have been stuffing ballot boxes, committing perjury, and here and there in the state carrying the elections by fraud and violence." Such a policy was almost bound to lead to "disaster" at some point, "as certainly as there is a righteous judgment for nations as men. No man can be in favor of perpetuating the election methods which have prevailed in Mississippi since 1875 who is not a moral idiot." Only the complete disfranchisement of African Americans could purify what Judge Chrisman conceded was a corrupt political process. Without apparent cynicism or irony Chrisman argued that ending the black vote would be a progressive political reform, for it would eliminate the need to rig elections. When black voters were banished, white voters would be able to conduct free and fair elections.[69]

Once again we hear the language of conservatism applied to a ruthless white-supremacist strategy. Indeed, most historians agree that the voice of 1890 was a radical voice, overtly and hatefully racist. And most agree that the period from the late 1880s until at least 1920 marked the nadir of American race relations, a time in which political terror was ever more widespread and blacks were systematically stripped of their rights and bombarded by the scurrilous rhetoric of overtly racist demagogic politicians.[70]

But one should not read back from the later period of legalized segregation and purely inflammatory political rhetoric to suggest that the Redeemers were more temperate because some of them used less vicious language when articulating their white-supremacist views. It was a scant twelve to fourteen years from the Redeemers to the radical acceleration of the late 1880s, and the latter movement was an extension, and in a sense a further rationalization of, the groundwork the Redeemers had laid. The Redeemers created the white-supremacist goals and methods that served as a counterrevolutionary terrorist matrix for the later forms of radicalism.

The principle of "peacefully if possible, forcibly if necessary" was a call for as much reactionary terrorism as was needed, and the White Liners had lived up to their word. They turned their evangelical fervor and outraged republicanism to the goal of white supremacy. Looking back at the South Carolina movement of 1876, Robert Wallace Shand, a Red Shirt militia leader, queried rhetorically, "Was all this justifiable? Yes—for unlike elections at other times our very civilization was at stake. We could not live in South Carolina if negro rule continued. . . . We had to fight as we could. Our plan of campaign was an evil, but its success overcame a greater evil."[71]

During the White Line campaign, no Democratic newspaper or major Democratic public figure expressed the slightest moral reservation about the plan of attack—to the contrary, they were fierce in their determination to sweep all before them. It is in this framework that one must read their self-serving claims to paternalism and their insistence that they sought peace and wanted to exercise a kindly direction over the black race. Of course, if their power were unquestioned, they would prefer to act in a gentlemanly fashion, a style in which the better bred of them certainly believed. But during that campaign, when dominance was the central issue, they willingly suspended paternalism when necessary, revealing the genuine threat of violent terrorist attacks they intended to make on anyone who questioned their authority. That is the context in which to evaluate their self-proclaimed conservatism, which was actually a rhetorical tactic in their fundamentally violent counterrevolutionary strategy. During the heat of battle, gentlemen of property and standing let drop their paternalist guise. When they had won their victory, they could resume that image, but forever afterward the use of systematic terrorism would lend a sinister meaning to their professions that they would "take care" of "their" black people.

One of the doomed Republican candidates during the election of 1875 was George T. Cook, a black schoolteacher from Pennsylvania who had settled in Aberdeen and was running for the lower house of the legislature. Cook was a highly literate and witty man who made a considerable impression as a person of substance even on white Democrats. Nevertheless, he was an enemy whose political role they had to destroy. On October 12, Cook received an anonymous letter that read, "You are known to be a vile, corrupt, and thieving scoundrel, unworthy to live in any community. You are an enemy of the white and the black race; your death would be a blessing to the civilized world, and you are hereby notified that you must resign your political aspiration and leave Monroe County . . . by October 15." Despite a barrage of continued threats, Cook continued to speak at Republican meetings. On election day, hearing that the White Line militia was gathering around the central polling station in Aberdeen, Cook rode seven miles out into the country to vote. "I voted there, and prudently retired after voting," Cook later told senatorial investigators. Asked why he "prudently retired," he replied, "Well, there were some four or five white men from Aberdeen walking around there, and one of them identified me as being 'the carpet-bag scoundrel Yankee nigger,' as they always used to call me; and he had a considerable of a good-size club, and looked as if he had the ability to use it."

During the campaign, several of the leading citizens of Aberdeen—"conservative gentlemen," Cook called them—had told him that "the white men intend to rule this county, and that they had submitted to negro and to military rule about long enough, and that we could not expect to have their friendship unless we either voted their ticket or refused to have anything to do with politics." After the White Line victory, these same gentlemen could relax a bit. Isaac Dodge, a "nice, clever gentleman" in Cook's reckoning, who kept the local livery stable, told Cook one day "that he thought I was the most genteel free nigger he ever saw, and he never heard anything bad about me, and that if I got into difficulty there without bringing it on myself—he says, 'If you behave hereafter as you have done before, I will protect you. Don't go away now; the radicals are beaten, and the democrats and conservatives—the white men—are going to rule the county, and now we want you to stay, and if you behave yourself you will be protected.'"[72]

Isaac Dodge was comfortable in his knowledge that the White Line had re-created a white southern republic where African Americans, put back in their place, could be subjects of humorous contempt rather than objects of fear. The counterrevolutionary victory had demanded a disciplined and bloody terrorist campaign: violence that was unifying, liberating, and cathartic as well as politically successful for its instigators, endlessly fearsome and humiliating for its victims.

The white tribe was back in the saddle.

CHAPTER 4

The Haymarket
Terrorism and Class Conflict

In the gathering gloom auguring a late-afternoon spring thunderstorm on May 4, 1886, at the Haymarket Square in Chicago, Samuel Fielden, a stone hauler and anarchist labor agitator, jumped down off the wagon from which he had been speaking. The dispirited crowd of ragged, mainly unemployed workingmen began to disperse, just as a phalanx of 176 policemen marched at double-quick time into the square. A few minutes earlier, Fielden had harangued his audience with strident revolutionary language delivered in his English working-class accent, "You have nothing more to do with the law except to lay hands on it and throttle it until it makes its last kick. It has turned your brethren out on the wayside and degraded them until they have lost the last vestige of humanity, and become mere things and animals. Keep your eye upon it, throttle it, kill it, stab it." Now the forces of the law formed ranks, military style. They were led by Inspector John Bonfield, a veteran of many savage attacks on workers, who had instructed his men, "Don't spare the powder," and by Captain William Ward, who commanded the crowd to disperse, something they were already doing. "But we are peaceable," Fielden insisted; "all right, we will go."

At that moment, a hissing spherical object sailed over the heads of the crowd into the ranks of the police and exploded with an enormous roar. As several policemen fell, wounded by the shrapnel of a dynamite bomb, the rest pulled out their pistols and fired wildly, hitting some of their fellow policemen as well as many in the crowd, a few of whom may have had pistols and returned fire. "Fire and kill all you can," Police Lieutenant James Bowler shouted to his men. Seven policemen were fatally wounded, along with an uncounted but similar number of workers, men who over the following days remained faceless and nameless to the press in death, as they had been in life.[1]

The movement that led to this explosion and the show trial of the anarchist leaders that followed together make up the most dramatic episode of class conflict–based terrorism in American history. Examining it with care can elucidate much of the underlying structure within which later terrorist events have been dealt with in the United States, where alien, revolutionary terrorism has often led to reactionary government responses that sacrifice freedom to the quest for security. Indeed, the analysis in this chapter is intended in part as a means to lay out a template for understanding the attacks of September 11, 2001, and the retaliatory actions of the Bush administration as an exchange between revolutionary and reactionary terrorism. To a considerable degree this history does repeat itself.

In 1875, while African Americans were being beaten into submission by Redeemer regimes in the South, a vast new proletariat, composed mainly of poor immigrants, presented what appeared to most ruling authorities in the northern states to be an enormous social and economic threat. These ethnic and religious aliens were also often virulently anti-capitalist, and thus almost unimaginably "anti-American." American society seemed to be dividing along class lines, pitting the middle and upper classes against the masses in an incipient industrial catastrophe of the kind that was previously thought to have characterized only Europe. Organized, if marginal, revolutionary terrorism became locked in a struggle with reactionary state terrorism. Each side in the conflict wrapped the mantle of liberty and morality around its shoulders while insisting that the corruption of all that was holy came from the subhuman and dehumanizing others. The scene of combat would be the courtroom and death row as well as the streets: at stake were human lives as well as proprietorship of the fundamental collective values of freedom, justice, and order.

Immediately after the explosion, with almost unanimous support from the mainstream press and the populace, the Chicago police embarked on a campaign of reactionary terrorism, a prolonged Red Scare to secure the republic from the subversive bombers. As might have been expected, the Chicago papers were the most sanguinary. "The anarchists are amenable to no reason except that taught by the club and the rifle," the *Chicago Daily News* insisted, and the *Chicago Times* urged that to deal with such "miscreants," the command should be "Fire low and fire quick . . . remorselessly."[2]

Across the nation, headlines screamed about "Bloody Monsters," "fiends" in human form. Likening them to Apache, the Saint Louis *Globe-Democrat* insisted, "There are no good anarchists except dead anarchists. . . . Let us whip these Slavic wolves back to the European dens from which they issue, or in some sense exterminate them." The *New York Times* suggested the appropriate remedy for the socially diseased of Chicago: "In the early stages of an acute outbreak of anarchy a Gatling gun, or if the case be severe, two, is the sovereign remedy. Later on, hemp [hanging], in judicious doses, has an admirable effect in preventing a spread of the disease."[3]

Overwhelmingly supported by public opinion as well as the press, and infuriated by the deaths of their comrades, the police immediately set out a dragnet. "Make the raids first and look up the law afterward!" Julius S. Grinnell, the Cook County state's attorney, instructed the police, and Mayor Carter Harrison, a long-time friend of the worker, issued draconian orders, amounting to martial law, prohibiting any public assembly of workers. Hoping to uncover evidence of what they believed was a huge, well-organized conspiracy, the police dispersed picket lines, beat up strikers, broke into labor halls and private residences, and arrested more than two hundred workers, throwing them into jail without charges or the right to secure an attorney. They beat many of the prisoners, hoping to elicit information, promising relief only if the prisoners turned state's evidence. Some did, telling the authorities what they wanted to hear even if it meant lying.

And then on May 27, three weeks after the bomb was thrown, eight of the prisoners—the leadership of the anarchist movement—were indicted for murder and criminal conspiracy. They were brought to trial on June 27, convicted on August 20, and all but one sentenced to hang, a punishment that was carried out on four of them on November 11, 1887. The drama of the trial and its aftermath revealed the depths of the divisiveness at the core of American industrial and social relations and the fear among the better off in the new industrial cities that their land was filling with frightening aliens toiling in satanic mills. Nothing had prepared the American citizenry for this suddenly invasive cityscape, where all the familiar, reassuring social ties appeared to have been cast off in ugly and often violent ways. Now was the time to resurrect the old values before it was too late. In the echo of the Haymarket bomb, the Red Scare and show trial amounted to legally sanctioned state terrorism, employed to combat the anarchist terrorism of the streets. The Golden Rule was reconstituted to read, Do unto others as you fear they will do unto you.

This event was a hyper-dramatic enactment of social divisions that had long festered in the United States. The dominant society—white, bourgeois and "respectable" working class, English speaking, established—articulated what one might call the official values of the day through its most significant social institutions: the press, the courts, the police, business organizations, and the Protestant Church. In opposition, the anarchists expressed a contrary set of values, often amounting to direct and violent attacks on those who dominated them. Both sides sought control of shared symbols that defined the moral ground for the future of American society. The struggle over values so fundamental to the social fabric lent special intensity to this class conflict, making a huge impact on the nation as a whole.

Although urbanization and immigration were as old as the American republic, and although the notion that an alien menace was polluting the big cities certainly dated from the mass immigration of Irish Roman Catholics that began in the 1840s (if not from the Alien and Sedition Acts of 1798), one event previous to the Haymarket affair in particular had galvanized Americans' fears of massive social change: the national railroad strike of 1877, when railway workers in major cities, subjected to deep wage cuts during a depression and often roughly treated by their employers, went on a spontaneous wildcat strike that shut down the essential artery of national commerce. In several places they also resorted to sabotage and violence. Unprepared and overwhelmed, mistrusting militias that had ties to the workers, local and state authorities called on the national government to break the strike, and in response President Rutherford B. Hayes sent out federal troops, the first time in American history federal soldiers had been used to quell an industrial disturbance (and the same year that he stopped the army from having any further involvement in securing black rights in the South). This shocking labor violence and the responses to it were to be repeated several times in the late nineteenth and early twentieth centuries.

As many of the workers in the most dangerous occupations were poor recent immigrants, the standard explanations for the industrial strife tendered by the wealthier native-born population were xenophobic. American workers had always made free contracts with their employers, they believed, and an ambitious worker retained the ability to become a master himself if he remained frugal, sober, and peaceful. This new form of collective labor violence, acted out in many episodes over the years, could only be explained as an un-American pestilential visitation from class-riven Europe.

In addition, in 1877, and again in 1886, the uprising of the Paris Commune in 1871, fresh in many people's minds, seemed to illustrate the anarchy threatened by the lower orders and the necessity of using draconian measures to quash their rebellions. At that time, after the empire of Louis Napoleon had collapsed following France's massive defeat in the Franco-Prussian War, socialists and anarchists had seized control of Paris. They held it for several months before the forces of the new Third Republic gathered troops and, with the Prussian army politely standing aside, entered Paris and slaughtered about twenty-five thousand Communards—men, women, and children. In response to the railroad strike of 1877, many newspapers called for the "grape and canister" policy that the French forces had used, as the *Philadelphia Record* put it. In Pittsburgh, the *Commercial Gazette* agreed that to quell the growing "spirit of the commune . . . [l]aw and order [must come] first, justice afterwards." The *Albany Journal* explained, with no apparent irony, that strikers would have to be taught "at the mouth of the cannon and the point of the bayonet, that this is a free country." The higher goal of maintaining social order by any means necessary trumped the Anglo-American tradition of liberty for all. Justice had to be suspended or redirected toward systematic purgation of the ogres of disorder. Freedom equaled social order. Thus, eighty years before McCarthyism, the American tradition of repressive anticommunism was born, a tradition that can embrace other enemies as well, for example, "Islamofascists."[4]

Such harsh applications of force were justified, the American establishment believed, because the threat had been imported in abuse of the American tradition of having open borders for freedom-seeking immigrants. As James A. Garfield of Ohio, minority leader of the House of Representatives and future president of the United States, put it in 1878, "It is not the proper and lawful refusal of laborers to be oppressed by the capitalists that threatens the public peace, but the red fool-fury of the Seine, transported here, taking root in our disasters, and drawing its life only from our misfortunes." No self-respecting American workingman would take up the cudgels of violence—such evil was extrinsic to the real American republic. "Socialism in America is an anomaly," the *Chicago Daily News* editorialized in January 1886, agreeing with Garfield, "and Chicago is the last place on earth where it would exist were it not for the dregs of foreign immigration which find lodgment here."[5]

A wide range of evils within America could be explained as the result of class-ridden, degenerate Europeans. In 1872, for example, following the Great Fire of Chicago a group of protesters marched behind the banner "Leave a Home for the Laborer," protesting a proposed City Council attempt to legislate a building code that would ban cheap—and inflammable—building materials, thus making it hard for workers to reconstruct their houses. A few of the protesters, many of whom were of foreign birth, heaved bricks through the windows of the temporary city hall. In response, the newspapers denounced "the scum of the community . . . mongrel firebugs, [who] never owned a foot of ground and never will, if they do not spend less money for beer and whiskey." Such a demonstration was but "a taste of communism." The City Council passed the building code and then set about regulating the beer gardens and saloons frequented mainly by foreign workers.[6]

Thus the language of loathing was used to blame un-Americans for social distress. America, in the establishment estimation, was essentially unitary in values, based on order and freedom, opportunity and democracy, while threats to that order came from outside, like disease to an otherwise healthy host. Militant foreign workers were widely perceived as desecrators of all that was good and republican and Christian in America, the agents of filth corrupting public purity. By the time the Haymarket bomb exploded, the explanation of any industrial evil was well in place—and for many Americans the explosion released them from their normal self-censorship, licensing extreme language in response. "The enemy forces [are the] rag-tag and bob-tail cutthroats of Beelzebub from the Rhine, the Vistula and the Elbe," declared the *Chicago Times.* Other newspapers called the anarchists "scum and offal . . . human and inhuman rubbish . . . the offscourings of Europe," who had come to "indulge in that license" forbidden them by European autocracies. It was high time for them to receive the punishment of "rope, bullet or ax," populist vigilante tactics that had now been delegated to the police.[7]

That such a brutal version of justice was likely to replicate European governmental tyranny was not significant for such writers. It was as if they believed that a scourging of the anarchist villains at hand could purge the nation of evil. But what if class tensions had complex causes that demanded long-term government solutions? The notion of building an activist state that would gradually regulate and reform industrial society barely existed, and it was certainly not part of mainstream values. Immediate action was necessary, and it would have to suffice: presumably, powerful acts of repression were needed to respond to powerful outbreaks of anarchism, as often as necessary. That this response might not deal with the underlying social problems, that it might lead to a cycle of terror that would undermine freedom in the name of freedom and thus let terrorism win, evidently was too abstract a concept. Then (as now), for those in political charge of American society, the stark, black-and-white war of good versus evil offered a kind of morality play, a repeatable ritual of violent class struggle. As the irrepressible and grizzled veteran warrior William Tecumseh Sherman put it in 1886, "There will soon come an armed contest between Capital and Labor. They will oppose each other not with words and arguments, but with shot and shell, gunpowder and cannon. The better classes are tired of the insane howlings of the lower strata, and they mean to stop them."[8]

For Sherman and many others like him, as well as for the workers who hated the social order, "Capital" was shorthand for those in power, led by businessmen, who controlled the state, and including churches, the courts, the army, and the police. Although these institutions were relatively small and disorganized by today's standards, they were strong enough to maintain political and social dominance when class antipathies erupted into violence.

"Labor," on the other hand, was so disorganized that it hardly had a collective identity at all. Workers came from many lands, spoke a number of languages, worshiped at separate churches, and lived islanded in ethnic communities among others like themselves. Unions were few and weak. Some skilled workers had organizations, and the Knights of Labor were attempting to organize all workers, industrial and craft, but they were swimming against a stream of worker dissimilarity and an individualist tradition in employment. Native-born workers and many from abroad were alike fearful of socialism, at the time a persuasion more than a coherent movement, which sought to further working-class consciousness, while many unionists were meliorists looking not for revolution or even heightened class consciousness but to simply improve working conditions and wages. Socialists prophesized that the day would come when the workers would seize the means of production and the state and would create a government of workers, for workers. But socialism itself contained many conflicting tendencies—from utopianism and reformism, which recoiled from strikes and strife, to more militant Marxism. Some socialists formed political parties to try to obtain power by legal means, but these met with limited electoral success. Almost all believed that their analysis of the situation was scientific and historically inevitable but that the workers' immense sufferings made finding a solution urgent. This left open the question of whether violence should play a role in bringing about a workers revolution.

It was precisely around the issue of force and the imminence of a cataclysmic showdown with Capital that anarchism developed as a movement among socialists, mushrooming both in Europe and the United States during the 1880s. Although there were many preconditions for its rapid development, perhaps the most telling was the high level of unemployment and poverty in the cities coupled with the increasing use of police brutality to suppress industrial workers. By 1885 the American economy was mired in a deep depression, leading employers to fire hundreds of thousands of workers and slash the wages of the remainder. Strikes were wildcat affairs that tended to last a few angry days while the bosses brought in scab labor and the police defended the plants and assaulted the picketers. Tens of thousands of impoverished men and women milled about the cities without work, sustained only by intermittent private charity, driven from pillar to post. A significant minority of these workers had become so desperate and angry that they sought to destroy the economic system and the men who ran it, whatever the consequences.

Bruce. C. Nelson, a close student of Chicago anarchism, posits that in 1886 there were between 723 and 861 anarchists in organized groups, of whom only about 175 were members of "American"—that is to say, English-speaking —units; the majority were primarily Germans and other central or eastern Europeans. These organizations were locals of the International Working People's Association (IWPA), a group founded in England in 1864 and re-born in American form in 1881.[9]

The manifesto of the IWPA dated from 1883; Johann J. Most, a German-born firebrand and international revolutionist, composed it for a Pittsburgh convention. Unlike many socialists, IWPA anarchists, who usually called themselves "revolutionary socialists," opposed the very existence of the state, denouncing both parliamentary government and institutional reform. In this they were close to Marxist socialists in both name and program. What distinguished them from other socialist groups was the millenarian intensity of their call for direct action to seize power, if not immediately then imminently.

Johann Most folded the 1883 Pittsburgh manifesto into the American republican tradition, beginning with the Declaration of Independence, in which Jefferson called it the right and the duty of the people to throw off despotism and create a new government. If Jefferson's foundational writing justified "armed resistance by our forefathers," Most insisted, the "necessities of the present time compel us to re-assert their declaration." Most found great value in Jeffersonian republicanism and sought to guide American workers who subscribed to those values to new ends. Jefferson-like, Most composed a list of current social evils, including "the exploitation of the propertyless by the propertied," those who enriched themselves by others' labor and claimed a greater and greater monopoly of wealth and power while workers were driven into ever-deeper poverty. All current laws were directed against workers, claimed Most. Schools for the poor supplied little but crude indoctrination producing "prejudice, arrogance and servility; in short, want of sense," while churches sought to make "complete idiots out of the mass and to make them forgo the paradise on earth by promising a fictitious heaven." The press and political parties were mere lackeys of the "capitalistic classes," who would never cede power voluntarily.

This was standard Marxian socialist analysis; it was the remedy and the social goal that set anarchists apart. To strike off their chains, Most wrote, workers must create "agitation for the purpose of agitation; organization for the purpose of rebellion." Knowing that no good could be expected from "our master . . . there remains but one resource—FORCE!" Only the destruction of the ruling class would lead to a "free society based upon cooperative organization, to exchange of products without merchant capitalism and without 'profit-mongery.'" This was relatively mild language for Most and for the Chicago anarchists as well. The emphasis on force, on a cataclysmic revolution that would simultaneously bring forth its cooperative alternative, inspired an escalating rhetorical and psychological fervor as anarchists began to perceive signs of the approaching revolutionary end time. The most obvious signal was increased police oppression, which created a special fury among the masses of unemployed and destitute workers. Sharing that anger, and often special targets of the police themselves, anarchists sought to articulate, amplify, and channel it into a revolutionary vanguard that could act as soon as possible with concentrated, overwhelming force. Revolutionary terrorism rose in tandem with reactionary terrorism.[10]

Through their speeches and in their newspapers, Chicago anarchists attempted to construct a superior counterculture—an alternative politics, a relevant faith—that would persuade downtrodden workers to join their revolution. *The Alarm* was their English paper, and their German-language *Arbeiter-Zeitung* (Workers Newspaper) reached a far broader audience of approximately twenty thousand (as many as read the mainstream German-language Republican Party paper published in Chicago). The IWPA also sponsored picnics and choral societies, poetry readings and dramatic societies, and members met in favorite taverns, in meeting halls, and along the shore of Lake Michigan for social as well as political events. Their largest gatherings were for the commemoration of the Paris Commune in March, and for the international labor holiday, May Day. Spontaneous (and carefully organized) fellowship offered a pleasant respite from the alienating experience of the big industrial city, a substitute for churches and political parties, and a seedbed for revolutionary terrorist training. Within the core group the IWPA also secretly discussed military tactics and formed rifle clubs, drilling for a showdown with authority.

Chicago's anarchists built their strength on root-and-branch opposition to bourgeois society. Not merely did they oppose capitalism; they opposed all the established tenets of the existing social order. "All political laws [are violations] of the laws of nature and the rights of man," William Holmes wrote in *The Alarm* in 1884, outlining the anarchist credo. "The more a man is governed, the less he is free." The anarchist "has no faith in the laws of man; but all faith in the laws of nature. . . . He therefore demands the abolition of all political laws, and the restoration of all the rights of man as nature has provided." Holmes, like John Brown—or Jefferson, for that matter—had great faith that because true revolutionaries understood the higher laws of nature, they could dispense with the merely customary and inevitably corrupt positive laws that governed ordinary people. They followed a theology of total human freedom. Albert Parsons, the leading native-born Chicago anarchist, always added when he reached this point in the credo: "Government is for slaves; free men govern themselves." The capitalists were the false law-making class, and so a root-and-branch revolution included the abolition of law and private property, which was rooted in law—institutionalized arrangements that Parsons called the "coward's weapon." Law was merely the less obvious arm of violent oppression.[11]

"No God, No Master," their banners proclaimed when they marched on public holidays; "No Priests, No Capitalists, No State, No Law." Religion was another social building block that needed to be removed. As Parsons put it in 1885, anarchy and religion were locked in a "struggle for supremacy between the real and unreal, between the known and the unknown, between the natural and unnatural, between knowledge and superstition." Anarchy was "armed with ideas only," while "all the material forces, 'brute force' of the established order," were arrayed on the side of religion.[12]

Anarchist agitators were well aware of the impact their anti-establishment theistic version of the higher law would have on the polite classes, many of whom were fascinated in a horrified sort of way at such utterly foreign ideas. On March 5, 1885, Parsons was invited to address the West Side Philosophical Society, an upper-middle-class organization, at a packed meeting at Princeton Hall on West Madison Street. "I am the notorious Parsons, the fellow with the long horns, as you know him from the daily press," Parsons began, playing with his public image as the devil, which was precisely how many in the audience viewed him. Parsons used the occasion to insult the "many gentlemen in white shirts and ladies wearing elegant and costly toilets" in his audience, telling them that their fine clothes were made by "*Sans Culottes*" who dwelled in misery and hunger, people who one day would awaken them with the "thunders of dynamite" if they did not mend their ways and "hearken to the voice of reason." Parsons was referring, of course, to the poor Parisian workers (who wore trousers instead of knee-breeches [culottes]) who had formed the most radical and violent element during the terrorist phase of the French Revolution. Certainly understanding the threat behind Parsons's revolutionary reference, the audience hissed, and two terrified young women fled in tears, but the rest sat riveted to their chairs.[13]

Whether consciously or not, Parsons, who had been reared in Texas and fought for the Confederacy, had both reversed the message and assumed the stance of an evangelical preacher. Bred in a Protestant religious system he now scorned, he understood that Christians would see him as the anti-Christ. In his counter-jeremiad, he threatened them with imminent damnation if they did not mend their ways. And in fact he brought to bear a sturdy knowledge of the Bible, which he often used when attacking organized religion and the other props of the social order.

On Thanksgiving Day, November 29, 1884, Parsons spoke to a crowd of three thousand, many of them unemployed, at Haymarket Square. Rich capitalists "were enjoying today the feast of Belshazzar . . . wrung from the blood of our wives and children, and the champagne thus obtained ought to strangle them," Parsons began. Fancy preachers in elegant churches were that day citing Scripture to reassure the capitalists, Parsons knew, and in response he quoted from those portions of the Holy Book that amounted to a sort of anarchist's alternative version of Scripture. Parsons's favorite verse was from the book of James, "Go now ye rich men, weep and howl for your miseries which shall come upon you. Your gold and silver are cankered . . . and shall eat your flesh as it were fire. . . . Behold the hire of the laborers which have reaped down your fields, and which you have kept back by fraud." Parsons also quoted from Amos, "Hear this, O ye that swallow up the needy, even to make the poor to fall from the land, that ye may buy the poor for silver shoes and the needy for a pair of shoes." And Isaiah, "Woe unto them that join house to house and lay field to field till there is no place that they may be alone in the midst of the earth." And Solomon, when that wise king proclaimed, "There is a generation that are pure in their own eyes, and yet is not washed of their filthiness; a generation, O how lofty are their eyes, and how their eyelids are lifted up." And Habakkuk, who had warned the Israelites, "Woe to him that buildeth a town by blood, and establisheth a city by iniquity." Parsons, the revolutionary anarchist, preached that unlike the poor among the Hebrews and Christians of old, "We do not intend to leave this matter in the hands of the Lord. . . . We intend to do something for ourselves, and do it in this world."[14]

Parsons was thoroughly conversant with the religion he both invoked and rejected (and after all, the Judeo-Christian God was said to love the down-trodden); his consciousness and that of most the workers listening to him had been formed in Christian churches. The anarchists deliberately extended their antiauthoritarianism to the strictures of church leadership, discipline, and creed; they knew that the God and the religious values they hated could be turned to revolutionary purposes if they were reworked for alternative, apocalyptic ends. Anarchist agitators preached a "scientific" faith grounded in the zealous republican and religious values they sought to turn upside down.

Defiance was the great anarchist motif, and it suffused their language. Repeated rituals of defiance helped them remake themselves as dedicated, almost superhuman revolutionaries who could join with their fellows through violent action to create invincible collective power. In an editorial mocking the pleas for moderation emanating from other working-class leaders, William Holmes celebrated the truly subversive anarchist by ironically assuming the voice of those he considered class cowards, frightened of the dangers the anarchist presented: "If you fall into his hands . . . goodbye contentment and peace and submissiveness and patriotism. [The anarchist breeds only] discontent and aggressiveness. He is an eternal rebel and glories in his rebellion. He is an advocate of . . . war against this God-ordained and capitalist-supported system. He acknowledges no country; has no creed; worships at no shrine; reverences no institutions; calls no man master. . . . He is an advocate of violence, retaliation and universal Anarchy."[15]

Disintegration would precede revolution. The poorest of the poor, exploited and alienated, were in the best position to shed all vestiges of past submission and claims to respectability for they had nothing to lose. Forged in anarchist consciousness, they would arise, able and ready to strike down the forces of order in one huge, terrorist-ignited revolution. An 1885 editorial in the *Arbeiter-Zeitung* created a literary conceit in the form of what one might call the emerging New Anarchist Man. When "Order and Justice" are maintained by traditional leaders, "harlequins given to treason, phariseeism and lying, and blood; devastation and destruction mark[ing] their course," life can appear to be impossible for the poor working wretches. But when all seems hopeless, "deep in the background" there emerges a "wholly different" class of leaders. These reborn anarchists "have serious faces which express courage, fearlessness, character and power of action." They carry weapons and "cannot have any good intentions; it is night so that their forms and movement can scarcely be seen." Are they criminals? No, their faces reflect a "higher radiance that surrounds their ideal features . . . frank, fiery eyes . . . proud self possession." When they come into focus, one sees, emblazoned on their flags, "death to the tyrants, death to all deception and lies." Soon their ranks will grow numberless; the "avengers" of the exploited generations will arise. A few months later, the same editorialist could foretell even more clearly the rapidly approaching revolution led by these brave new anarchists. Soon they would build "the temple of the unveiled Goddess of Liberty upon the whole face of the globe. But to this end," admonished the writer, stressing the necessarily violent means that lay at the core of revolutionary terrorism, "you must be wolves, and as such you need sharp teeth. Workingmen arm yourselves!"[16]

Unlike the other union and socialist movements with which the anarchists were in effect competing for recruits, it was never clear whether the means and the goal of anarchism were collective. Indeed, anarchists disagreed on this point among themselves, as they did on participation in wider labor movements, such as the common front then pushing for an eight-hour workday. The majority of Chicago anarchists did believe in using group formations and tactics that linked them to other workers organizations; indeed, many of them were also union members. But the most extreme of these rebels, who called themselves Autonomists, rejected the tendency toward bureaucratic domination that they found in *all* permanent associations. They feared the pollution of power even within their own ranks. And for this minority within a minority, freedom demanded spontaneity of individual action—the inspired anarchist would know what to do in any given situation and would act on his own. At the expense of his life, he would blow up the oppressor. He was the exalted and unruly enactor of true freedom, the godlike metaphysical revolutionary terrorist come to earth.[17]

The IWPA chapters and the Chicago leadership managed to retain the Autonomists at the same time that they carried out more collective activities. Their organization did have structure—there were organized groups, as well as speakers and writers who were identified by mainstream journalists as leaders. Planning social events, rallies, and actions collectively, the leaders nevertheless did not seek to control independent individualist expressions of anarchist truths; on the contrary, they encouraged them.

Anarchists nurtured the ideal of freely willed, correctly informed individual action. In 1884, in her frequently reprinted and widely distributed one-page
parable "To Tramps: The Unemployed, the Disinherited, the Miserable,"
Lucy Parsons, the wife of Albert Parsons, composed a fantasy of political
revenge by the downtrodden. She vividly described the lot of many working
people, "harnessed to machines" for up to sixteen hours a day, their products
stolen by the bosses, their mean lives keeping them at best "but a few days
ahead of the wolves." Workers remained in their chains "at the caprice of
[their] employers," who, when it suited the necessities of their profit margin,
mercilessly threw them onto the streets, leaving each "a tramp, with hunger in
your stomach and rags on your back." Cold, wet, starving, miserable, and
homeless, the tramps may be tempted to dash themselves "into the cold
embrace of the lake rather than longer suffer thus." "Stop!" Parsons insisted.
Instead of killing yourselves, walk up the streets of the wealthy and deliver a
petition "by the red glare of destruction." These exploitative class robbers have
never yielded power or wealth to peaceful petitions. They understand only one
language, the speech that comes "from the cannon's mouth." Furthermore,
"you need no organization when you make up your mind to present this kind of
petition. In fact an organization would be a detriment . . . but each of you
hungry tramps . . . avail yourselves of those little methods of warfare which
Science has placed in the hands of the poor man, and you will become a
power . . . in this land. *Learn the use of explosives!*"[18]

Posing the meaning of life for the dispossessed in this way, anarchists like
Lucy Parsons arrived philosophically at nihilism—the absolute destruction of
authority and even, if need be, of oneself. The nihilists' assassination of Tsar
Alexander II in 1881 was a thrilling example of revolutionary anarchy. An 1885
editorial in *The Alarm* argued that no government could exist without a head;
repeated assassinations would therefore destroy government. By this means,
"all governments will disappear forever. Those governments least offensive to
the people should be destroyed last." There would always be natural leaders,
teachers, and advisers, "but bosses, jailers and drivers are unnecessary." Nihilism appears immoral or amoral to the uninitiated, but the theorist concluded
in self-justification that "assassination properly applied is wise, just, humane
and brave. For freedom, all things are just." If you are about to be destroyed,
destroy your would-be destroyer first, or at least take him with you. This was
the freedom fighter of the last resort, ancestor of today's suicide bomber.[19]

Though anarchists insisted that it was the industrial system that caused
misery, they always personalized that system. They talked about a general

social revolution, but they most often advocated individual deeds that would lead to more individual deeds that would, in an additive and accelerating way, bring about the collapse of government. The connecting thread in this revolutionary terrorist reasoning was destruction—the terrorist act.

The means to ignite this process, as Lucy Parsons indicated, had been handed to the poor everywhere by modern science: dynamite. Indeed, the anarchists made a veritable fetish of dynamite. More than any other topic, dynamite and its use appealed to their imagination. Their publications carried repeated, detailed descriptions of dynamite bomb production; their speeches frequently concluded with paeans of praise to dynamite.

The men in power were aware of this new technological danger. In his annual report of November 10, 1884, General Philip Sheridan, commander-in-chief of the U.S. Army, warned, "This nation is growing so rapidly that there are signs of other troubles which I hope will not occur, and which will probably not come upon us if both capital and labor will only be conservative. Still it should be remembered [that] destructive explosives are easily made, and that banks . . . public buildings and large mercantile houses can be readily demolished, and the commerce of entire cities destroyed by an infuriated people with means carried with perfect safety in [their] pockets." Only three weeks later, *The Alarm* reprinted Sheridan's warning in an editorial entitled "Dynamite: The Protection of the Poor Against the Armies of the Rich." With considerable sarcasm, the editorial suggested that "a hint to the wise is sufficient. Of course Gen. Sheridan is too modest to tell us himself that an army will be powerless in the coming revolution between the propertied and the propertyless classes. . . . One dynamite bomb properly placed, will destroy a regiment [with a weapon] easily made" and concealed.[20]

Dynamite seemed so perfect: all that concentrated destructive power, cheaply made, easily concealed and used, terribly deadly. Dynamite seemed to level the playing field of political violence. Properly used, it made one worker as strong as whole regiments. Then as now, dynamite and its variants were the most powerful weapons available to individuals and groups that lacked the wealth, the armies, and the massive firepower of established states. This remains the weapon of choice for those practicing what terrorism experts call asymmetrical warfare.

Anarchists rhapsodized about the new weapon. After reprinting more of Sheridan's annual report, *The Alarm* sang out, "Dynamite is the emancipator! In the hand of the enslaved it cries aloud: 'Justice or annihilation!' But best of all, the workingmen are not only learning its use, they are going to use it."

Dynamite would destroy private property and government—and using it would eradicate all vestiges of submission. The following year, in the same publication, an Indianapolis anarchist almost swooned: "Dynamite! Of all the good stuff, this is the stuff . . . this sublime stuff." And a Mr. Gorsuch rhapsodized,

> But now labor, strong and mighty, doth arise and claim her own;
> Steady roll the wheels of progress crushing money, king and throne.
> Then our battle-cry re-echo, "dynamite shall free the slave!"
> All ye men who fear not, forward! Tho' ye fill a martyr's grave;
> Yet the tyrant private property dethrone, the coming race
> Bright with glowing fire of freedom shall thy name in honor trace.[21]

Images of dynamite filled anarchist speeches as well. On April 28, 1885, the evening of the grand banquet to open the elegant Board of Trade building in Chicago, the IWPA called a protest meeting at the Haymarket. How could capitalists build a "Temple of Usury," Samuel Fielden demanded, contrasting the workers' fifteen-cent meal (with a piece of pie thrown in) with the twenty-dollar dishes of the rich. It was high time to "destroy from the earth every unproductive member of society." Then Albert Parsons, the last speaker to take the stand, concluded that to achieve emancipation, "Every man must buy a Colt's navy revolver (Cheers from the crowd and 'that's what we want'), a Winchester rifle ('and ten pounds of dynamite—we will make it ourselves!') and learn how to make and use dynamite. (Cheers and cries of 'Vive la Commune!')," reported *The Alarm*.[22]

With such call-and-response rituals, speakers and audience shared an exhilarating vision of the coming destruction of capitalism, brought about by Lord Dynamite. Whether this rhetoric of revolutionary terrorism amounted to actual preparation for revolution or was merely a verbal safety valve for the violent resentments of the dispossessed is impossible to determine. We do know, however, that the police had spies among the anarchists taking down every word for possible future use as they built their case for the unleashing of reactionary terrorism. Indeed, some of the police were almost certainly agents provocateurs who took it upon themselves to amp up the anarchist rhetoric and encourage the most violent elements in the movement, the better to discredit it when they acted. In this context, Captain Bonfield, the police commander of the labor beat, had been bragging to the press that his policy of clubbing workers was all that kept Chicago from insurrection, while he fed his alarm and anger with every report he solicited.

In the spring of 1886, during a long depression marked by increasing unemployment and wildcat strikes, the Chicago police became increasingly anxious, while the anarchists grew in confidence. All across the nation more and more desperate workers flocked to the eight-hour-workday movement, including a wide variety of unionists and socialists. After initially staying away from the movement, which most of them considered reformist and thus part of the problem, the anarchists joined it once they recognized its growing strength and potential for class agitation. Not merely did they join, but with their fervor and their powerful orators they moved to the center of the movement in Chicago. On April 25 about twenty-five thousand workers gathered at the lakefront for a rally called by the Central Labor Union, at which the most effective speakers were anarchists. On May 1, the international Labor Day, three hundred thousand men and women went on strike nationally, forty thousand in Chicago alone, and eighty thousand workers, led by Albert and Lucy Parsons, marched up Michigan Avenue in the heart of the city's elegant shopping district. Such numbers were unprecedented; suddenly the anarchist message appeared to be triggering a mass response. Although the marchers were nonviolent, the anarchists had faith that militant organization would soon turn the masses to their revolutionary purposes.

Many anarchists believed that the great day was fast approaching when the workers revolution would begin. Before May Day they warned in their papers, "The capitalist sluggards are thirsty for the blood of working men." And this time, they insisted, "the working men will not permit themselves to be kicked by them like dogs any more. . . . They want vengeance and they cry for blood." They urged the workers, "Clean your guns, complete your ammunition. The hired murderers of the capitalists, the police, the militia, are ready to murder. No working man should leave his house . . . with empty pockets." Despite such talk, May Day passed peacefully.[23]

But on May 3, as the anarchists conducted a rally near the McCormick reaper plant, strikers in the crowd broke off to taunt the scabs who had taken their jobs. The police intervened, firing on the crowd, killing at least two workers—although some reports put the number as high as six—wounding about twenty-five more, and scattering the rest.

Inspired by the memory of eighty thousand massed marchers just three days earlier, infuriated by another egregious police assault on workers, August Spies, the leading German-American anarchist, rushed back to the offices of the *Arbeiter-Zeitung* and dashed off a furious broadside, which was widely distributed around Chicago that night. "**Revenge!** Workingmen, to Arms!!!"

the headline blared (fig. 2). After briefly summarizing the nefarious activities of the murderous Chicago police and the years of humiliation and iniquity workers had suffered, Spies cried out, "If you are men, . . . you will rise in your might, Hercules, and destroy the hideous monster that seeks to destroy you. To arms we call you, to arms!" The German version on the bottom half of this violently revolutionary broadside was even hotter. "Slaves, we ask and conjure you, by all that is sacred and dear to you, avenge the atrocious murder that has been committed upon your brothers today, and which will likely be committed on you tomorrow. . . . Annihilate the beasts in human form who call themselves rulers! Uncompromising annihilation to them." By the next morning, the anarchists had decided to call a mass meeting at the Haymarket for 7:30 P.M. The circular they pasted up around town included the final phrase "*Workingmen arm Yourselves and Appear in Full Force,*" though a printing later that day omitted that adjuration (fig. 3).[24]

Approximately fifteen hundred workers came to the square that evening to listen to more speeches. But with a storm approaching, and without any outlet for action, the outdoor meeting fizzled, and the crowd began drifting away, perhaps as few as six hundred remaining when the phalanx of police quick-marched into the square. Armed insurrection seemed distant, however much the anarchists roared their defiance, however near cataclysm had appeared just days earlier.

And then the bomb exploded, the police opened fire, and the Haymarket affair became an iconic event in American history, as the two forces of terrorism, revolutionary and reactionary, violently collided.

No one ever established who the bomb thrower was, or demonstrated that a conspiracy had been involved. It was, in fact, a classic Autonomist act: an individual anarchist had acted on his own initiative against the monster of the state, seeking vengeance against the police. Or perhaps the bomb thrower was an agent provocateur, familiar with the Autonomist ideology and seeking to discredit the entire anarchist movement with that bomb. In either event, the act and the police deaths that resulted from it provided the perfect justification for the forces of the state to crush the anarchists with more concentrated and efficient political violence—police raids, judicial prosecutions, executions —than their enemies could ever bring to bear against them. All those anarchist calls to arms followed by a real bomb had created the necessary basis for a campaign of governmental reactionary violence.

In the weeks following the bombing, as several policeman died painfully from their wounds at the Haymarket while their colleagues arrested more

REVENGE!

Workingmen, to Arms!!!

Your masters sent out their bloodhounds — the police —; they killed six of your brothers at McCormicks this afternoon. They killed the poor wretches, because they, like you, had the courage to disobey the supreme will of your bosses. They killed them, because they dared ask for the shortening of the hours of toil. They killed them to show you, "Free American Citizens!", that you must be satisfied and contended with whatever your bosses condescend to allow you, or you will get killed!

You have for years endured the most abject humiliations; you have for years suffered unmeasurable iniquities; you have worked yourself to death; you have endured the pangs of want and hunger; your Children you have sacrificed to the factory-lords — in short: You have been miserable and obedient slave all these years: Why? To satisfy the insatiable greed, to fill the coffers of your lazy thieving master? When you ask them now to lessen your burden, he sends his bloodhounds out to shoot you, kill you!

If you are men, if you are the sons of your grand sires, who have shed their blood to free you, then you will rise in your might, Hercules, and destroy the hideous monster that seeks to destroy you. To arms we call you, to arms!

Your Brothers.

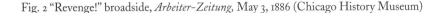

Rache! Rache!

Arbeiter, zu den Waffen!

Arbeitendes Volk, heute Nachmittag mordeten die Bluthunde Eurer Ausbeuter 6 Eurer Brüder draußen bei McCormick's. Warum mordeten sie dieselben? Weil sie den Muth hatten, mit dem Loos unzufrieden zu sein, welches Eure Ausbeuter ihnen beschieden haben. Sie forderten Brod, man antwortete ihnen mit Blei, eingedenk der Thatsache, daß man damit das Volk am wirksamsten zum Schweigen bringen kann! Viele, viele Jahre habt Ihr alle Demüthigungen ohne Widerspruch ertragen, habt Euch vom frühen Morgen bis zum späten Abend geschunden, habt Entbehrungen jeder Art ertragen, habt Eure Kinder selbst geopfert — Alles, um die Schatzkammern Eurer Herren zu füllen, Alles für sie! Und jetzt, wo Ihr vor sie hintretet, und sie ersucht, Eure Bürde etwas zu erleichtern, da hetzen sie zum Dank für Eure Opfer ihre Bluthunde, die Polizei, auf Euch, um Euch mit Bleikugeln von der Unzufriedenheit zu kuriren Sklaven, wir fragen und beschwören Euch bei Allem, was Euch heilig und werth ist, rächt diesen scheußlichen Mord, den man heute an Euren Brüdern beging, und vielleicht morgen schon an Euch begehen wird. Arbeitendes Volk, Herkules, Du bist am Scheideweg angelangt. Wofür entscheidest Du Dich? Für Sklaverei und Hunger, oder für Freiheit und Brod? Entscheidest Du Dich für das Letztere, dann säume keinen Augenblick; dann, Volk, zu den Waffen! Vernichtung den menschlichen Bestien, die sich Deine Herrscher nennen! Rücksichtslose Vernichtung ihnen — das muß Deine Losung sein! Denkt der Helden, deren Blut den Weg zum Fortschritt, zur Freiheit und zur Menschlichkeit gedüngt — und strebe, ihre würdig zu werden!

Eure Brüder.

Fig. 2 "Revenge!" broadside, *Arbeiter-Zeitung*, May 3, 1886 (Chicago History Museum)

Fig. 3 "Attention Workingmen!" broadside, *Arbeiter–Zeitung* May 4, 1886 (Chicago History Museum)

than two hundred anarchists and trashed the union offices and meeting places of Chicago workers, the press and civic and merchant leaders demanded swift and savage vengeance. The prosecutor, Julius S. Grinnell, and the judge, Joseph E. Gary, were eager to comply, bringing eight defendants—George Engel, Samuel Fielden, Adolph Fischer, Louis Lingg, Oscar Nebbe, Albert Parsons, Michael Schwab, and August Spies—to trial. What ensued was a classic show trial leading to death sentences that amounted to judicial murder.

To begin with, the jury was stacked. Rather than choosing names at random from a box, the usual practice in criminal cases, Grinnell appointed Henry L. Ryce special bailiff to summon such jurors as he saw fit. With these broad discretionary powers, Ryce went down to the Board of Trade and collected the names of clerks, merchants, and manufacturers, middle-class men who were most likely to detest anarchists. A year after the trial and a week before the convicted men were to be hanged, Otis S. Favor, a Chicago businessman and old friend of Ryce's, deposed under oath that while he had been selecting jurors Ryce had said to Favor, "I am managing this case and know what I am about. Those fellows are going to be hanged as certain as death. I am calling such men as the defendants will have to challenge peremptorily and waste their time and challenges. Then they will have to take such men as the prosecution wants." In the end five salesmen, five clerks, a hardware dealer, and a school principal composed the jury trying the radical workers.[25]

While questioning men from the pool Bailiff Ryce had collected, Judge Gary, using more efficient methods than Ryce had predicted, made doubly sure that the jury would convict the anarchists. The pattern of voir dire was nearly uniform. A potential juror would admit to extreme prejudice against anarchism and prejudgment against these defendants in particular. William P. Black, the defense attorney, would then challenge the juror, and Judge Gary would interrogate him, badgering him until he stated that despite his preconceptions he believed he could decide the case impartially in accordance with the law and the evidence. Gary would then overrule the objection.

For example, H. N. Smith, the hardware dealer, told Black that he had a decided opinion on the guilt of the defendants, one that he had expressed to many others, and that some of the injured policemen were personal friends of his. During the trial, "you would be willing to have your opinion strengthened and hate very much to have it dissolved," Black suggested. "I would." "Under these circumstances do you think that you could render a fair and impartial verdict?" "I don't think I could." "You think you would be prejudiced?" "I think I would because my feelings are very bitter." "Would your prejudice in any way influence you in coming to an opinion, in arriving at a verdict?" "I think it would." Challenged for prejudice, Smith was then interrogated by the judge until he agreed that he would try to act fairly and on the evidence, at which point the challenge was overruled.

James H. Walker, a dry goods merchant, admitted to Black that he had formed an opinion on the guilt of the defendants and had expressed to others —that he was prejudiced. Assuming that Judge Gary would ask Walker the same questions he was asking everyone else, Black queried, "Assuming your present opinion, that you believe the defendants guilty, would you believe your present opinion would warrant you in convicting them?" "I presume it would," Walker agreed. Judge Gary then examined Walker closely, pressing him to give the right answer to the question "Do you believe that you can sit here and fairly and impartially make up your mind, from the evidence, whether that evidence proves that they are guilty beyond a reasonable doubt?" "I think I could, but I should believe that I was a little handicapped in my judgment, sir." Whereupon Judge Gary replied, in the presence of other potential jurors not yet examined, "Well, that is a sufficient qualification for a juror in the case of course; the more a man feels that he is handicapped the more he will guard against it."

Whether he was being cynical, ironic, or stupid with this particular statement and his whole mode of interrogation, Gary ensured even before the trial proper began that the jury would convict. Another potential juror, railroad clerk John B. Geiner, declared that "it is evident that the defendants are connected with that affair from their being here," while G. W. Adams, a traveling salesman, made it clear that "I have an opinion in my mind that the defendants encouraged the throwing of that bomb," precisely the conclusion the state intended to establish.[26]

During the trial, the state tried every argument it could to gain a conviction. To prove a direct connection between the men arrested and the bomb thrower, M. M. Thompson, a clerk at the department store Marshall Field, was called to testify that he had seen defendants August Spies and Michael Schwab go up an alley near the square, and, after whispering about whether "one is enough," pass something to another anarchist, Rudolph Schnaubelt. Another witness, Harry L. Gilmer, a painter (who had a record as a petty criminal in Iowa), swore that Spies had conspired with Adolph Fischer in that alley and that then Spies had lit the bomb. Neither witness spoke German, the language Schwab and Spies always used with each other. In rebuttal, the defense brought many witnesses who testified that Spies had never left the wagon from which he was giving his speech, and that all the other indicted anarchists had either been at home or at various taverns when the bomb was thrown. As for Schnaubelt, whom the state never connected with the bomb through the introduction of evidence, he had disappeared from Chicago.

After perjured and discredited testimony failed to make a direct connection between the anarchist leaders and the crime, Grinnell fell back on his secondary position, that these leaders had met the night before the bombing and conspired to blow up several newspaper offices and police stations. But in fact, as defense lawyers demonstrated, only two of the defendants, Fischer and George Engel, Autonomists who had frequently expressed violent opinions, had attended that meeting, and no other element of this supposed battle plan had transpired, no other bombs had been thrown. Another defendant, Louis Lingg, *had* made bombs, which the police found in his rooms, but no witness connected him to the square on the fatal day, and Lingg's bombs did not closely resemble the remnants of the Haymarket missile.

Undeterred, Grinnell fell back on a third argument to make his case, that the anarchist leaders had continually advocated violence against the police as agents of the state and had encouraged the construction and throwing of bombs in principle. Therefore the leaders had incited the admittedly unknown bomb thrower to do the deed, which made them guilty of the murder of the policemen. Anarchist ideas were on trial, not acts but words that Grinnell insisted had provoked the acts: the defendants ought to be hanged for expressing opinions that threatened social peace, regardless of whether they took part in the actual bombing.

In his summation to the jury, Grinnell made the state's connection of ideas to acts explicit: "Law is on trial. Anarchy is on trial. These men have been . . . indicted because they were leaders. They are no more guilty than the thousands who follow them. Gentlemen of the jury, convict these men, make examples of them, hang them and you save our institutions, our society." Interpreting the law in a manner he thought necessary for conviction, Judge Gary instructed the jury that if "by print or speech" the defendants "advised or encouraged the commission of murder, without designating time, place or occasion at which it should be done," and if some person "induced by such advice and encouragement" then threw the bomb, whether he could be identified or not these "conspirators are guilty of murder." Unsurprisingly, the jury thus picked and thus instructed convicted seven of the Haymarket defendants of murder: as one juror told the press, "Every man on the jury was an Ameri-

can. [None of us suffered] toleration for imported preachers of assassination."
The judge then sentenced them to be hanged.[27]

But far from being a simple legal matter, this trial, conviction, and punishment were deliberately constructed as a morality tale to warn would-be revolutionaries of their inevitable punishment and to reassure the general public that the government would stamp out violent, antisocial ideas by all means necessary, however much sacrifice of civil liberties and counter violence that might entail. Not mere acts, however heinous, but essential social values were at issue.

The trial of seditious ideology in Judge Gary's courtroom was surrounded, as it were, by a far larger body of public opinion, or at least the opinions of the overwhelming majority of persons of standing within the community. In Chicago even voices that were usually calmer than those of the popular press responded with loathing to the Haymarket anarchists. Three surviving speeches given less than two weeks after the bombing, one by a leading attorney and the other two by prominent Protestant clergymen, demonstrate the level of panic the revolutionary terrorists had aroused.

On May 9, David Swing, pastor of one of the largest Protestant congregations in Chicago, gave a sermon in which he declared that he doubted the capacity of American republicanism to deal with an underclass controlled by subversive values lacking even "one ray of religious, social or political truth." Now was the time, said Swing, to consider a far more efficient form of police state: "We need a careful definition of what freedom is. If it means the license to proclaim the gospel of disorder, to preach destruction, and scatter the seeds of anarchy . . . the sooner we exchange the Republic for an iron-clad monarchy the better will it be for all of us."[28]

On May 16, Charles Carroll Bonney, a lawyer and the president of the Citizens' Law and Order League of the United States, spoke to the Chicago Sabbath Association at the Union Park New Jerusalem Congregational Church on "The Present Conflict of Labor and Capital." Taking as his text the biblical admonition that "they that take the sword shall perish with the sword," Bonney sought to reinforce Capital by insisting that the full force of the law must immediately and always attack "infidelity and anarchy" at its root. The anarchists—and the "tens of thousands of foreign people in our midst" for whom the anarchists were speaking—had demonstrated complete "ignorance of our language and . . . our civilization[,] . . . of the nature and purposes of our government." Respectable members of society had abandoned these masses of ignorant aliens to demagogic politicians and "anarchist leaders who want to live upon their toil, rule them with rods of iron, and finally lead them to destruction. . . . The war cries of those who follow the red flag of murder and arson are: No God! No Master! No Law! No Property! NIHIL! Nothing!" Before May 4, Bonney argued, these forces of "riot and murder" had been permitted to walk the streets of Chicago like "conquerors, [while] Law and Order meekly submitted," in toleration of their vile public outbursts, tacitly conceding such sedition an equal right of expression with that granted constructive ideas. Bonney praised the police dragnet then sweeping the city. "There is no lack now of lawful authority to suppress red-flag meetings, raid anarchist dens, and seize nihilist arms." The law had not been dead after all, "but only asleep. The Haymarket bomb awoke it, and the deadly fire of policemen gave it instant execution." Now the law would move from bullets to the noose. A swift trial and execution of the anarchist leaders would be the next righteous step of an "outraged law." The path of justice was plain: "The bomb was a waiver of trial and a plea of guilty." ·

On May 3, the day before the bombing, August Spies had cried out for the vengeance of the poor against the rich; now, on May 16, Charles Carroll Bonney replied in kind for the rich—"It is the nature of law to retaliate. It is the Gospel, not the law, that returns good for evil." Draconian law, "well and fearlessly enforced," alone could subdue anarchists. "They would not strike the law if they believed it certain that the law would at once strike back." Bonney was speaking for all those who felt under attack by anarchists, who were now engaged in working themselves up to a fever of reactionary terror-ism. The law as defined by Bonney enabled a kind of blind destructiveness aimed not at specific criminals but at the world of sedition in which they operated, if need be at the expense of actual criminal law and the freedom of speech and assembly guaranteed in the Constitution. By a brutal counter-attack they sought to strike fear into the hearts of future revolutionary terror-ists and anyone who might sympathize with them. When under fire, liberty defined as public safety displaced liberty as free expression.

Toward the end of his oration, Bonney adopted a somewhat cooler tone in a search for a longer-term solution beyond the immediate summary justice that the Haymarket anarchists would receive. He proposed establishing "Law and Order Missions" in the slums to teach the patient spirit of legal change to the ignorant masses of immigrant workers. Bonney insisted that "the people . . . are the sole source of executive power, [that] the law is their king. Justice is his throne. Self-government is their glory." The police and the courts would utterly destroy anarchism, and then, after appropriate reeducation, the newly disciplined, submissive, and fully assimilated masses might one day be accepted into the benign embrace of the American republic.[29]

On May 9, five days after the Haymarket bombing, and a week before Bonney enunciated his doctrine of legal vengeance, the Reverend Frederick A. Noble preached a sermon titled "Christianity and the Red Flag" to his congregation at New Jerusalem Congregational Church. Noble took Isaiah 59:7–8 as his text: "Their feet run to evil, and they make haste to shed innocent blood: their thoughts are thoughts of iniquity; wasting and destruction are in their paths. The way of peace they know not." In rhetoric more explicitly biblical than that of Bonney, if parallel to it, Noble read the anarchists out of the human race. He found these "fiends . . . fresh from European jails," to be "unparalleled in modern times" for their "cool, calculating and satanic maliciousness." Such men sought neither reform nor even revolution but to unleash the "disastrous fury of a cyclone" to ruin government, law and property, home and church, school and business—all the mainstays of civilization. Without hesitation, "these miscreants [who proclaim] No God, no law, no master . . . must be made to feel the crushing weight of the authority they have outraged and defiled."

In religious language at least as heated as that used by the anarchists, Noble called for blood revenge against them—Christian retribution was the fit punishment for their sins. "They have rolled their garments in blood; let them suffer the legitimate consequences of their doing. Let them drain the dregs of the cup of their own spilling. They have said with fiendish deliberation, that blood must be spilled; blood has been spilled; let their own veins and arteries furnish the further supply. They have said that heads must fall; heads have fallen . . . let these men now have the privilege of furnishing a few heads for the basket. . . . I know of no cause more in need of martyrs. Let them have a few as speedily as possible." Noble was handing back the language used by the anarchists that he had read in the press. He not only understood them and took them at their word, he also literally wished to treat them as they had threatened to treat him. Noble felt that they deserved the same fate accorded the French Communards in 1871 at the hands of law and order. (His words also referred to the justice meted out by the guillotine during the Terror of the French Revolution, ironically, if unintentionally, against the established order by the revolutionaries.)

American liberty had been born in revolutionary violence, Noble preached, and the Civil War had been a rebirth of that liberty in collective political violence. Indeed, that war had inspired ruthless responses to later civil threats, providing continuity to what Noble would not have recognized as reactionary terrorism. "The Old Flag has been bathed in blood over and over again, that it might mean liberty," Noble argued. Americans were warriors who must never hesitate to use righteous and cleansing political violence. For now, "No more Sunday-afternoon assemblages on the Lake Front, in which threatening and slaughter are threatened without stint. No more toleration for a press whose sole mission is to move to madness . . . dagger and dynamite." Noble believed that for as long as it took, "bloody rioters" would have to be "smitten down in the streets[,] . . . haranguers of sedition . . . ruthlessly silenced," and "murderers and abettors of murderers . . . hung." Death to the seditious; there would be no redemption for them. But for their children and deluded followers, firm but loving reeducation into American values might be possible. However, Noble warned at the end of his sermon, "moral and religious training is not the shortcut to the suppression of a mob. For that—guns." Thus did Noble invoke the warrior traditions deep within Americanism and Christianity, the ideological bases of reactionary terrorism.[30]

Spokesmen for the polite classes such as Noble and Bonney, acting in ideological concert with the police and courts, succeeded in isolating the revolutionary anarchists, dividing workers through a campaign of fear and violence, further consolidating their domination by such means. And not only citizens of property and standing called for the extirpation of anarchism and anarchists; under enormous social and ideological pressure so, too, did most of organized labor. Dreading that they would be hanged with the same rope awaiting the anarchist necks, deeply concerned that their larger reformist cause would be discredited by association with anarchist actions—as in fact proved to be the case—moderate workers organizations denounced the anarchists. In Cincinnati, the Bricklayers Union declared that "the carrying of the red flag at the head of the procession that pretends to represent the laboring class is acting a lie, for a red flag does not mean honest labor, but money or blood, and should not be tolerated in America." Other Cincinnati unions disavowed the "red flag of the Commune," while the Knights of Labor called the red flag "un-American . . . an open proclamation against the Government and its institutions."[31]

Terence V. Powderly, national head of the Knights, disowned the anarchists, whose "red flag is the emblem of blood and destruction," and urged workers to "condemn the outrage committed in Chicago in the name of labor." The *Knights of Labor*, the Chicago newspaper of the organization, had no sympathy for this "band of cowardly murderers, cut-throats and robbers

Fig. 4 Thomas Nast, "Advice to So-Called American Socialists: 'You Had Better Not Attack This Club,'" *Harper's Weekly,* February 27, 1886 (Chicago History Museum)

. . . who sneak through the country like midnight assassins . . . causing riot and bloodshed . . . They are entitled to no more consideration than wild beasts. The leaders are cowards and their followers are fools." This editorial insisted that the Knights expel anarchist infiltrators from their ranks, and shun them, refusing even to engage them in conversation. Such "monstrosities" needed to be "blotted from the surface of the earth."[32]

Almost every rhetorical depiction of the anarchists, before, during, and after the trial, included the images of the beast, the un-American, the unchristian, the other, the very devil. Editorial cartoons, even more powerfully than written denunciations, offered clear images of anarchists as subhuman

LIBERTY (to go if you do not like the institutions of our Republic) OR (commit murder and you will be punished with) DEATH.

Fig. 5 Thomas Nast, "Liberty or Death," *Harper's Weekly*, June 5, 1886 (Chicago History Museum)

destroyers. Some of the most strident came from the pen of Thomas Nast and were published in *Harper's Weekly*, the most widely read weekly news magazine of the day. Himself a former Catholic German immigrant, Nast had been a reformer, deeply committed to the advancement of blacks and to Reconstruction, but he had long since turned reactionary, excoriating labor, immigrants, and especially Roman Catholics. His images of the Chicago anarchists turn them into devils. In one cartoon, published on February 27, 1886, ten weeks *before* the Haymarket affair, Nast clearly supports the policeman whose upraised club represents the legitimate authority of the United States and whose gun is drawn and ready to shoot down the subhuman anarchist, perhaps modeled on Most or Spies (fig. 4). The hair of the anarchist leader is twisted on the top into two horns, and he is trailing a "Bloody Red Flag" behind him like a tail. Nast urges the policeman to crack that anarchist's skull with American righteousness or perhaps to shoot him; he must act more boldly than had the ineffective London police in a recent riot in which a mob of unemployed workers had trashed several gentlemen's clubs on Pall Mall. Nast had already created his stereotype of the godless un-American anarchist by the time the Haymarket bombing occurred.

The same devil anarchist reappeared in a Nast cartoon on June 5, 1886, a month after the Haymarket (fig. 5). Now he waves a black-lettered flag and

Fig. 6 A. R. Cassidy, "Justice Hurling a Bomb," *Graphic News,* June 5, 1886 (Chicago History Museum)

brandishes a pistol, a bomb lies between his feet, and his heavy boots are desecrating the Stars and Stripes. Nast offers him the alternative of a hanging at the hands of Uncle Sam or returning to Germany on the next steamer. Miss Liberty points to the ship, while she (or Nast) tells the anarchist, "Go if you do not like the institutions of our republic or commit murder and you will be punished with death." The slogan "America, love it or leave it," has had a long life in the history of American political reactionism.

Miss Liberty, the spirit of the American republic, was on people's minds at the time, for the Statue of Liberty, a gift from the French republic, was just then being constructed in New York Harbor, to be dedicated on October 28, 1886. In a cartoon by A. R. Cassidy in the *Graphic News,* also published on June 5, 1886, Miss Liberty stands on her pedestal, towering above a fleeing mob of workers, many carrying pistols in their hands, in a city square that resembles the Haymarket (fig. 6). She is preparing to hurl a bomb inscribed "Law" into the mob. In the background stands a memorial statue of a policeman, his pistol drawn, whose death Miss Liberty will avenge through mass destruction of the crazed, alien workers. Cassidy clearly espouses state terrorism.

In one of the most powerful cartoons he ever drew, "Liberty Is Not Anarchy," which appeared in *Harper's Weekly* on September 4, 1886, Nast depicts an enormous Miss Liberty—so huge that only her hands and part of her cloak fit in the frame of the drawing (fig. 7). She grasps the Chicago anarchist leaders between the fingers of one hand, ready to squash them like beetles, while with the other she holds a huge sword marked "U.S.," a ring embossed "Union" on her finger. The hilt of the sword makes a mighty cross with the blade—Christianity united with republicanism to avenge liberty.[33]

Thus did reactionary terrorism spring from the fears induced by revolutionary terrorists. Violent reaction greeted the social threat posed by the frightening anarchist rhetoric and the bomb that followed. A terrorist attack born of horrific working conditions led to terrorist revenge by the state, supported by the middle class and much of the working class as well as by the wealthy.

Following much the same path John Brown had forged thirty years earlier, the anarchist leaders, aware of the nearly unanimous condemnation their acts had aroused and cognizant that they were on trial for their ideology, began to shift their rhetorical emphasis during their trial from defiant cries for violent revolution to appeals for freedom of speech and social justice, values in which they had always, in fact, believed. Violence, they now insisted, had always been intended only as the means to obtain a fair shake for all humanity, no matter how poor. Now the anarchists sought to downplay the ideology of force still further and focus attention on their goal of a glorious millennium of everlasting social harmony. In part this softening reflected their situation: they were being tried for their lives before a hostile court and thus were powerless to act independently on their own behalf. But they also grasped that their prophecy about the barely sublimated violence of the legal system was coming true for them: the most telling presentation of themselves that they might make was as martyrs to freedom crushed by the law operating as blind force, not blind justice.

To aid in their mythic reconstruction, they needed to emphasize that the state had all the worldly power and they none at all; they had only the transcendent and everlasting power of moral truth. They produced the warmest, most affirmative version of themselves they could sustain, doubtless believing that their underlying humanism, rather than the violent tactics they had advocated, reflected what was fundamentally true about them. They knew that this affirmation of beneficent goals would offer the best chance for the wider acceptance of their ideas and would at the same time highlight that it was the state that was behaving monstrously. Because the prosecutor and

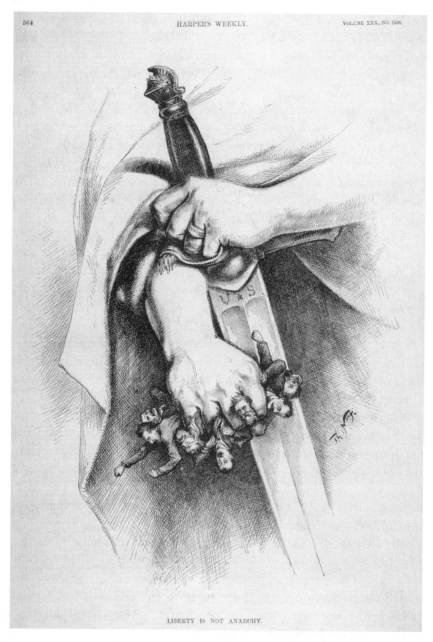

Fig. 7 Thomas Nast, "Liberty Is Not Anarchy," *Harper's Weekly,* September 4, 1886 (Chicago History Museum)

the judge acted with such unbridled vindictiveness against the defendants' ideas and goals, this humanized version of anarchist morality made considerable sense during the drama of the show trial. The dialectic thus created echoed the drama devised by John Brown and the state of Virginia.

While he was listening to Julius Grinnell expound his conspiracy theories, Albert Parsons wrote in his notebook, "The enemies of Liberty strive to create the belief that an anarchist is a dynamiter. I deny it. I say it is a villainous slander—a malicious, premeditated falsehood. I'll tell you what an anarchist is. Anarchists are people who know their rights and dare maintain them. If this makes me an anarchist then put me down as such, and if this makes me a dynamiter than count me as one." Parsons believed that he was merely asserting the rights to self-defense and to bear arms guaranteed by the Second Amendment to every American citizen. He then added, "If dynamite can protect me I will *use* it," but scratched out this last sentence. Parsons almost certainly realized that such a defiant statement, if made at the trial, would make him appear to be the overt advocate of terrorism the prosecution claimed he was, and could undermine an appeal based on the true Americanism of his libertarian beliefs.[34]

Taking the stand in his own defense, Parsons recounted what he had said at the Haymarket that fatal day. In his reconstruction, Parsons claimed that during his speech he had asserted that the anarchists had carried the "red flag of liberty, fraternity and equality for labor all over the world." But he had borne this flag as the emblem of universal humanist values, he also had declared to his listeners that in the United States no one should starve or give up the "inalienable fight to life and liberty and the pursuit of happiness. . . . Rather than being "cut down like dogs in the street" by the "armed hirelings [of monopoly], in the interest of your liberty and independence [you should] arm yourselves . . . arm yourselves." Capital had formed a "gigantic conspiracy" against Labor. If Capital refused to concede the eight-hour workday, "it meant war, not by the working classes . . . but by monopolists."

It is impossible to know how much Parsons changed his words in his courtroom reconstruction of his Haymarket rhetoric, although he had certainly given far more aggressive and virulent speeches in the past. Even on trial he burst out into denunciation from time to time, at one point asserting, "Dynamite is the diffusion of power. It is democratic; it makes everybody equal." And he also told the judge that executing the anarchists would amount to "judicial murder." But on the whole his appeal was to justice and fair play. When pressed by Julius Grinnell as to whether he had said the present social system must be changed, Parsons replied, "Yes, in the interest of humanity." Questioned as to whether he had argued that violent rebellion was the indispensable means to bring about social change, Parsons replied, "No sir, because I don't know myself. . . . I think I told the audience that the existing order . . . was founded upon . . . force, and I think I said the actions of the monopolists and corporations . . . would drive the people into the use of force before they could obtain redress. I might of stated it—I am not sure."[35]

Similarly, Samuel Fielden, whose speech immediately before the bomb went off had caused a police spy to run to the nearby station and fetch John Bonfield's shock troops, muted the fierceness of his words as he recalled them at the trial. His courtroom version, a rather abstract analysis of the corruption of capitalism, amounted to backpedaling, far less bold and captivating as well as less clever than the powerful image John Brown had constructed at his trial twenty-seven years earlier. As for the single inflammatory phrase he did recall using, he now said that his intent had been to reiterate to working people that the only thing they could do to "get any satisfaction . . . from the law would be to throttle it. I used that word in a figurative sense. I said to throttle it, because it was an expensive article and could do them no good." This gloss, a dilution of his original intention, amounted to a prescription for avoiding the law rather than assaulting it through direct action.

Under cross-examination, Fielden denied any connection between his words and the advocacy of violence. He had never owned a pistol. While it was true that he drilled with the International Rifles, the unit had never armed and had soon disbanded. (Later historians have suggested that the group drilled frequently, sometimes with arms.) Grinnell then quoted newspaper versions of Fielden's Haymarket speech, something he evidently did not possess for Parsons's words. According to their reports, Fielden had said, "The law makes no distinctions. A million men own all the property of this country. The law is of no use to the other fifty-four million. You have nothing more to do with the law except to lay hands on it and throttle it until it makes its last kick. It has turned your brethren out on the wayside and degraded them until they have lost the last vestige of humanity, and become mere things and animals. Keep your eye upon it, throttle it, kill it, stab it." At first Fielden admitted that he thought had might have used such language, but as Grinnell read further from the report of his speech, Fielden insisted that such accounts were garbled and taken out of context. "I think I used that language, but you haven't got the sense of it at all quoting it in that way, and I don't accept that as my speech at all." Grinnell then asked Fielden with mock incredulity, "You considered there was nothing inflammatory about your speech, nothing incendiary?" Fielden replied that he did not think so: "I spoke generally, from a general stand point." Grinnell was trying to demonstrate conspiracy—that is, conspiracy defined as collective encouragement to violence. Fielden insisted that he had been speaking in generalities rather than urging concrete action. Given the court's broad definition of sedition, Fielden could never win the argument. Without disowning his general principles, which he was not prepared to do, Fielden tried to present the softest and most humane possible interpretation of his language.[36]

This change in the anarchists' interpretation of the language they had used, from fire to calm criticism, was part of a general strategic shift as they approached the verdict they knew the state soon would impose on them. Facing death, they wished to assert their own humanity and their service to all humanity, to make their deaths as meaningful and useful as possible to the great and imminent revolution they were certain they were serving. They believed they were testifying before the court of public opinion and for the future, and they wanted to turn their trial into something glorious and inspiring to as many people as possible, to broaden their base far beyond anarchist circles. It is impossible to know whether they experienced a genuine change of heart about the use of terrorism or whether their courtroom stance was simply the best propaganda position available under the circumstances, or both. At an instinctive level they also may have been trying to save themselves from hanging, although they certainly knew they were appearing in a kangaroo court and before a judge who was eager to make their deaths an example for other potential revolutionary terrorists.

Railroaded by the state, their comrades beaten and shot down on the streets, the anarchists in the dock sought to reverse the definition of who was savage and who civilized. After the trial, at which all the defendants but Nebbe (who received fifteen years) were condemned to hang, Adolph Fischer wrote that although the *Chicago Times* had called the anarchists "Apaches," it was the "police Apaches who . . . spilled the workingmen's blood [and] thirsted for more. . . . Geronimo Bonfield measured his wigwam and said . . . 'I wish I could have three or four thousand of them in a bunch, without their families, and then I could make short work of them.'" After describing the terrible childhoods and working lives imposed on the poor by their uncaring and exploitative rulers, August Spies quoted and reframed the language used against the anarchists: "The wretch who condemns the order of things! He is an 'enemy of civilization,' and 'society must protect itself against criminals.'" Who did "the star-spangled Mephisto, Bonfield" and the "Sicilian brigand" Grinnell, "the hireling juror" and the "vast horde of social vultures" in the Chicago public think they were, claiming to speak for all of society when they crushed dissent? "Unisono [Unison] is the anathema. Unisono is the cry—'To the gallows.'" No, the men on trial insisted, *they* were the repositories of eternal democratic ideals, expressed through their protests against a system that was devouring workers and preparing to slaughter the workers' anarchist servants after a farcical "trial." Albert Parsons wrote to his wife, after proclaiming his love for her and their children, "For the people—humanity—I cry out again and again in the doomed victim's cell: Liberty—Justice—Equality."[37]

Facing execution for what they were certain was their humanitarian faith, the anarchists embraced the notion of their martyrdom. (And, it must be noted, by so doing they also avoided any sense of responsibility for the killing they had encouraged.) The more the state reviled them, the more the cowed masses howled, the more certain were the anarchists that their deaths would contain deep meaning. "Bonfield . . . this fiend, in order to justify his murderous attack upon [the Haymarket], said . . . Anarchists! Oh, horror! The stupid mass imagined that Anarchists must be something very bad, and they joined in the chorus with their enemies and fleecers: 'Crucify! Crucify!'" Though a proud atheist, Spies sought through such language to identify himself with the murder of Jesus as a way of demonstrating both his suffering and his eternal commitment to humanity.[38]

Martyrdom as a partially secularized Christian parable also described Fischer's vision of the meaning of his death. "The social revolution must have its impetus, and our noble anarchist cause its martyrs. So be it. I am ready to lay down my life on the altar of our ideal." Another Chicago anarchist added, "The blood of martyrs is the seed of the church."[39]

Surely the end time was fast approaching, surely the anarchists' martyrdom signaled the imminent arrival of the millennium. As Albert Parsons put it, "This is the seed time. The harvest is near. We are sowers now, but we will reap very soon." With apocalyptic—and histrionic—faith, Parsons insisted, "It must be **Liberty** for the people or **Death** for the *Capitalists*. . . . I love humanity, and therefore die for it. No one could do more. Every drop of my blood shall count an avenger, and woe to America when these are in arms." At the same time, Parsons rejected organized religion as the tool of Pharisees. He could not believe that there was a Supreme Being who would allow human beings to make war and establish false states. Parsons proclaimed, "There is but one God—Humanity. Any other kind of religion is a mockery, a delusion, and a snare." And yet he too imagined himself as Jesus before the Sadducees, and he believed that according to the higher law of nature, service to humanity was worship of an alternative Supreme Being: Parsons was convinced that his death for his soon-to-triumph ideals would have permanent meaning.[40]

Sharing much of the civic and religious culture that they also sought to destroy, the Haymarket anarchists believed they were living and dying in a great tradition of Christian and libertarian martyrdom. As Spies wrote, "If death is the penalty for proclaiming the truth, then I will proudly and defiantly pay the costly price! Call your hangman! Truth crucified in Socrates, in Christ, in Giordano Bruno, in Huss [Jan Hus, a fourteenth-century religious dissenter], in Galileo, still lives—they and others whose number is legion have preceded us on this path. We are ready to follow!" Spies also compared himself to the Anabaptist incendiary Thomas Müntzer, whose sixteenth-century version of the gospel, according to Spies, "commanded equality and brotherhood. . . . The champions of law and order and Christendom chopped his head off."[41]

Martyrs to liberty had trod American as well as European soil. Fischer compared himself to other so-called "cranks" such as "Socrates, Christ, Huss, Luther, Galileo, Rousseau, Paine, Jefferson, [Wendell] Phillips," and, last but not least, old John Brown, a hero who had "endeavored to enlighten [his] fellow man [and] was put to death for it." In 1887, as the condemned men's appeals worked their way through the court system, Lucy Parsons called a mass meeting to commemorate John Brown's legacy and to protest the forthcoming execution of the Haymarket anarchists. And John Brown, Jr., sent a basket of Catawba grapes to the anarchists, reminding them of his father's great words as he faced his own execution, "It is a great comfort to feel assured that I am permitted to die for a cause,—not merely to pay the debt of nature, as all must."[42]

Defining meaningful death through the long tradition of Christian and libertarian resistance to a corrupt and murderous state, the anarchists knew that they were addressing a broader audience than they had ever reached before. By choosing to present a dehumanizing picture of the anarchists, by committing judicial murder, the press and the court had in effect allowed the anarchists to offer a plausible rewrite of the social and humanist meanings of the great drama all were enacting together. Both sides claimed the moral high ground, just as each side insisted that the other was composed of subhuman fiends. At stake were not opposing values but alternative versions of shared values, including shared terrorist sensibilities. In their words and deeds anti-state and state mirrored each other. Despite the xenophobia of the prosecution and the German origins of most of the defendants, there was nothing foreign about this drama of terrorism, nothing imposed from outside. The trial was intrinsically American, a major demonstration of the way in which, as it threatened to break out everywhere and not just in Chicago, class war had been Americanized.

It must be stressed that a persistent note of defiant terrorism underlay the anarchists' adoption of the cloak of martyrdom. Speaking in own his defense in the courtroom, the bomb maker Louis Lingg, the angriest, least sophisticated, and, at twenty-two, youngest defendant, declared that he rejoiced that the triumph of the dynamiter was fast approaching. "I despise you," he told the court. "I despise your order, your laws, your force-propped authority. HANG ME FOR IT." Lingg did not wait to be executed by the state he detested. The day before he was scheduled to hang, he lit a dynamite cartridge that someone had smuggled into the prison, put it in his mouth, and blew his head off.[43]

As the day of death, November 11, 1887, approached, all over Chicago, thousands of supporters of the condemned men pinned tiny gold-and-silver gallows to their clothes, like relics of the true cross. Soon a mass subscription would fund a monument to the martyred anarchists of the Haymarket in one cemetery, while the merchants of Chicago would build another to the martyred police in a different graveyard. In both places, the imprimatur of God and the republic forever memorialized the martyrs in cold marble, that is until the Weathermen—latter-day underground leftist terrorists —blew up the monument to the police in the 1970s.

A few people, appalled by the Haymarket verdicts, were willing to stand up against public opinion and denounce the hangings. Several labor unions supported the anarchists against the state, as they continued the eight-hour workday movement that because of the Haymarket affair had lost most of its traction with the public. Terence Powderly of the Knights of Labor, on the other hand, continued to call for the blood of the anarchists, who had hijacked socialism and the union movement and ought to be purged, every vestige of them. Some writers and intellectuals also protested the show trial and the verdict as the products of a deeply fearful, witch-hunting atmosphere. The University of Wisconsin economist Richard T. Ely called the immediate post-Haymarket events in Chicago "a period of police terrorism," while the journalist and novelist Brand Whitlock later characterized the climate of opinion as "one of the strangest frenzies of fear that ever distracted a whole community."[44]

Most noteworthy among the dissenters was the mild-mannered, utterly respectable middle-class novelist William Dean Howells, one of the most prominent American men of letters of his era. To use the terminology of a later day, Howells was radicalized by the experience. A few days before the execution, Howells wrote to the New York *Tribune* pleading for clemency for the Chicago anarchists. Howells's mild language, written in the spirit of Christian forgiveness, urged that "all those who believe that it would be either injustice or impolicy to put them to death" petition the press and the pulpit and take to the agitator's platform as well as appeal directly to Illinois governor Richard J. Oglesby to use his power to overturn the unjust act of the court, "in the only direction where power can never be misused, for the mitigation of their punishment." Whitelaw Reid, the editor of the *Tribune*, disagreed with his old friend and tried to dissuade him from publishing the letter. A few months earlier, Howells had tried to enlist George William Curtis, editor of *Harper's Weekly*, which had published Thomas Nast's vitriolic cartoons, to the cause, sending him a petition for his signature condemning guilt by association as the route through which "fear and hatred . . . seem to have debauched this nation" and proclaiming that men of conscience opposed such public hysteria. Curtis angrily rejected the position assumed by his old friend: "They are not condemned for their opinions, but for bitterly inciting, without any pretense of reason, to a horrible crime which was committed with disastrous results." Howells found no signers for his petition among the other senior men of letters.[45]

Several other middle-class reformers did rally to try to save the anarchists' lives. Prominent among them was Henry Demarest Lloyd, the former financial editor of the Chicago *Tribune* now embarked on a muckraking antimonopoly career, and, most notably, William M. Salter, a trained Congregationalist minister who, after losing his faith, had become Chicago leader of the humanist Ethical Culture Society. Lloyd and Salter orchestrated an amnesty campaign, primarily directed at Governor Oglesby. Quite forceful in private, Salter argued in public that there was a "kernel of truth to the claim of the anarchist sympathizers that the anarchists were tried for murder and are to be hanged for anarchy" but conceded that there still was a case for treasonable conspiracy. Instead of demanding a general pardon, he tried to separate the true incendiaries from the merely strident among the Haymarket leaders. On these grounds, Salter argued that Oglesby ought to commute the sentences of Schwab, Parsons, and Fielden.[46]

On November 10, Oglesby commuted the death sentences of Fielden and Schwab to jail terms, but he did not do so for Parsons, who had gained considerable public sympathy for having left his sanctuary in Wisconsin, where he might have chosen to remain incognito, and marching into the courtroom to surrender on the first day of the trial in order to stand in unity with his brothers. It is unclear why Oglesby made the choices he did, but after Lingg's suicide, Spies, Parsons, Fischer, and Engel hanged on November 11. In its next issue *Frank Leslie's Illustrated Newspaper* printed a gruesome artist's rendering of the four anarchists standing on the scaffold with nooses around their necks, draped in white like ghosts, the moment before the executioner dropped them to their deaths. The caption read, "The Law Vindicated— Four of the Chicago Anarchists Pay the Penalty of Their Crime" (fig. 8).[47]

After the hangings, Howells grew even more agitated about the miscarriage of justice. To William Salter he wrote, "I do not think the men should have [had] *any* sentence at all under that *bouffe* trial, with its cock-and-bull pretense of a conspiracy." In an even angrier letter written for the New York *Tribune,* Howells insisted, "They died, in the prime of the first Republic the world has ever known, for their opinion's sake. . . . Their trial has not been a trial by justice, but a trial by passion, by terror, by prejudice, by hate, by newspaper." Angry though he was, Howells never mailed or published this letter.[48]

In Chicago the often hysterical reign of law and order continued for several years during the mayoralty of John Roche. In July 1888, the police arrested three Bohemian anarchists, charging them with conspiracy to kill Bonfield, Grinnell, and Gary, and the police once more cracked down on all anarchist meetings, despite that fact that few self-proclaimed anarchists remained. But in January 1889 the *Arbeiter-Zeitung* and the Chicago *Times* independently revealed widespread corruption among the police, beginning with Bonfield himself. In response, Bonfield arrested the editors of both papers and charged them with libel. Calling him "an evil genius" and a "despot," the *Times* counterattacked: "To create the impression that Roche and his favored police officers alone stand between the city and destruction, and that to defeat his re-election is to encourage an uprising of anarchists, the department has resorted to extremes with the satisfaction of finding that its inventions are swallowed in certain credulous quarters as momentous facts."[49]

By this time, with revolutionary terrorism no longer an apparently imminent threat, some among the increasingly self-confident middle class in Chicago had had enough of the violent repression of the workers, and this easing of fears eroded the ideological domination of the reactionary forces. Indeed, the historian Richard Schneirov argues that from the post-Haymarket cli-

Fig. 8 "The Law Vindicated: Four of the Chicago Anarchists Pay the Penalty of Their Crimes—Scenes in the Cook County Jail Before and at the Moment of the Execution," *Frank Leslie's Illustrated Newspaper,* November 19, 1887 (Chicago History Museum)

mate a "new liberalism" was born in the city, based on antimonopolism and on the inclusion of labor, and accepted within what Jane Addams, the Chicago settlement-house founder, called the spirit of "social love," which could lead all citizens, rich and poor alike, into the embrace of "organic democracy." As evidence of this, in 1893, when George Pullman's mistreatment of his workers provoked a strike that turned nasty and violent, many of the new generation of middle-class reformers sided with the strikers against Pullman and President Grover Cleveland, who sent in federal troops to break the strike (killing at least thirty-four workers, a greater death toll than at the Haymarket).[50]

Nevertheless, reformers remained a distinct minority, and most Americans supported Cleveland's repression of the strikers. In this incident and later cases, the strikers were not anarchists, and none of them threw bombs. Still, organized labor continued to be regarded as a menace into the 1930s. The state cultivated and acted on fears raised by the entire labor movement, even though all mainstream unions eschewed violence, a situation that had some parallels to the Redeemer counterrevolutionary terrorism, which had been enacted even though the revolutionary terrorism they feared had been only a myth.

In many ways, the reaction against the Haymarket trial and executions climaxed in the message Illinois governor John P. Altgeld, a Democrat, issued on June 26, 1893, when he gave a full pardon to Fielden, Nebbe, and Schwab. That this pardon came from the pen of a conservative German-American governor, a lawyer, and a major speculator in Chicago real estate, was surprising at the time. So outraged was he by the miscarriage of justice during the Haymarket trial that not only did Altgeld condemn the jury packing that had preceded the trial testimony, he also attacked Judge Gary as colossally prejudiced and insisted that the root cause of the deaths at the Haymarket had been the consistently brutal police methods that had provoked the bombing. "While some men may tamely submit to being clubbed and seeing their brothers shot down, there are some who will resent it and will nurture a spirit of hatred and seek revenge. . . . The bomb was thrown by someone who, instead of acting on the advice of anybody, was simply seeking personal revenge for having been clubbed," Altgeld argued, without citing any evidence for this conclusion. "Capt. Bonfield is the man who is really responsible for the death of the police officers." Altgeld could have issued the pardons on the basis of jury packing alone, but he had gone on to excoriate the police and the courts, blaming them for a fundamental miscarriage of justice. In this he was addressing the wider issue of official abuse of liberty, not just the question of an unfair trial.[51]

Not missing a beat, the Chicago *Tribune* savaged him the next day. A "simple pardon" would have sufficed, but Altgeld's "un-American feelings got the better of him . . . in this hysterical denunciation of American principles, law, judges, executive and judicial officers and of people who deliberately and conscientiously approve of them." Soon editorial cartoonists let loose on the governor. Victor in *The Judge* depicted an apelike Altgeld, holding high the banner of anarchy, leading a blindfolded Miss Liberty over a cliff. In a later issue, Victor showed Altgeld using the knife of his pardon power to cut loose the mad dogs of Socialism, Anarchy, and Murder and set them on a defenseless Miss Columbia and her two young children—the offspring of the Republic—thereby tarnishing the memory of the Chicago police martyrs. Altgeld's reputation was destroyed, along with his career. Subsequently he became a hero to generations of liberals, including John F. Kennedy, who wrote about Altgeld in *Profiles in Courage*.[52]

Although the Haymarket affair might have contributed to the birth of progressive reform in which working people were respected (though unions were not), it also remained a prime precedent for those who believed in hard-nosed law and order, who deployed the blunt instruments of coercion to suppress the un-Americans, particularly organized workers, aliens, and racial others. Reformers acting to eradicate or at least ameliorate the underlying conditions that produce political violence exist (most of the time as minority dissenters) in a perpetual tension with law-and-order advocates. And for even a suspicion of a potential outbreak of revolutionary terrorism, the ideology and practice of reactionary terrorism remains in place as a deeply structured response ever ready to be reactivated.

Often, usually at crucial and highly publicized moments, the more punishing form of law and order has expressed the prevailing view of how liberty must be protected and enhanced. Those professing Christian and republican virtues, when embattled, can reorient their faiths to justify violent punishment of dissidents, in the name of justice, liberty, truth, and order. The frightening Chicago anarchists and the brutally repressive Chicago authorities did not talk past one another. They conducted a ruthless struggle for the allegiance of all citizens. However you look at it, terrorism won.

CHAPTER 5

The Philippines War
Terrorism and Empire

At the end of the nineteenth century, when Americans ventured abroad they were prepared militarily and ideologically to subdue, with a clear eye and a strong arm, those they considered lesser peoples. Although the United States conquered a distant colony for the first time only in 1898, Americans were far from uninitiated in colonial warfare when they reached across the Pacific Ocean for new territory in the Philippines. For nearly three hundred years, ever since Europeans first began settling the vast North American continent, they had fought what amounted to a protracted colonial war against the Indians who had been there for twelve thousand years: the last open battle with the Indians (a massacre), at Wounded Knee, was fought in 1890. So it should be considered no surprise that when it came time to conquer another nonwhite people eight years later, the United States made use of the template of Indian warfare. In his 1901 essay "Philippine Ethnology" published in *Harper's Weekly*, Frank D. Millet, a famous artist and war correspondent, made the connection when he asserted that "our North American Indians so thoroughly interpret [for] us this type of humanity [that we may find] that some of our present hostiles are blood-relations to the poor foes of the Pilgrims and Puritans."[1]

Whatever European Americans thought they knew about their long-term Indian enemies—that they were at best malleable children, at worst ferocious savages—was directly applicable to the strange people they now were confronting on the field of battle in the Philippines. As Lieutenant Jesse Lee Hall testified at the Senate hearings on the Philippines War held in 1902, Filipinos reminded him of Indians (and Mexicans as well, for that matter), "and dense ignorance is the worst thing against them. What enlightenment will bring is the question. I think they have some admirable traits." Bishop

James M. Thoburn, head of the Methodist Church in India and Malaysia, who had spent six weeks investigating Protestant possibilities in Catholic Manila, added in his testimony to the senators that the Filipinos were much "like our American Indians. . . . They have no cohesion whatever among themselves. . . . They go off into tribes and clans, and the biggest man is called a sultan, and his jurisdiction is limited. . . . I am afraid they are a treacherous people." American dominance over the Filipinos was to be justified the same way it had been over the Indians, Thoburn believed: "They have fallen to us by what we call the fortune of war. . . . We [should act] as we have acted on the theory for a hundred years with regard to the American Indians, that no matter what they wish or what government they desire we will hold them by force."[2]

Most of the veteran American officers commanding in the Philippines had spent nearly their entire careers fighting Indians; it was not surprising that they applied the analogy of Indian warfare to the fight against another hostile people. Furthermore, when, after losing a disastrous conventional military struggle, the Filipinos resorted to guerrilla warfare, similar to the strategy Indians had employed, the combat grew increasingly savage. At this juncture, Colonel Jacob H. Smith told reporters in Manila that dealing with these "natives" was "worse than fighting Indians," and that without waiting for direction from his commanders, he had naturally adopted tactics that he had learned fighting America's own "savages." The constraints of conventional warfare had vanished; fighting crossed over from war to war crimes, much as had been the case in the race and guerrilla warfare of the American Civil War and the Indian wars. Restraints off, terrorism became the general policy for both sides, with the far better armed and organized American colonizers capable of using force more lethally, particularly as they believed themselves licensed by nature and by God to do so in order to subdue this strange and inferior people. For Vice President Theodore Roosevelt, the Filipinos were only a "jumble of savage tribes," which he likened to Apache, while General Charles King explained that "the Filipino" was "utterly without conscience and as full of treachery as our Arizona Apache," who finally had been subdued in 1886, after decades of ferocious small-scale battles.[3]

It was not that the Filipinos (or the Indians before them) passively submitted to American conquest. They fought back, using terrorism both to discipline their own people and to push back and kill the invaders; in response, American soldiers behaved with equal or greater brutality. Once it became a matter of revenge for enemy savagery, each side felt entitled to employ retributive slaughter and other forms of wartime terrorism, and the cycle continued unabated until the war was finally ended.

Back on the American Plains in 1866, one cold December morning Captain William J. Fetterman's company of eighty-one officers and men had ridden out in pursuit of Sioux near Fort Kearney. They were ambushed and annihilated, and the Sioux then mutilated the troopers' bodies. Immediately after the massacre (a term Americans reserved for the slaughter of their own troops or white civilians), General Sherman, at that time commander of the army in the West, wrote to U.S. Grant, the commander-in-chief, "We must act with vindictive earnestness against the Sioux, even to their extermination, men, women and children." Although Sherman rarely used such genocidal language, he was not speaking abstractly. Two years earlier, a Colorado regiment of 700 men had surprised and destroyed a peaceful band of Cheyenne at Sand Creek, killing at least 28 men and 105 women and children. They then mutilated the corpses, gathering fingers and ears to take back to Denver as trophies, several soldiers cutting out the genitals of the women and stretching them over their saddlebows.[4]

Such episodes had continued, off and on, for countless decades as white settlers pushed westward across the continent. But in the thirty years it took to suppress the Plains Indians in post–Civil War America, army strategy was not mere slaughter, nor was genocide the goal. Militarily, the plan, first fully formulated in 1868 and refined in practice over the remainder of the century, was to herd nomadic Indians into concentrated areas where they would be fed and protected by the U.S. government as the railroads pushed through their lands, bringing buffalo hunters and settlers, and remaking the West as a "progressive" and "civilized" land. The Indians who refused this solution and left the reservations to hunt and raid became aliens entering what amounted to free-fire zones, fair game for the military to hunt down, return to the reservations, or kill.

So long as bands of Indians continued to leave the reservations, the enforcement of this concentration policy amounted to unstoppable war, including selective extermination when expedient. It must be stressed, however, that the other aim of the government's Indian policy was assimilation. Reformers, often in conflict with the military, urged a peaceful program that would suppress Indian forms of family life, economic livelihood, community organization, and religion and replace them with nuclear Christian farming families. The reformers placed special emphasis on retraining Indian children, if necessary taking them away from their parents by force and sending them to boarding schools, where they were compelled to speak only English and to obey their Christian masters. In time, communal land was to be privatized in the hands of these newly minted "white" Indians. Thus were nomadic, hunter-warrior societies to be blended into Christian, capitalist Anglo-Saxon America. As Richard Henry Pratt, the leading Indian educator and founder of the Carlisle Indian School in Pennsylvania, proudly declared, the reformers' aim was to "kill the Indian and save the man." This position, offered without apparent irony, was intended to obliterate the otherness of the other in the name of an impossible assimilation.[5]

What we might call culturcide was, in the context of late-nineteenth-century social values, the *progressive* response to the treatment of the Indians, strenuously objected to by most settlers and military figures, who preferred to use direct and violent force to eliminate any trace of the Indian threat, rather in the manner that they hunted down wolves. There was nothing relativist or pluralist in this aspect of mainstream American nationalism—white Americans were a people on the march, creating a nation dedicated to liberty, in part by eliminating the clearly understood forces of evil they confronted along the way. But even on the kinder road to nationality the goal was assimilation, not the encouragement or even sufferance of separate value structures and ways of life.

The softer choice of assimilation was difficult enough where African Americans and Indians were concerned—after centuries of struggle they remained a despised, often brutalized underclass—but it became even harder to accomplish when the United States began expanding past its continental borders. Could missionary work extend assimilation to non-Protestant, non-white peoples far from the continental United States, or would conquest demand brute suppression and exploitation? When the Grant administration had sought to annex Santo Domingo in 1871 as a means of extending U.S. power into the Caribbean, waves of protest prevented the acquisition of a nation whose alien populace could never be welcomed as equal members of the American family. Meanwhile, polyglot southern and eastern European immigrants were showing up in ever-increasing numbers at Ellis Island, pouring into the burgeoning and unsettling new cities, organizing strikes and anarchist dynamite brigades. During the same hectic decades the European powers, America's rivals, were all engaged on massive imperialist enterprises, frequently using the most brutal means to overwhelm indigenous populations and rapaciously exploiting the labor and natural wealth of their new colonies.

While many of their elders hesitated to undertake imperialist actions, younger Americans who were rising to positions of power at the end of the nineteenth century often found the prospect of high adventure abroad enticing. They usually referred to themselves as expansionists rather than imperialists, and in a sense this word lent an aura of continuity to their project. "Manifest Destiny" at home naturally led to "American Mission" abroad. The United States had expanded across the continent; now Americans would move farther west, across the Pacific. In 1898 a long campaign in the press and the more activist echelons of the Republican Party rallied the nation to come to the aid of the Cubans, who were fighting a desperate war of independence against Spain. When the battleship *Maine* blew up in Havana harbor (probably because of an accident), expansionist voices swelled in outrage, in a sense forcing the McKinley administration into war against the tottering Spanish Empire. The Spanish-American War proved to be a spectacular success: Cuba fell rapidly to U.S. expeditionary forces, while the U.S. Navy shelled the rickety Spanish Navy into oblivion off Cuba, Puerto Rico, and at Manila harbor as well, the seat of the major Spanish possession in the Pacific.

Admiral George Dewey's triumph in Manila on May 1, 1898, was no accident—careful planning had sent off a modern fleet to destroy Spanish interests in the Philippines. But what would come next remained unclear. Dewey had not been accompanied by a sizable army or marine force, and the Americans at first found it expedient to support local insurrectionists who had been fighting the Spanish occupiers since 1896. In fact, Dewey sent a ship to Hong Kong to transport the Filipino leaders in exile there, including their leader Emilio Aguinaldo, back to Filipino lines outside Manila, and he supplied their forces with guns and ammunition. In Washington, and in the press across the nation, strident voices, stimulated by the easy and heady triumph in Cuba, pushed for the annexation of the Philippine Islands, which came to pass with the Treaty of Paris, signed on December 10, 1898, when the Americans "bought" the islands from the Spanish Crown for twenty million dollars. While the Senate was debating the treaty, with the outcome in considerable doubt, war broke out between the Filipino independence forces and the small American expeditionary force that had been sent out a few weeks earlier. Whoever fired the first shot, open conflict was highly useful to administration operatives in rallying Senate votes; the Treaty of Paris was approved on February 5, 1899. Cuba was freed, while Puerto Rico and the Philippines were taken as dependencies rather than territories in the traditional sense, thus remaining outside the constitutional protections accorded other Americans.

United States troops were sent to Asia in increasing numbers as the war against the Filipinos escalated, reaching sixty-five thousand in 1901.

The subjugation of the Philippines started not in the name of military conquest and economic domination, then, but in the spirit of the other pole of American expansionist ideology: assimilationist idealism. The United States was bringing Christianity and universal libertarian ideals to a poor, oppressed people for their own good rather than for selfish American ends. On December 21, 1898, President William McKinley set the high moral tone of the war to come in his proclamation accompanying the dispatch of the first sizable contingent of troops. "It should be the earnest and paramount aim of the military administration to win the confidence, respect, and affection of the inhabitants of the Philippines by assuring them in every possible way that full measure of individual rights and liberties which is the heritage of a free people, and by proving to them that the mission of the United States is one of *benevolent assimilation,* substituting the mild sway of justice and right for arbitrary rule."[6] Given their history of liberty for all, Americans colonizers would not be like European imperialists—they intended to be Christian emissaries bringing justice and freedom rather than materialist exploiters imposing tyranny. This Christian libertarianism, American-style, proved to have a long ideological life. With modest refinements it remained in place for Vietnam and Iraq.

McKinley himself, a product of the Civil War generation that had experienced the horrors of battle at first hand, was something of an agonized expansionist, fearing what foreign conquest might entail, but not so fearful that he was unable to act decisively. And there were sizable contingents of domestic anti-imperialists who loathed European-style wars of conquest, particularly when alien races were involved. So the first U.S. imperialist war was fought in the context of political division on the home front, an extended public argument over the implications of such ventures and who expressed bedrock American values.

Across the Pacific, for the next three years military commanders and civil governors refined the peculiarly idealistic American approach to colonization even as they developed brutal forms of military repression. Out in the jungle and along rugged mountain ranges, given considerable latitude by their commanders, junior officers and enlisted men, acting out of racial prejudice and hunger for revenge against the Filipinos, applied the savage forms of war they had learned in their conquest of the Indians. When their often-horrific means collided with the idealistic ends of the missionary imperialists and news of what was happening filtered back home through soldiers' letters and reporters' stories, anti-imperialist forces gathered sufficient strength to put the war itself on trial in the form of Senate hearings in 1902, as well as to compel a series of military court-martials for the most egregious offenders. Administration authorities had to contend with searching criticism, which they did through both denial and highly selective punishment of the worst malefactors, whose actions, they insisted, were rare exceptions to the rule of kindly colonization. The existence and meaning of extralegal terrorism was at the core of this public debate. Conquest could not be accomplished without brute force, a means that contradicted democratic and peaceful goals and presumably benevolent motives. American military and political authorities, using every means necessary for conquest, and learning to "manage" what therefore appeared to be state terrorism while at the same time reaffirming American idealism, provided much of the ideological tension that has accompanied U.S. imperialism ever since.

Precisely at the moment when the Treaty of Paris hung in the balance in the Senate, the British poet Rudyard Kipling rallied American public opinion toward expansionism. He reaffirmed from a friendly outsider's perspective America's great new mission in his poem in *McClure's Magazine* entitled "The United States and the Philippine Islands, 1899." Now was the time for Americans to don the European imperial mantle and make imperialism a universal liberator. No longer could Americans sit on the sidelines, congratulating themselves on their isolated continental greatness, taking potshots at European power politics while remaining aloof from a world that called out for their leadership.

> Take up the White Man's burden—
> Have done with childish days—
> The lightly-proffered laurel, the easy ungrudged praise.
> Comes now, to search your manhood
> Through all the thankless years,
> Cold, edged with dear-bought wisdom,
> The judgment of your peers!

For Kipling, the ostensible goal was neither power nor wealth but a higher education and liberal government for benighted peoples in accordance with the standards of European civilization. He called on the best Americans to enlist in an extremely difficult but indispensable social mission, though he acknowledged that the racially inferior natives they served would be unappreciative. Indeed, bearing with ingratitude would be one further proof of the disinterested service men of honor were performing when they uplifted "ignorant peoples":

> Send forth the best ye breed—
> Go bind your sons to exile
> To serve your captives' need;
> To wait, in heavy harness,
> On fluttered folk and wild—
> Your new-caught, sullen peoples,
> Half-devil and half-child.

The superior race had no choice but to use imperialist means to demonstrate its inner mettle, "In patience to abide" when tried by those "sullen peoples / Half-devil and half-child." It would be necessary to test the limits of civilization to know what civilization really was. The truly civilized man had to conquer his own inner demons by testing his core values: "To veil the threat of terror / And check the show of pride." And the paramount goal of this heroic self-control and self-sacrifice, which the natives never would understand, was the selfless development of their good: "To seek another's profit, / And work another's gain. . . . Fill full the mouth of Famine / And bid the sickness cease." The white man's burden was "no tawdry rule of kings, / But toil of serf and sweeper."[7]

Many younger Americans thrilled to Kipling's Nietzschean challenge—although he spoke in a British voice, they could Americanize his racial triumphalism by adapting his ideals to the spread-eagle oratory that was rampant on every Fourth of July and during every political campaign. At this moment of the new millennium, the shiniest trumpet sounding the call for the new American empire was the stentorian voice of a handsome young senator from Indiana, Albert J. Beveridge, whose oratory electrified Americans. On January 9, 1900, at a time when some were becoming discouraged by reports of persistent Filipino resistance and stronger and uglier military measures being used against them, Beveridge spoke to a packed Senate chamber—and to the nation as a whole—capturing the meaning of American expansion with clarion justification.

"The Philippines are ours forever," Beveridge began, and beyond those islands lay the vast Chinese market ready to be opened. To secure that future, "we will not renounce our part in the mission of our race, trustee, under God,

of the civilization of the world." As Kipling urged, Beveridge professed himself grateful "for a task worthy of our strength" and gave "thanksgiving to
Almighty God that He has marked us as His chosen people, henceforth to
lead in the regeneration of the world." Beveridge stressed the commercial as
well as the religious aspects of this holy task. Future wars, he believed, would
be fought over commerce, and the power that ruled the Pacific would dominate the commercial world; that power, holy as well as capitalist, should be
American.

At times this great struggle, of which the Philippines War was but the
opening round, would demand drastic methods, which Americans would have
to employ without hesitation and without guilt, Beveridge believed. "Our
Indian wars would have been shortened, the lives of soldiers and settlers saved,
and the Indians themselves benefited had we made continuous and decisive
war. . . . We acted toward the Indians as though we feared them, loved them,
hated them—a mingling of foolish sentiment, inaccurate thought, and para-
lytic purpose." The need for decisive ruthlessness ought to be the lesson of
those earlier expansionist struggles; such warfare "needs to be finished before it
is stopped." Responding unashamedly from his belief in white racial supremacy to the charge that "our conduct of the [Philippines] war has been
cruel," Beveridge insisted: "We are not dealing with Americans or Europeans
[but] with Orientals [who] mistake kindness for weakness, forbearance for
fear." We must remember that "in dealing with Filipinos we deal with children. . . . Savage blood, Oriental blood . . . Spanish example—are these the
elements of self-government? . . . These people who are not capable of
'consenting' to any form of self-government must be governed."

Ruling this low oriental race required American supermen who could
countenance ruthless methods while remaining dispassionate, disinterested,
and subservient to the higher good they embodied, "the highest examples of
our civilization . . . men of the world . . . not theorists or dreamers . . . brave
men, physically as well as morally . . . as incorruptible as honor, as stainless as
purity, men whom no force can frighten, no influence coerce, no money buy."
Whether and how to usher in the new era of American world domination was
not in the end a political or constitutional issue but something more "elemental"—a "racial" matter. "God has not been preparing the English-speaking
and Teutonic peoples for a thousand years for nothing but vain and idle . . .
self-admiration. No! He has made us the master organizers of the world to
establish system where chaos reigns. . . . He has marked the American people
as His chosen nation to finally lead in the regeneration of the world."[8]

Beveridge attuned American ears to European militant imperialism; his strident evocation of race mastery was in the vanguard of such thought in the United States, although he was not a fringe actor. He was close to Vice President Roosevelt and a clique of activist, imperialist Republican insiders who agreed with everything he was saying—although his language was more inflamed than they were used to—and this group had sufficient power to steer the administration in the direction Beveridge wanted. The best evidence of this influence was the way they had persuaded the older, extremely cautious, normally passive President William McKinley to undertake the annexation of the Philippines. In his muted and hesitant but increasingly committed way, McKinley accepted and carried out their imperialist imperative. McKinley had experienced great ambivalence about annexing the islands. He consulted widely before signing the 1898 treaty, and while the dominant elements in his own party urged annexation, many whom he respected asserted that the price of becoming a colonial power would outweigh the potential benefits, setting the United States on the path of European imperialism and away from the freedoms of American self-governance. No would-be racial superman, not even a typically ruthless man of power, McKinley fully realized that he and his nation were approaching a great turning point in U.S. foreign policy.

Whatever he may actually have thought at the time, a year after making his choice McKinley shared the memory of his agonizing decision-making process with the Methodist General Missionary Committee, which visited him at the White House. The committee was about to leave when McKinley called out, "Hold a moment longer. . . . Before you go I would like to say just a word about the Philippine business. . . . When . . . I realized that the Philippines had been dropped into our laps I confess I did not know what to do with them. I sought counsel from all sides—Democrats as well as Republicans—but got little help." Rather than take responsibility for having made a political choice among available options or praise his own strong leadership abilities, McKinley instead described a religious experience, in which the Lord had made his decision for him: "I walked the floor of the White House night after night until midnight; and I am not ashamed to tell you, gentlemen, that I went down on my knees and prayed Almighty God for light and guidance more than one night. And one night late it came to me this way . . . : (1) That we could not give them back to Spain—that would be cowardly and dishonorable; (2) that we could not turn them over to France or Germany—our commercial rivals in the Orient—that would be bad business and discreditable; (3) that we could not leave them to themselves—they were unfit for self-government—and they would soon have anarchy and misrule over there worse than Spain's was; and (4) that there was nothing left for us to do but to take them all, and to educate the Filipinos, and uplift and civilize and Christianize them, and by God's grace do the very best we could by them, as our fellow-men for whom Christ also died."[9]

A skeptical Methodist might have noted that talking with God tends to reinforce choices leaders want to make for other reasons. Yet however phrased, this pious submission elicited the Lord's instruction to act as a proper expansionist. Even if reluctant, the president must take up the burden of the time in the national interest. But even in McKinley's kindly language, the project was a matter of uplifting a lesser people incapable of self-government, and the agenda was annexation of the Philippines regardless of how much American and Filipino blood that might take. McKinley would never choose to see expansionism in such a harsh light, and his softer version of the American imperialist mission would lead to ideological and moral contradictions more convoluted than those imagined by uncomplicated imperialists. McKinley's formulation would sound better to the ears of skittish voters, allowing them to maintain traditional American republican modesty while celebrating traditional national expansion at the same time.

Having been inwardly reassured that he was acting not out of personal or political motivations but from clear Christian duty (which just happened to comport with American self-interest), McKinley never looked back. He told the Methodist missionaries during their visit about the aftermath of his vision, "Then I went to bed, and went to sleep, and slept soundly, and the next morning I sent for the chief engineer of the War Department (our map-maker), and I told him to put the Philippines on the map of the United States, and there they are, and there they will stay while I am President!"[10]

Though McKinley played down his role as agent of change and put the responsibility on God, unlike such strident imperialists as Albert Beveridge, Beveridge and his Republican allies had helped guide and reinforce his decision. As long as he lived, McKinley believed that the U.S. domination of the Philippines was providential, and that his motives, and American motivations in general, were good. In his 1899 State of the Union Address, he preached that America's duty was to reconstruct and reform the Philippines. Americans should not wait until the end of the war to begin the "beneficent work. We shall . . . open the schools and the churches, . . . set the courts in operation, . . . foster industry and trade and agriculture, and in every way in our power . . . make these people whom Providence has brought within our jurisdiction feel that it is . . . their liberty and not our power, their welfare and not our gain, we are seeking to enhance." The American flag always waved "in blessing," and the Filipinos soon would acknowledge the "gift of benediction" that had been brought with it to their shores.[11]

Two years later, in his second inaugural address, McKinley insisted, as had American authorities from the onset when they termed the Philippine resistance an *insurrection* against the United States rather than a *war for independence,* that benevolent American authority was already building a peaceful and rich colony. "We are not making war against the inhabitants of the Philippines. A portion of them are making war against the United States. By far the greater part of the inhabitants recognize American sovereignty and welcome it as a guaranty of order and of security for life, property, liberty, freedom of conscience, and the pursuit of happiness." With no plebiscite and no opinion polls to back him up, McKinley had to base this claim entirely on his faith in American goodness, to which he believed the Filipinos were bound to respond. McKinley's reasoning resembled the way adults surmise the consent of children.[12]

While serving the long-range American mission of moral uplift, the army spent three years in increasingly ruthless warfare to suppress the Philippine "insurrection." After their armies were decimated in the first few months of conventional warfare, the Filipinos adopted a decentralized guerrilla strategy. This was a brutal war: the islands were numerous, largely covered in jungle and impassable mountains, with a hot, unhealthy climate and tenacious and hostile local populations attacking U.S. forces at unexpected moments. At home a vocal anti-imperialist minority was opposing the entire affair, rightly assuming, given press reports and letters from soldiers in the field, that something terrible was taking place.

By February 1902, Democrats in the Senate had managed to force an investigation of the war, and the record of those hearings gives us a searing picture of what the guerrilla war necessitated and how its imperatives challenged the American conception of benevolent assimilation. The Republican majority, chaired by the enthusiastic expansionist Henry Cabot Lodge of Massachusetts, brought the official spokesmen for the war, both civil and military, to the witness stand, along with expert witnesses of the religious and "scientific" ethnological persuasion, to bolster the official case concerning the conflict, while the Democratic minority focused on junior officers and enlisted men, who had seen up close what the army was doing from day to day. Tensions were sometimes evident between the civilian and military leadership, the military stressing coordinated attacks, the civilians pacification, and military officers occasionally quarreled among themselves. The lower military grades, meanwhile, demonstrated their impatience with both sets of leaders—their mandate had been to take whatever action necessary whenever they perceived themselves to be under threat.

The lead witness for the administration, questioned for nearly the entire month of February 1902, was the Philippine Commissioner, William Howard Taft, the former governor of Ohio, whose performance as the civil governor of the Philippines was one of the main reasons the new president, Theodore Roosevelt, chose him as his successor in 1908. Taft generally presented an upbeat picture of the grateful conversion of the Filipino people to American rule. He was reputed to have called them his "little brown brothers," an opinion few troops shared. Yet Taft was no fool, and he saw the negative side of the American occupation as well as its hope for the future. As he wrote to Secretary of War Elihu Root in 1901, "The severity with which the inhabitants have been dealt would not look well if a complete history of it were written out." But that was not the message he wanted to share with the senators or the public.[13]

As had McKinley, Taft generally expressed the warmest version of imperialism, though this kindliness masked a darker version of the Filipino "character." In a sophisticated fashion, which included an understanding of the way powerful colonizers project images on those they dominate, Taft described the way Americans viewed the Filipinos, especially their reputed "treachery"—their apparent welcome of Americans that had masked their extreme hostility. "It is said that this is an oriental people . . . that loves siestas; that seized every occasion to have a joyful gathering, and therefore that we, blind optimists, have been misled," Taft analyzed. "Well, of course, if you assume that the individual with whom you are dealing has none of the elements of human nature with which you are acquainted, is a different animal, is engaged in every thought in deceiving somebody, no matter how ignorant he may be, no matter how simple in appearance, you can reach any conclusion you desire in construing those evidences of welcome . . . and confidence that we have every day." Rather, Taft argued, the average Filipino "is moved by similar considerations to those which move other men." If "violent crimes, ambush, assassination" are more common in the Philippines than in European countries, "it is also true that kindness" toward the Filipinos reduces the violence against Americans if used regularly instead of "abrupt and unconciliatory" methods. Taft professed a creed in which struggling to win the allegiance of the Filipinos rather than sponsoring or permitting war crimes in the name of domination would be the order of the day.[14]

Naturally peaceful people though they were, Taft believed that the "terrorism of the guerrilla campaign" had distorted the Filipinos' normal character, for it was "indispensable" to such warfare that "murder and assassination" of their own people as well as Americans had to be practiced. Here Taft argued that guerrilla conflict produced cruelty regardless of race. "War, of course, provokes cruelty in everyone," he asserted. But there was something— a sort of innate racial characteristic—in these people that rendered them particularly open to becoming horrific warriors. "The uneducated Filipino is a docile person, but left to the natural ferocity which war and hostility of that sort provokes, he becomes very cruel." The guerrillas were "ignorant, uneducated and cruel men, for the uneducated native, I am sorry to say, is cruel to animals and has little regard for human life." Here was Taft's version of the negative side of the docile and cheerful " little native."[15]

In response to the provocations of the ruthless guerrilla war being waged on them, Taft reassured the committee, Americans had used "more compassion and more restraint and more generosity" than had any other colonial power in any other war against "inferior races." And yet Taft conceded that when Americans saw evidence of Filipino savagery in the mutilated bodies of their dead comrades, "it is not to be wondered at that . . . small bodies of American soldiers . . . should possibly at times have yielded in their outraged feelings . . . and resorted to [brutal] methods which under the circumstances they regarded as more or less justified." From his office in Manila, he had heard many references to the practice of torture, though he had never tracked them down. "Of course it was no duty of mine. That was a military responsibility," Taft explained. Nevertheless he did not condemn Americans' torture of Filipinos outright. Imagine that a soldier finds his "Bunkie" dead in the field, his body mutilated, Taft reasoned. Revenge would be a normal response. "You must understand that a soldier has human nature and that things are done which a commanding officer would not approve and yet cannot be prevented because of the outrage of feelings. That is the explanation of a great many things." Terrorism, Taft implied, flowed naturally from colonialist military invasion, however well-intended.[16]

This at least partly honest and probably unplanned admission of U.S. atrocities, however infrequent Taft believed them to be, caused a considerable reaction in the anti-imperialist press. But in the balance of his testimony, Taft reverted optimistically to a description of the civilizing mission he believed he had been leading. He was certain that granting independence to the Filipinos would bring chaos and tyranny while driving out capital and development. Alternatively, no matter how long it might take, "It is in my judgment the duty of the United States to continue a government there which shall teach those people individual liberty, which shall lift them to the point of civilization of which I believe they are capable, and which shall make them rise to call the name of the United States blessed." This intervention "is the best possible thing for the Filipino people. . . . Probably the United States is only taking its burden of civilized peoples in helping out uncivilized peoples," he said, echoing Rudyard Kipling and Albert Beveridge. However reluctant he might have been initially for U.S. engagement in the region, "going as far as I have gone now, and feeling the missionary spirit as I think I may say I have it," Taft concluded that Americans had no choice but to stay the course and expand the blessings of liberty to this hitherto uncivilized Asian people.[17]

For the military leadership, staying the course had meant growing frustration and ever-increasing ruthlessness in response to the kinds of assaults that were intrinsic to guerrilla warfare. General Robert P. Hughes, a capable division commander who had served in the Philippines for three years, noted in his testimony to the committee his own change in attitude toward the Filipinos, from generosity of spirit to hardness. As a professional officer, he believed that war "should be made entirely civilized and just as light as possible to succeed. I went there supposing these people to be sufficiently civilized to follow the ordinary rules of civilized warfare. I became convinced, greatly to my sorrow, that they would not follow the rules of war." Although conceding that the best of the Filipino men the army employed as laborers did a full day's work and improved in regularity of habits under "our system of honest dealing," Hughes found that most were "lazy" and sneaky. "They want at least three days in the week [off] and they want to go to cockfights, and they want to gamble, and they want to whet up their bolos." Somewhat comic in this rendition, these same Filipinos, when they turned on their masters and fought as guerrillas, "were indifferent to every other man's life . . . absolutely indifferent to taking life. . . . These people are not civilized."

Therefore, responding to the "treacherous" and "savage" characteristics of the Filipinos, American military practice "became stiffer as we went along," Hughes admitted. Under endless duress, men in his command gradually turned from civilized warfare into forms of terrorism they understood to be beyond the rules. They burned villages and shot down increasing numbers of enemy men they suspected of being insurrectionaries. Asked whether the huge disparity of Filipino to American casualties suggested unnecessary slaughter, Hughes replied with contempt for his enemy, "I always felt as if we were hitting a woman in fighting those people. They did not know the first thing about how to fight." That so many of them had died was a result not of their bravery or stoicism but of the stupid obstinacy of their leadership. Hughes denied categorically that his men tortured their enemies, or that he had ever instructed them to kill prisoners, or that he knew for certain whether that practice had ever been used in the field. Here Hughes revealed the way a commander can give his men license to kill prisoners while maintaining his ability to deny to his superiors (including congressmen), and perhaps to himself, that he bore any responsibility for that killing: "My instruction, given with caution—because you cannot bind by an absolute rule a man who meets an enemy—was not to kill unnecessarily: that killing the . . . ordinary man, accomplished nothing . . . but if they could pick out the leaders and kill them they were accomplishing something."[18]

Privately, writing in his diary even this battle-hardened veteran was shocked by some of the activities practiced by men under his command, though his instructions had licensed extreme violence, and though he too despised the enemy he considered uncivilized and worthy of elimination. His soldiers became so quick to torch villages that Hughes confided, "It is not our usual way of making war." He was appalled at "the amount of robbery and looting done by these rowdy troops. . . . They would steal the sandals of a native who had died of smallpox." Hughes did nothing to change this behavior—the occasional private protest in his diary was a means of trying to reinforce his self-image as a humane man and civilized soldier even as he recognized that fighting a guerrilla war such as he was leading was bound to take American soldiers along a morally descending course. For public consumption Hughes insisted that the American army maintained its essential humanity when confronted by this dastardly enemy.[19]

Hughes's commander during the first phase of the war, Elwell S. Otis, insisted to the Senate committee that only an iron hand could discipline the Filipino people. Should the Americans leave, "it would be anarchy or military despotism." Because the Filipinos could not divorce liberty from license they were "not fitted for self-government," of which they had not the "slightest conception."[20]

It followed in the minds of many military officers that whatever his patriotic protestations, "the Filipino" was essentially a primitive and apolitical other meriting harsh punishment. Colonel Arthur L. Wagner, with the

U.S. Adjutant-General's Office, who insisted that he knew of absolutely no torture of Filipinos, also noted that if a town were "notoriously a nest of ladrones [bandits]," and if the rest of the people in the town were unwilling to give them up, "it would be justifiable and proper to destroy the town, even though we destroyed the property of some innocent people. The Almighty destroyed Sodom, notwithstanding the fact that there were a few just people in that community." To which Senator Beveridge responded, "How strange; I was thinking of Sodom and Gomorrah."[21]

The expert witnesses called to buttress the official analysis of the Filipino people and the necessity of staying the course, ethnologists and clergymen, applied a similar biblical sensibility to the "little people" of the Philippines and to the American mission, though usually in a less blood-curdling way than as a reenactment of the Lord's punishment of Sodom and Gomorrah. A. Lester Haslett, investigator of soldiers' morals in Manila for the Women's Christian Temperance Union, expressed the opinion that the vast majority of the Filipinos "are but children who must sit at our feet and learn [the] lessons of self-government." The Manila elite he found rather cultivated, progressive, and quite promising, "fully as bright as the Japanese." Although he had gone to the islands "an ardent anti-expansionist" he had returned a "firm believer" in U.S. policy. He had seen the light: the racial main chance was there. "God has given us a wonderful opportunity, for which I am sure he will hold us strictly accountable. To refuse to accept the heaven-bestowed privilege to elevate to a like plane with ourselves a people" ready to learn to build their nation would be to prove "unworthy of so high an honor." And besides, the natural resources were "wonderful," large lodes of gold, silver, and other metals cropping right out of the ground, vast coalfields, a huge rubber industry awaiting development. Haslett's dreams of natural wealth just waiting to be gathered failed to pan out, at least in the short run.[22]

Interestingly enough, few spokesmen making the semi-official case for empire stressed potential wealth, deep-water ports, access to the China market, or other forms of American strategic self-interest. Not realpolitik or economic exploitation but doing good in the world was the advertised American way, the American gift.

The Methodist bishop James M. Thoburn, who compared Filipinos to American Indians as inferior races incapable of self-government, placed American Mission in a geopolitical context. As the bishop of India and Malaysia, he was well acquainted with British methods of governing the heathen. Thoburn would have the Americans adopt the "spirit of English policy" but adapt it "according to American ideals" which were a "little better"—that is, Americans were kinder and less rapacious than the British. He was certain that in the next hundred years all "outlying uncivilized or half-civilized" peoples would come under the jurisdiction of five or six "great governments"—the new imperial world order.

There was no doubt in the bishop's mind that uncivilized peoples needed rigorous domination. The Filipinos, like the Malays he knew so well, were "treacherous," "restless," "very defective" in their capacity for self-government, inferior in moral and intellectual abilities. When held firmly but fairly as a "subject race under fixed rights that are assured to them," this lesser race could be lifted up spiritually by American missionaries and brought to Jesus under the protection of the American flag. Thoburn ignored the fact that 90 percent of Filipinos were already Christians, the only Asian population that had almost completely converted. But they were Roman Catholics—Christians of the wrong sort. Even if they were properly brought to Christ, they should never be "amalgamated" into the United States, Thoburn believed. (McKinley's phrase about benevolent assimilation was contaminated, he implied, by overtones of degenerative race mixing.) The inferior peoples should remain separated, inferior and "protected."[23]

For sheer patriotic grandiloquence and breadth of vision, no other American spokesman compared to Arthur MacArthur, commanding general in the Philippines from 1900 to 1901. Americans were now embarked on a "heroic age of History," MacArthur declared. The Aryan race had, over a thousand years, expanded westward, first across Europe; then over the Atlantic; and now, with "relentless vigor . . . this magnificent Aryan people," was moving ever westward across the Pacific, "back almost to the cradle of its race." Conquering the Philippines was the American racial destiny: "We have been committed to a position by a process of spontaneous evolution." This lightly scientized version of McKinley's divine mission, probably based on reading contemporary racial theories in the popular press, reinforced U.S. expansionism from another ideological angle.

Aryans all the conquering races were, yet Americans were better than the rest, MacArthur went on. "All other governments that have gone to the East have simply planted trading establishments [and] systematized living conditions, but they have not planted an idea that would be self-sustaining." Only force kept European colonies in line—if they departed their subjects would revert to savagery within five years. How unlike this was the promise of American conquest, for "we are planting in those islands imperishable ideas."

And that core idea of Americanization was "republicanism, [because] inspiration and hope go with our flag." In the conquest of the Philippines, Americans were "instruments" changing the world to a greater extent than had anyone since Europeans discovered the North American continent. Withdrawal from this mission would bring about the "permanent failure of Republicanism in the East," a collapse into anarchy for the Philippines and all the other potential Asian republics if the less enlightened world powers "initiated a struggle for supremacy" that could lead only to world war, widespread decay, and renewed barbarism. The good news was that "once planted" properly, American republicanism could never be eradicated.

MacArthur felt confident that the Filipino people had "rudimentary republican ideas and aspirations, and that they [were] therefore in an essentially plastic condition" that could lead to great success if the Americans governed the islands as a "tuitionary annex." Unlike many other American colonizers, MacArthur rather admired the Filipinos. He hoped to see them develop as independent craftsmen and smallholder farmers instead of being forced onto huge and exploitative labor plantations such as those the Dutch were imposing on Java. They should rather be encouraged to develop their natural artisan talents. "In art, [when] deft touch is an element they excel. . . . They are imaginative, full of romance and poetry," gifted actors and musicians. They had a natural pride in work and an eager ability to learn. In almost mystical fashion, half Thomas Jefferson and half Richard Burton, in love with the natural wealth and the mysteries of the East, MacArthur foresaw an American-style republic developing under the patient guidance of sensitive American colonizers, the most evolved of the Aryan peoples. "A magnificent and mighty destiny awaits us in the East."

As for the behavior of the American occupying army, though he conceded that "individual men have committed individual outrages," MacArthur insisted: "I doubt if any war—either international or civil, any war on earth—has been conducted with as much humanity [and] self-restraint, in view of the character of our adversary, as have been the American operations." This humanity did not derive merely from orders given by commanders but from "the spontaneous generosity of our soldiers, who have uniformly displayed that kindness which is characteristic of American soldiers." Pervading the army was the imperishable idea that Americans were "representing the highest stage of civilization" and needed to act in ways worthy of the "approbation of public opinion at home."[24]

This was the high point of the defense of U.S. policy presented to the senatorial investigating committee in 1902. In his way, expressing without apparent cynicism or irony a view that approached primal innocence, Mac-Arthur had outlined better than any other figure the basic value system that justified occupation. (It is also possible, one must consider, that MacArthur was being guileful, and that all his testimony was given tongue in cheek.)

Not all the senators were supportive of the MacArthur line however—the anti-imperialists, mainly Democrats, cross-examined him about his position, often sharply. Although much of their questioning concerned such issues as torture, the burning of towns, and the shooting of prisoners, MacArthur's grandiose Americanism, his belief in the purity of American motivations, led Senator Charles A. Culberson of Texas to interrogate the general closely about the ways in which the principles of republicanism were being planted in the archipelago.

Opening this line of inquiry, Culberson led MacArthur to agree that these fundamental values were embodied in the Declaration of Independence and the Constitution. One of the principles of 1776 was no taxation without representation. "We have not yet planted that idea . . . have we?" Culberson asked MacArthur, who replied, "That will come in due time, I think." Mac-Arthur then pointed out that there were three native Filipinos sitting on the governing commission of the U.S. occupation authority.

> CULBERSON: Care is taken, however, to have the Americans in the majority?
> MACARTHUR: That would be necessary at present, of course.
> CULBERSON: Those Filipinos, of course, are not selected by the Filipino people, but by the American authorities?
> MACARTHUR: They have been selected with all considerations possible to get the best representative men; not by a public expression through the ballot, however.
> CULBERSON: They are selected by the American authorities?
> MACARTHUR: Precisely so.
> CULBERSON: And not by the Filipinos?
> MACARTHUR: But not by any eccentric or capricious method. With a view of satisfying the Filipinos themselves.

Culberson did not remark that a similar form of "virtual representation" had been advanced by British authorities in the struggle leading up to the American Revolution and rejected by the Americans; instead he concluded that the Filipinos were indeed being taxed without representation, contrary to American republican ideas.

Self-government was another essential republican principle Culberson touched on, and MacArthur admitted that the Filipinos were as yet completely under U.S. rule: "They are after personal rights, essentially so, and not forms of government." Senator Edward Carmack, Democrat of Tennessee, then intervened: "Do you think personal rights can be secured without political rights?" To which MacArthur replied, "I think they can under the American flag most decidedly [if we treat the Philippines as a] tuitionary annex, [our having] acquired absolute sovereignty over everything Spain owned" through the Treaty of Paris.

Culberson returned to the questioning: "I will ask you if the Filipinos have freedom of speech? . . . Have they freedom of the press?" And then, without really waiting for a reply, Culberson himself pointed out that neither was possible under the current sedition law (which, MacArthur was happy to point out, was passed after he had left his command). For example, no Filipino speaker or journalist was permitted to advocate political independence.

Moving on, Culberson asked: "Are the people . . . entitled to keep and bear arms?" MacArthur's reply: "I should say not, and hope not most sincerely." Culberson asked about grand juries and trial by jury and received the same responses. And this:

> CULBERSON: [Are American] soldiers not quartered in the houses of the people without the consent of the owners?
> MACARTHUR: Most undoubtedly. There is a state of war there, and that is one of the necessities of field operations.

Culberson concluded this line of questioning by noting that he had read out practically the entire Bill of Rights, "and in each case you have answered that it has no application to the present conditions in the Philippines." In response MacArthur could only object that he was being misrepresented and that Culberson had failed to capture the "fine shades" of his opinions.[25]

Culberson's pointed questioning was indicative of the disbelief and frustration experienced by many who opposed imperialism in general and the war in the Philippines in particular. Anti-imperialists, who represented a long American tradition from which the imperialists had broken, gathered together in and outside Congress, and they made themselves heard. But they were relatively ineffective, however sharp their opposition to the war. Most were old men, arguing in what seemed to many to be old-fashioned ways, while the race for empire made an exciting, youthful appeal to patriotism and idealism. Harder heads among the expansionists, it must be added, were afraid of being shut out of trade at a time when the U.S. economy demanded cheaper raw materials and new and bigger markets for the flood of goods being produced by American industry, and for these people too anti-imperialism connoted stagnation.

And the anti-imperialists' political timing was off. By 1902, when the worst cases of American brutality were fully aired in the Senate, the war was already winding down. In a daring raid in March 1901, General Frederick Funston had captured the Filipino leader, Emilio Aguinaldo, who almost immediately embraced U.S. domination, and the resistance was shrinking, even though American military measures remained harsh, perhaps harsher than ever. Because the British had become fully engaged in a big and extremely nasty guerrilla war against the Boers in South Africa, public opprobrium had shifted to focus on someone else's imperialism, that of "perfidious Albion," which was using reprehensible methods against another "white race" and was traditionally regarded as the worst international evildoer by Americans.

In 1900, when the war had increased in brutality and was not going well, many Democrats had urged William Jennings Bryan to make anti-imperialism the center of his second presidential campaign. Bryan's standing on the issue, however, was undercut by the fact that in 1898 he had urged his supporters in the Senate to support the Treaty of Paris. And when war had broken out between the Americans and the Filipinos as the treaty neared ratification, Bryan had publicly supported the efforts of the U.S. Army "to defend American interests at any cost."[26]

Now in 1900, in his speech accepting the Democratic nomination for president, Bryan argued anti-imperialistically that the war threatened to corrupt the nation by swelling the military and overtaxing the poor, by imposing rule on another people through undemocratic means, and by pretending to uphold Christianity when in fact certain scheming and powerful capitalists were only serving their own interests. But when it came to demanding that the United States withdraw from its imperialist enterprise, Bryan equivocated. "If elected," he pledged, "I will immediately convene Congress . . . and recommend an immediate declaration of the nation's purpose . . . to establish a stable form of government in the Philippine Islands [and] to protect the Filipinos from outside interference while they work out their destiny," just as the United States under the Monroe Doctrine had long protected the states of Central and South America. "Since we do not desire to make them a part of us or hold them as subjects, we propose the only alternative . . . to give them independence and guard them against molestation from without." But for how long would the United States continue to "protect" the Philippines through occupation? Even most enthusiastic expansionists argued that the occupation would end some day when the Filipinos had been sufficiently schooled in republicanism, though they pushed back the projected date of departure fifty or seventy-five years, or even more.[27]

Through his imprecision, Bryan hoped to capture anti-imperialist voters while not offending more patriotic flag-wavers among his potential constituency. As would prove to be the case for later antiwar presidential candidates, he found it politically difficult not to support an ongoing war during an election year. Bryan's somewhat equivocal version of anti-imperialism, which fell short of becoming a referendum on empire, did not catch fire with the electorate in 1900—most American voters were proud to see their flag waving in the great new outpost in Asia.

If anti-imperialism failed to gather steam at the propitious moment, neither did it go away, William Jennings Bryan notwithstanding. The anti-imperialists all agreed that imperialism was corrupting the United States and imposing draconian rule on a people who did not want it and that the United States should get out of the Philippines immediately and resist any future imperialist adventures. But although many anti-imperialists believed as strongly as did the imperialists that the United States was the greatest republic in the world and that the white race ought to be dominant, others criticized those assumptions.

Finley Peter Dunne ("Mr. Dooley") and Mark Twain, the two greatest political satirists of the day, were in many ways the most cutting opponents of the American policy in the Philippines. Dunne, adopting the Irish-American voice of "Mr. Dooley," excoriated administration policy in his widely read syndicated newspaper column and books compiled from his newspaper work. In 1898, Mr. Dooley offered an account of how President McKinley had come to annex the islands that eerily anticipated the hand-wringing explanation McKinley later gave to the Methodist missionaries, a statement that became public knowledge only in 1904. "We can't sell thim, we can't ate thim, an' we can't throw them into th' alley whin no wan is lookin.' An' 'twud be a disgrace f'r to lave before we've pounded these frindless an' ongrateful people into insinsibility. So I suppose . . . we'll have to stay an' do th' best we can."

Dunne listened closely to the paternalism, racism, and underlying menace of the supporters of the war, about which Mr. Dooley observed, "Whin we plant . . . the starry banner iv Freedom in th' Ph'lipeens . . . an' give th' sacred blessin' iv liberty to the poor, downtrodden people iv thim unfortunate isles,—dam thim!—we'll larn thim a lesson. . . . We say to thim: 'Naygurs,' we say, 'poor dissolute, uncovered wretches,' says we, 'whin th' crool hand iv Spain forged man'cles f'r ye'er limbs . . . who was it crossed th' say an' sthruck off the' comealongs? We did . . . an' now, ye mis'rable, childish-minded apes, we propose f'r to larn ye th' uses iv liberty. [Then] we'll treat you the way a father shud treat his childher if we have to break ivry bone in ye'er bodies. So come to our arms.' "[28]

On October 15, 1900, stepping off the boat on his return from his ten-year self-imposed exile in Europe, Mark Twain joined the anti-imperialist cause. "I left these shores . . . a red-hot imperialist. . . . But I have thought more since then . . . and I have seen that we do not intend to free, but to subjugate the people of the Philippines. We have gone there to conquer, not to redeem." Twain then used a metaphor, probably for the first time, that would be applied to later American colonial wars. "We have got into a mess, a *quagmire* from which each fresh step renders the difficulty of extraction immensely greater."[29]

For the unusually well-traveled Twain, the United States was using republican pretenses to enter the European imperialist game. For the rest of his life (he died in 1910), Twain remained enraged at what the European powers were doing in Asia and Africa, as well as what he considered identical American behavior in the Philippines. In his caustic 1901 essay "To the Person Sitting in Darkness," Twain assumed the mentality of a cynical snake-oil peddler to attack the current American project within a larger European context. The Filipino revolutionaries at first had greeted the Americans as liberators, Twain wrote, believing as they did in the spirit of the Declaration of Independence. "Then we showed our hand" of military conquest. "To them it looked un-American . . . foreign to our established traditions. And this was natural too; for we were only playing the American game in public— in private it was the European one." Twain was inflamed about the material and ideological means the imperialist powers were using and the rationalizations they made without shame, even without apparent awareness that they *were* rationalizations. "Would it not be prudent to get our Civilization-tools together, and see how much stock is left on hand in the way of Glass Beads and Theology, and Maxim Guns and Hymn Books, and Trade-Gin and Torches of Progress and Enlightenment (patent adjustable ones, good to fire villages with, upon occasion)." Ninety percent of the heads of state and legislative bodies in "Christendom," including the American ones, "are members not only of the church, but also of the Blessings of Civilization Trust. This world-girdling accumulation of trained morals, high principles, and justice, cannot do an unright thing, an unfair thing, an ungenerous thing, an unclean thing. It knows what it is about. Give yourself no uneasiness; it is all right."[30]

At the core of anti-imperialism lay a premonition that by entering the international chase for empire, the United States would fatally go off course. For anti-imperialists, the danger had been present at least since 1871, when the Grant administration had tried to annex Santo Domingo. Averted when the Senate rejected that treaty, the threat had reappeared in other Caribbean and Latin American adventures and in the long fight over the seizure of Hawaii; now the Rubicon had been crossed into what appeared to be the first stage of large-scale colonialism.

The most eloquent anti-imperialist in the fight against the Grant treaty and afterward had been Carl Schurz, a German-American politician, a journalist, a Union general during the Civil War, and an agitator of considerable public standing. Schurz believed that to be true to its fundamental republican values the United States should never govern a people undemocratically, and that any territory it acquired should eventually be admitted as a state. But the United States also had to stay racially homogeneous (by which he meant white) to remain a nation, and "tropical peoples" were unassimilable because they shared nothing with Americans, "neither language, nor habits, nor institutions, nor traditions, nor opinions nor ways of thinking; nay, not even a code of morals." In the past Schurz had been unable to imagine a person "of the Latin race mixed with Indian and African blood" sitting in the U.S. Senate, and now he could not imagine Filipinos sitting there either, nor could he see Americans assimilating into the national fabric "millions of persons belonging partly to races far less good-natured, tractable and orderly than the negro is." Blacks and the new immigrants from eastern and southern Europe were bad enough; imagine the problems of incorporating "unspeakable Asiatics, by the tens of millions" into the country.[31]

As might be expected, many southern Democratic politicians were even more outspoken than Schurz in their racist objections to a potential American empire—on this ground they made a loose coalition with the independent Republicans who ran the anti-imperialist cause (the Mugwumps). E. L. Godkin, editor of the *Nation*, the leading reformist magazine of the day, was as virulent in his language as were the southerners: he had in the past referred to Mexicans as "greasers," and Nicaraguans as "slightly Catholicized savages." During the Philippines War, learning that missionaries were translating the Bible into various Filipino languages, Godkin wrote in the *Nation* that they ought to include his verse, "Mow down the natives like grass and say unto them, the Syndicate has arrived." Godkin had no more sympathy with corrupt businessmen and politicians at home than he did with the "savage races" abroad, and he thought that expansionism mixed them together in a toxic foreign policy.[32]

If anti-imperialists like Schurz and Godkin were essentially unsympathetic toward the Filipinos while opposing the war, others expressed more fellow feeling, even if their liberalism remained tinged with racial condescension. On May 22, 1902, several clergymen in Boston called a public meeting of protest against the "atrocities in the Philippines." At the meeting the Reverend Robert J. Johnson, of the Gate of Heaven Church, argued that "we did not even treat the Indians" as badly as we were treating the newly conquered race. At least on occasion the government paid attention to the requests of Indians and negotiated treaties with them. Now, in the name of Christian virtue, the United States was oppressing the only Christian nation in Asia. "It is only against these Filipinos, who are neither savages nor half-savages, but a Christian people, whose only crime is that they have read our Declaration of Independence, believed it to be true, and tried to live up to it, that we have taken this high and haughty position." The Reverend Francis H. Rowley of the First Baptist Church, added, "It is honor, not dishonor, to withdraw the flag from every foot of ground where it cannot float save in violation of the rights of man."[33]

It is likely that more Christian clergymen supported the conquest than opposed it, however. This public meeting was poorly attended, as were most other anti-imperialist gatherings. At the same time, missionaries successfully raised large sums of money to finance their campaign to convert the Filipinos to Protestantism.

Especially infuriating to many anti-imperialists was the way in which, to their way of thinking, the celebrants of empire used abstract ideology to cover up and dismiss their deeds. Charles Francis Adams detested such phrases as "white man's burden," and "lifting up inferior races," especially considering the "unchristian, brutal, exterminating" treatment of the Indians and the "long, shameful record" of abuse of blacks and Chinese within the continental United States. What qualified Americans to govern even-less-familiar people of other races, Adams asked. William James, who wrote to Adams in 1902, "God damn the U. S. for its vile conduct in the Philippines," was certain that American intervention would end Filipino national life: "We can destroy their old ideals, but we can't give them ours." Talk of educating and eventually liberating the Filipinos was only "sniveling . . . loathsome cant." In an op-ed piece in the *Boston Evening Transcript* in 1899, James declared that the United States had come upon "an intensely living and concrete situation," and had ruined it with "bald and hollow abstractions," about good government, upholding the American flag, and the "unfitness" of the Filipinos for self-government. "Such bald abstractions as Reason and the Rights of Man, spelt with capitals" were now being used in "stark-naked abstract" ways to kill Filipinos. "Could there be a more damning indictment of that whole bloated idol termed 'modern civilization' than this amounts to? Civilization is, then, the big, hollow, resounding, corrupting, sophisticating, confusing torrent of mere brutal momentum and irrationality that brings forth fruit like this?"[34]

The anti-imperialist who was the least negative or ambivalent about racial matters during the Philippines War was not a clergyman, a philosopher, or a Mugwump but a crusty old Republican warhorse, Senator George F. Hoar of Massachusetts, who found a vein of commonality with oppressed peoples that led him to make a general criticism of the Philippines policy in the context of American race relations in general. On January 9, 1900, speaking in the Senate, he argued that his imperialist colleagues simply could not understand that "God who made of one blood all the nations of the world [made all men] capable of being influenced by the same sentiments and the same motives—a love of liberty [that] does not depend on the color of the skin but . . . on [a shared] humanity." In 1904, writing his memoirs, Hoar challenged the whole notion of racial hierarchy and racial uplift, arguing that they were just so much self-serving projection by white men with power. "The Indian problem is not chiefly how to teach the Indian to be less savage in his treatment of the Saxon, but the Saxon to be less savage in his treatment of the Indian. The Negro question will be settled when the education of the white man is complete." Accepting that the Americans had been victorious in the Philippines and were ensconced in power, Hoar mourned what he believed had been lost. The United States had perverted the Monroe Doctrine from a policy of "eternal righteousness and justice" to one of "brutal selfishness." In victory "we crushed the only republic in Asia. We made war on the only Christian people in the East. . . . We vulgarized the American flag. We introduced perfidy into the practice of war." We tortured unarmed men, killed children, and established concentration camps. "We baffled the aspirations of a people for liberty."[35]

Whatever the ideological debate in the homeland, however the argument over Christian and republican values was conducted, whatever the army brass claimed about the general conduct of the war, men in the field set the actual terms of combat. Their attitudes and their behavior as they experienced the terrors of guerrilla warfare—vicious ambushes and raids by small groups of men on both sides—expressed the actual American presence in concrete ways. Evidence about their behavior came out in the testimony of junior officers and enlisted men at the Senate hearings. And in the songs they sang, the jokes they told, the opinions they expressed in their letters, we can uncover widely shared attitudes toward the enemy and the war they were conducting, as their beliefs were subjected to the coruscating pressures of guerrilla combat.

As in every war, to counter their anxieties and express solidarity while on the march, men adapted old songs to new situations, songs that rapidly spread throughout the army. In this war, through this collective folk art, the soldiers often indicated their awareness of the hostility of the Filipinos and the dreadful nature of guerrilla war and of everyday life in fetid jungles and on bleak mountainsides. They also expressed their contempt for leaders who used grand abstractions to justify the war and offered rosy predictions about a quick victory. To the tune of "Son of a Gamboleer," foot soldiers sang:

> I'm only a common soldier in the blasted
>   Philippines.
> They say I've got brown brothers here,
>   But I dunno know what it means.
> I like the word fraternity, but still
>   I draw the line.
> He may be a brother of Big Bill Taft,
>   But he ain't no brother of mine!

So much for Taft's sense of mission and cheery optimism. As far as the men were concerned, the enemy was an enemy: brotherhood was reserved for the band of soldiers with whom the individual enlisted man was fighting. A soldier's other best friend was his rifle (in this case the weapons were Krags). The soldiers wanted to destroy an enemy they detested and return to their normal lives back home as quickly as possible. That was *their* sense of mission. Thus, to the tune of "Tramp, Tramp, Tramp, the Boys Are Marching," soldiers joined in singing:

> Damn, damn, damn the Filipinos
>   Cut-throat khakiac ladrones!
> Underneath the starry flag
>   Civilize them with a Krag
> And return us to our beloved home.[36]

Jokes revealed similar attitudes, though most of these have been lost. One joke that was recorded in a soldier's newspaper revealed something of the racial complexity, the irony, and the absurdity of the war. When the 25th Infantry regiment, one of four black units sent over, showed up in Manila late in 1899, many white troops, having had no notion they were coming, were surprised. According to the story, one white volunteer from a western state called out to a newly arrived black soldier, "Hello, nig. Didn't know you'd come. What do you think you're going to do over here?" The black soldier replied, "Well, I doan know, but I ruther reckon we're sent over heah to take up de White Man's burden!"[37]

In such songs and stories, the men expressed their uncertainty about what the U.S. Army was doing so far away from home. They were risking their health and their lives for a cause that meant little to them as they fought the actual fight. When their period of service was extended without prior notification, volunteers in particular were furious that they were being kept in a vicious guerrilla conflict for no apparent good reason. As one Nebraska volunteer wrote home in 1899, "We feel that every man of ours that's lost is worth more than the whole damned island. . . . We don't know what we are fighting for hardly." Self-preservation was the paramount goal rather than American glory or Western Civilization. As one junior officer put it, in the most immediate sense of combat, "I'd sooner see a hundred niggers killed than one of my men endangered."[38]

Whatever else motivated soldiers, virulent racism was perhaps the belief that most united them. While senior officers and some men often referred to Filipinos as Indians, the usual names for the enemy were "niggers" or "Gugus" (a slur that sixty years later would evolve into "Gooks"). As one soldier pointed out to his parents, "Almost without exception, soldiers, and also many officers, refer to the natives as 'niggers'; and the natives are beginning to understand what the word 'nigger' means." Contemptible enemies like niggers, Indians, and Filipinos could be combined into a single image, linking together a long lineage of enemy others to be obliterated in ways outside the standards of conventional warfare. As one Kansas volunteer put it, "The country won't be pacified until the niggers are killed off like the Indians."[39]

For accuracy of reportage, letters from the front are hardly to be trusted, but even when one makes allowances for the distorting braggadocio of embattled young men wishing to appear powerful to the folks back home, the letters reveal much about the soldiers' attitudes toward the enemy. Letters depicted events in an intellectual and ideological context that soldiers believed their families shared and admired. One Washington State volunteer claimed that in the wake of his regiment after one battle, "There were 1008 dead niggers, and a great many wounded. We burned all their houses. I don't know how many men, women and children the Tennessee boys did kill. They wouldn't take any prisoners. . . . At the best, this is a very rich country; and we want it. My way of getting it would be to put a regiment into a skirmish line, and blow every nigger into nigger heaven." Whether or not the Tennessee regiment involved in the battle really shot every Filipino civilian, this Washington volunteer certainly expressed genocidal desires, as did another soldier who wrote, "The boys say there is no cruelty too severe for these brainless monkeys."[40]

Often the young soldiers described their fighting style as a "Gugu hunt." Better than going off on one's own to shoot game, hunting Filipinos could deepen group solidarity and heighten the meanings of the sport for each member. A volunteer from Washington reported on the sense of collective blood lust that accompanied one such hunt: "Our fighting blood was up, and we wanted to kill 'niggers.' This shooting of human beings is a 'hot game,' and beats rabbit hunting all to pieces. We charged them and such a slaughter you never saw. We killed them like rabbits; hundreds, yes thousands of them. Every one was crazy." Such a tall-tale rendition of whatever might have actually happened nevertheless indicated something authentic about the Gugu hunt. Another soldier stepped slightly back from his similar report of martial blood lust and individualized his emotional responses when he concluded, "I am probably growing hard-hearted, for I am in my glory when I can sight my gun on some dark skin and pull the trigger."[41]

If that soldier had vestigial moral doubts about becoming the killer of these strange and alien enemies, Minnesota volunteer George Osborn seemed to suffer from none when he described a skirmish in which "we just shot the niggers like a hunter would rabbits." Although perhaps not describing exactly what transpired, Osborn's account sounds close to the language soldiers were likely to have used on the field of battle: "The Capt yelled out 'Remember the name of the fighting Sixth' and Lieut Nesbitt says 'Give em hell boys' . . . and as the Col had told us to take no prisoners *we did not* . . . we just shot niggers every which way and at last we had to use our bayonets and in about 3 min after we drew our steel the niggers began to run. . . . In all the fight we took 1 prisoner who 'died' before we got back to [the base]. And when we got back . . . we had a good chicken dinner . . . and I tell you it was good."[42]

American troops in the field faced long periods of boredom, malaria, dysentery, foot diseases, and psychological alienation punctuated for many by brief episodes of great terror when they were ambushed by enemy fighters or attempting to root them out. Filipino guerrillas fought a hard war, hoping to wear down the morale of the Americans through frequent raiding, cutting off supply lines, killing stragglers, and striking when least expected. And they often used vicious methods, including torture and mutilation of corpses, to spread terror among their enemies. After one slaughter of a company of American troops, Private William J. Gibbs returned with another unit the next day to find the corpse of an American lieutenant with his eye sockets dug out and jam shoved in his orifices, while other men's bodies had been flung in a well or hacked apart with bolos, their fingers and genitals cut off.[43]

Filipino forces also used terrorism against their own people to keep them from collaborating and to discipline them in the struggle for independence when gentler suasion did not work. General MacArthur was well aware that Filipinos were afraid to speak with Americans in any comfortable manner lest they be singled out for destruction by their own forces later on. "These people were terrorized in such a way that they would not even walk across the street to speak to an American officer who could give them protection." Of course MacArthur did not note that many Filipinos hated the Americans for reasons of their own. In a guerrilla war, however, where winning over the occupied people is crucial to pacification, providing more personal security than the indigenous force can offer often leads civilians to shift their allegiance to the occupiers. But while the war was ongoing, terror for terror was the usual military response by Americans, as it was by other invading forces in other colonial wars.[44]

When describing the behavior of their comrades toward the Filipinos, many soldiers recalled that revenge had driven them to what they knew were illegal terrorist actions. Asked by Senator Louis E. McComas whether the "voyage across the sea," had transformed the normally "humane and considerate, and not cruel" American soldiers into something bestial, Sergeant Mark H. Evans replied, "No it did not change them at all. Of course when occasionally we found some of our men piled up dead, ambushed, we were ready to do anything." Senator Beveridge chided another witness who had written to the newspapers about American atrocities against Filipinos for failing to record "outrages that were committed on Americans by natives," atrocities that would have put American actions in understandable (and perhaps justifiable, once can infer) contexts. Most of the time Beveridge dismissed or downplayed reports of brutal American actions.[45]

Especially considering that to their way of thinking these dangerous guerrilla enemies were members of a despised race, it should not be surprising that embattled American soldiers resorted to extreme measures when attempting to suppress them. Torture, burning of villages and towns, sometimes killing many civilians at the same time, shooting prisoners, and creating concentration camps and free-fire zones all characterized this colonial war, where military action blurred into terrorism. The testimony of many junior officers and enlisted men at the 1902 Senate hearings, even when read skeptically for bias and exaggeration, demonstrates the widespread pattern of such actions; these were not aberrations, as the administration and army wanted to suggest they were, but standard operating procedure, if rarely stemming from direct orders from the top. Commanders gave their subordinates considerable latitude, and the enlisted men as well pushed for intense action against an enemy they both feared and despised.

The "water cure" (in our day revised and renamed "water-boarding") was the most common and most talked-about form of torture; in fact, it became emblematic of the conduct of the whole war in the eyes of anti-imperialists. At the Senate hearings, when they had their day in "court" many soldiers testified, often in graphic detail, about the use of the water cure by the army.

Charles Riley, for example, described the torture of the presidente of the town of Igbaras on the island of Panay, a place of about two or three thousand people, in front of two companies of about eighty American soldiers, under the command of two captains. At the head of the stairs in the town hall was a raised galvanized water cistern holding about a hundred barrels of rainwater. Four or five soldiers stripped the presidente to the waist, tied his hands tied behind him, threw him to the floor, wedged open his mouth with a bayonet and placed him under the tank. "The faucet was opened and a stream of water was forced down . . . his throat [that was] held so he could not prevent swallowing . . . so that he had to allow the water to run into his stomach." This lasted somewhere between five and fifteen minutes. Then one of the soldiers stomped on his stomach with his foot, or punched him, so that the water spurted out in gushes two or three feet high, "like an artesian well." The presidente then gave the Americans some information and agreed to lead them into the hills to find the local militia. Once outside, when asked for more information, he balked, whereupon the men threw him on the ground and started over, this time with water poured from a five-gallon jerrican. At this point Dr. Lyons, a contract surgeon attached to the regiment, intervened. He took out two syringes, putting one up the presidente's nose and another in his mouth. "Then the doctor ordered some salt, and a handful . . . was thrown into the water." Finally, after being pumped full of water and pounded in the stomach again, the man gave in, and with a mounted company went after the Filipino soldiers. Before leaving the next morning, the Americans burned the town.[46]

About a dozen other soldiers testified in similarly graphic detail about the water cure. Corporal D. J. Evans described a prisoner filled with water being tied to a post while one American soldier, "who was over six feet tall, and who was very strong too, struck this native in the pit of the stomach as hard as he could strike him, just as rapidly as he could. It seemed as if he didn't get tired of striking him." Private Leroy Hollock testified that after several courses of water cure and punching, "I have seen blood come from their mouth after they had been given a good deal of it." Others noted that in several cases soldiers knocked out several teeth when jamming a bayonet in the mouth of a prisoner, and at least one testified that he knew for certain of a prisoner who had died after being tortured this way.[47]

Several units, including the Gordon Scouts of the 18th Infantry, had regularly designated "water details." A number of soldiers claimed that they knew personally of up to fifty cases of water cures, sometimes a dozen in one day in a single locale, and that the water cure was a well-established practice of the American expeditionary force, at least in the latter stages of the war in particularly difficult provinces. In several military departments, the local judge advocate ran the water cure procedures. At his court-martial in 1900, Captain Cornelius M. Brownell admitted that under his command, the water cure was used "several times on different natives," always proving, he claimed, a useful means of eliciting valuable information. Many other officers knew what he was doing and in fact used the same procedure. "There was no secrecy about it; every officer and every man [in] every regiment with which I served, knew when it was given, and I was never criticized by any officer . . . for administering it."[48]

The clearest description of the standard means employed by junior officers when using water torture came from Lieutenant Grover Flint, a Harvard man. Flint claimed to have personally witnessed more than fifty such cases during one two-day period. While the water detail did its task, officers such as he and the major in command of the battalion sat under a tree a long way off—sixty or eighty yards. Rather than giving direct orders to do a water cure, "our attitude was entirely passive." Asked whether the prisoners had been questioned before they were tortured, Flint replied, "No; they seemed to be put through [it] as a matter of routine." Some prisoners would give out information quickly, while others, braver or more ignorant, "would be put through the state where they were almost unconscious or almost drowned." Pressed about why he had not objected to the water cure, Flint admitted that he had become uncomfortable only when the prisoners were "obviously non-combatants." In any event, even if he had disapproved of the water cure, which he did not at time (a position he seemed to be rethinking now that he was far from the combat zone), Flint testified that he would not have protested to the commander of the unit, "because a subordinate has no suggestion to give in the presence of his superior officers. . . . It would be improper, just as it would be improper for your servant to suggest things to you." His superior's attitude was studiously detached: "He kept away. He did not like to see it at all, I know." It did not take direct orders to elicit the use of torture, which clearly was the understood policy of this unit. For the record American officers could stand apart and later deny that they had ordered torture.[49]

Expansionist senators sought to downplay the amount of torture that was practiced and to insist that it was contrary to both policy and the American character. The high command who testified denied that the water cure was used by American troops, or admitted only that it was used rarely, and then just by a few bad apples among the junior officers who had departed from the overall policy of benevolent kindness toward Filipinos. Senator Beveridge for his part belittled the severity of the water cure (just as the highest authorities in the Bush administration denied that water-boarding amounts to torture). "Of course this word 'torture' is used here referring to . . . water cure. . . . But I wanted to make the word 'torture' clear. No soldier uses the word torture in speaking of the water cure." To which Senator Thomas M. Patterson, Democrat of Colorado, replied, "When I use the word torture I mean the water cure." "That is your construction of water cure?" Beveridge asked with skepticism, to which Patterson replied, "Some people call murder homicide."[50]

As far as the men in the field were concerned, the water cure got results, and using it did not bother most of them. One soldier thought to update the "Battle Cry of Freedom," a favorite of Civil War soldiers both north and south:

> Get the good old syringe boys and fill it to the brim.
> We've caught another nigger and we'll operate on him.
> Let someone take the handle who can work it with a vim.
> Shouting the battle cry of freedom.
> Chorus:
>> Hurrah, Hurrah, We bring the Jubilee
>> Hurrah. Hurrah. The flag that makes him free.

Shove in the nozzle deep and let him taste of liberty.
Shouting the battle cry of freedom.

. . . .

Oh pump it in him till he swells like a toy balloon.
The fool pretends that liberty is not a precious boon.
But we'll contrive to make him see the beauty of it soon.
Shouting the battle cry of freedom.

. . . .

Keep the piston going boys and let the banner wave.
The banner that floats proudly o'er the noble and the brave.
Keep on till the squirt gun breaks or he explodes the slave.
Shouting the battle cry of freedom.[51]

Although the most commonly used form of torture, the water cure was not the only one. Several soldiers testified to the use of rattan whips, about the thickness of a human finger, to administer bloody beatings, often during a water cure. Other prisoners were threatened with loaded pistols held to their heads, with the sounds of gunfire going off nearby, presumably marking the shooting of another prisoner, though the shot might have been fired in the air. Private Isadore Dube testified that one woman prisoner was confined among male prisoners, the most degrading form of sexual humiliation he could imagine. Another soldier told a Norfolk, Virginia, newspaperman that he had witnessed a prisoner being stripped to the waist and tied up so that only his toe tips reached the ground, and then "a detachment of soldiers . . . gathered around their victim and burned his body with cigars, to make him tell them where they could find the bodies of five American soldiers killed in an ambush had been hidden." And several soldiers testified to watching their comrades ducking prisoners in the ocean and holding them under for a minute or two, in a sort of variation of the water cure. Senator McComas asked Sergeant Evans about this practice. "You have gone swimming in your boyhood days?" "Yes, sir." Have you not ducked a boy, or have you not been ducked in your experience in going in swimming?" "I don't recall any of them." And then Senator Beveridge chimed in with incredulity, "What, you never were ducked?" "No, sir," Evans replied, refusing to go along with the senator's trivialization of torture, his interpretation of it as a good old American boy's game.[52]

American units frequently linked torture to the burning of villages and towns as a means of ridding an area of Filipino guerillas. While some authorities who testified to the Senate denied that villages were burned, and others suggested the practice was unusual, several soldiers who had spent considerable time in the field concluded that it was a standard collective punishment. As Private Seiward J. Norton put it, burning barrios was used, "I think, to intimidate the natives." Leroy Hollock was willing to generalize in order to indicate what he thought was common policy: "If the soldiers wanted to get any information out of the natives they gave them the water cure, and in any town where there was any evidence of being insurgents the town was burned."[53]

In one well-documented case—the burning of Bauan, a town of some fifteen thousand people—Captain George D. Boardman testified that a young Filipino man named Thomas, who had been openly cooperative with the American forces, had been murdered by guerrillas at a Saturday morning market in front of two hundred witnesses, none of whom would give evidence against the four suspects Boardman's company had captured. The Americans threatened to burn the town the next day at noon, and still "they would not tell. At 12 o'clock we set the market on fire and there was a heavy wind, and it blew over and destroyed quite a portion of the city." Similarly, Edward J. Davis told the Senate committee that in another sizable town the mayor, who, according to Davis, was hated by the local population, most of whom were friendly to the Americans, was tortured until he admitted he was a partisan, at which point the American soldiers burned down the town.[54]

Most rural Filipinos lived in small villages, in houses of light bamboo construction, ten feet by twelve feet, on four posts, and this material burned readily when Americans marching through met any hint of support for the guerrilla resistance. At one point Senator Beveridge asked Captain Fred McDonald, who admitted that his company often burned villages, how long it took an owner to build such a "nipa shack." "Less than a week," McDonald reckoned. And how much would it cost, Beveridge inquired. "I should say less than $10," McDonald replied, adding that arson was a regrettable "military necessity." Senator Culberson turned on Beveridge, who, he said, "seems to justify burning [these dwellings] because of their very slight value . . . but they were the only houses the people had to sleep in and live in." Beveridge replied, "I do not undertake to justify anything."[55]

Rumors swirled back from the Philippines that in addition to the use of torture and the burning of towns and villages, it was understood procedure in many hotly contested locales to take no prisoners. Quoting from official army records when quizzing General MacArthur, Senator Patterson noted that the documents cited casualties in the guerrilla war between November 1, 1899, and September 1, 1900, of 268 killed, 750 wounded, and 55 captured among the American forces, while Filipino losses for the same time were 3,227 killed, 694 wounded, and 2,864 captured. Although the latter figure suggested that the army took many Filipino prisoners, Patterson wanted to know why the level of killed relative to the number of wounded was "in such immensely greater disproportion than the records" of any other known war. Senator McComas, getting the point, lashed out that he deeply resented Patterson's inference, which obviously was meant "to impute barbarity to the American soldiers and humanity to the Filipinos." MacArthur answered that the Americans shot straighter and the Filipinos did not know how to sight their guns, which meant that American troops could charge to within fifteen feet of them without being hit. Also, the Filipinos could easily haul their wounded into the dense bamboo thickets for hiding.[56]

Although he did not offer a complete explanation of this highly unusual killed-to-wounded ratio, Corporal Richard J. O'Brien indicated a plausible way in which the order to take no prisoners might be given without any officer directly implicating himself in what he knew to be an illegal command. Asked whether there were any orders given before American soldiers shot two elderly men carrying flags of truce as well as at least two women with their babies when his company had marched into a town on Panay one morning, O'Brien replied, "No, sir. In regard to that order being issued, we would go along in Indian file, the word would pass along 'take no prisoners.' Nobody would know where it emanated from." O'Brien stated that because such an order was not unusual, he did not bother to ask who issued it. Later, he heard Sergeant Conway report to the company commander, "that he had killed two more niggers." Asked whether his humanity did not revolt at such acts, O'Brien said, "It was none of my business." When pressed as to why he did not report illegal actions, including an instance of rape he described to the committee, he replied, "I knew that if I had done so I would have been dogged until I was mustered out of the army. They would have made my life hell." As for the prevalence of such incidents, he concluded that "some officers were more humane than others; every officer had a law to himself." The officer commanding this part of Panay, Captain McDonald, "was generally known as a 'nigger hater.'"[57]

In various court-martial depositions and testimony, other men related memories of the arbitrary and seemingly random shootings of both enemy soldiers and civilians by officers. In one of several such stories, William Moore, the orderly to Major Wilder F. Metcalf, and John F. Hall, first lieutenant in the 20th Kansas Volunteers, Metcalf's unit, both deposed, in

Moore's words, corroborated by Hall, that on February 10, 1899, when a group of Filipino soldiers surrendered in their trenches rather than flee with their unit following an American attack and "begged for mercy," Metcalf ordered Moore to load his gun and shoot the prisoners. "I refused to do it. One of the prisoners threw himself on his knees before Major Metcalf, threw his arms around Metcalf's legs and appeared to beg for his life, when Major Metcalf drew his revolver and killed the prisoner." Called before the Senate committee, Metcalf denied that he had even been at the place where the shooting allegedly occurred.[58]

Enemy combatants taken prisoner might be shot later according to the whim of the local unit commander charged with guarding them. As had been the case in counterinsurgency during the Civil War, the standard verbal formulation used to justify such killings was, as Leroy Hollock said of twelve Filipinos after they had been given the water cure and then confined to the guard house—"Some of them escaped and some of them were killed while trying to escape." Another soldier reported the same fate of nine other prisoners. Asked whether this attempt to escape was aided by the American authorities, Hollock replied, "I do not know. . . . All I know is that it was reported that they were killed while trying to escape." The passive voice indicated once more that either this soldier did not know who gave the direct order or that he was afraid to reveal his knowledge of who did, or possibly that he was ashamed.[59]

During the last two years of the war, in order to clear out the worst guerrilla areas, the army resorted to concentration camps in which to house the civilians among whom the guerrillas moved. The American press noted this development with considerable alarm, as such camps had been the cardinal policy of "Butcher Weyler," the Spanish commander in Cuba, that had done so much to arouse the American populace to support invasion of that island for humanitarian purposes in 1898. Colonel Arthur L. Wagner, assistant adjutant-general of the army, had just toured several such camps before he told the senators about them. They were constructed to be as humane as possible, Wagner said. In one of the camps, about eight thousand people had been gathered in an area about two miles by one mile. People were assembled according to their home barrios, sanitary conditions were carefully inspected, and the streets were "scrupulously neat." The people "seemed to be surprisingly contented." It was true that there was a "dead line drawn in a perimeter drawn 300 to 800 yards out from the camp," but otherwise the inmates had "perfect liberty" within. And really the camp was necessary to cleanse the area of cruel warfare: "I do not see how we could have stamped out the trouble otherwise. . . . The island was practically in the possession of a blind giant: strong, but unable to see where to strike." These model American concentration camps were more evidence that the war was being conducted, Wagner insisted, "as humanely as any war that was ever waged."[60]

Other reports suggested the camps were far from the ideal Wagner depicted. Senator Culberson read into the record the anonymous letter from a West Point graduate who had paid a visit to one camp. This officer wound eight miles up a "slimy, winding bayou" in a navy tug until he reached "a piece of spongy ground about 20 feet above the sea level. . . . This little spot of black sogginess is a reconcentrado pen," replete with "corpse-carcass stench" and fetid sewer odors. "I found 30 cases of smallpox and fresh ones on an average of 5 a day, which practically have to be turned out to die. At nightfall crowds of huge vampire bats softly swirl on their orgies over the dead. . . . It seems way out of the world . . . like suburb of hell." In fact, however lurid this picture appears to be, the most careful modern study suggests that an extremely high mortality rate owing to poor sanitation, disease, and demoralization was characteristic of these camps.[61]

After most civilians were removed from the countryside and committed to the camps, American troops, under orders to effect "the complete clearing out of every vestige of animal life and every particle of food supply," then swept the countryside, confiscating and destroying crops, horses, and cattle, burning all the houses and killing the occasional guerrilla. As they probably knew from the Boer War as well as from Spanish policy in Cuba, food shortages, poor sanitary conditions, and bad water supplies would lead to massive death rates, yet American authorities never acknowledged these dangers. After several weeks of this operation, most of the remaining guerrillas surrendered, the concentration camps were disbanded, and the civilians were sent back out to rebuild their lives as best they could. Such effective terror tactics produced utter demoralization as well as great physical privation for guerrillas and civilians alike.[62]

Using the volunteer army in this innovative manner, including employing as much terrorism as was necessary to subdue an alien population, was the traditional means of constructing an empire, which the United States was now doing. These means included large-scale atrocities—there were rumors in the papers about the slaughter of up to a thousand Filipino prisoners of war in one incident and many stories about the shooting of as many as forty prisoners at a time, but most of these were poorly documented. Under extreme duress and eager to get results, soldiers sometimes acted out their murderous impulses, even though this was apparently never organized above the company or regimental level.[63]

One of the horrors for soldiers fighting a guerrilla war, and one of the reasons genocide is always imminent in such conflicts, was their inability to distinguish enemy civilians from enemy combatants because men and women frequently slip between these two roles, often without changing uniforms. Before long every person becomes a potential guerrilla, and so the safest (and most coarsening) tactic is to shoot whoever is at hand. Asked whether he thought it was "in accordance with the rules of enlightened civilization to burn the private houses of the noncombatants," Private Seiward Norton replied, "They did not prove themselves noncombatants." And how could they? Therefore many, perhaps most, soldiers in such a war commit acts that they know will be judged illegal and immoral in the context of the lives lived by the folks back home.[64]

Implicated together, the soldiers lived by a pact of mutual silence toward the outside world. This bond was also a shared wound, an agreement to cover up brutal deeds that had alienated them from their common sense of humanity —in fact, from the core values of the civilization that they had been sent to protect and extend as military missionaries. Captain George Boardman defended his silence when asked to testify about terrible military events by explaining, "It is an unwritten law that one soldier shall not talk against another soldier, and I am a soldier. . . . A man who has been with his comrades for three years through the privations of war would be considered a pretty low man who would come and testify against his comrade." Such an attitude of implicit covering up pervaded the army from bottom to top, and was prevalent among the chief administrative officers directing the war from Washington.[65]

It was hard to impress on those at home, who had experienced none of this conflict firsthand, just how dirty the war was, how much it had emptied young soldiers of their youthful ideals. Showing considerable courage by standing up to several U. S. senators, Private Gibbs tried to explain what such a morally ambiguous war did to the inner spirit, the character, of the average American soldier sent to fight it. Three senators, including the chairman, Henry Cabot Lodge, pressed Gibbs to answer the question "Was the general conduct of our officers and soldiers kind?" Gibbs replied, "It was in some cases kind." "What was the general course of conduct of your comrades?" Senator Beveridge insisted, to which Gibbs responded, "It changed from day to day—there was no general course. . . . The whole tendency of the Army is to make the men anything but pleasant toward the natives, because every soldier realizes that war is hell and they are going to give the Filipinos hell. . . . And they use the guns to shoot with rather than to preach the gospel; but it is an unwritten code that one soldier would not talk against another." Beveridge insisted, Wasn't their treatment generally one of "kindness and consideration?" and Gibbs again stood his ground, depicting the realities of colonial warfare rather that endorsing the ideological disguise expansionists wanted the American people to believe: "The people were very much pacified. . . . Military rule, Senator, is a very poor thing to give anybody. . . . A soldier is a soldier anywhere."[66]

Although the Republican administration and its senatorial backers had long persisted in downplaying, when not denying, extreme military behavior of the sort Gibbs outlined, the Senate hearings and newspaper depictions generated much antiwar pressure by uncovering what appeared to be an extensive pattern of illegal behavior. In response, immediately after the hearings concluded, President Theodore Roosevelt fired Jacob H. Smith, now a general, for his actions the previous year when subduing the island of Samar, the last major holdout of guerrilla resistance. In a sense Smith was sacrificed so that the administration could appear responsive to the problem of illegal American actions while at the same time suggest they were isolated events, the better to justify the overall record of conquest and occupation.

Smith's downfall began with his response to the "Balangiga massacre" of September 28, 1901, during which the police chief and townspeople of Balangiga, together with guerrillas who had infiltrated the town, wiped out forty-eight of a seventy-four-man American garrison in a surprise attack and then mutilated the soldiers' corpses. Although not a concentration camp as such, Balangiga had been designed as a fortified town. Captain Thomas W. Connell had set up a tent village and shoved in hundreds of villagers as well as other men who came to town to serve as laborers, many of whom proved to be guerrillas. Connell stole from the villagers and treated them brutally; his men perpetrated at least one rape. On the fatal Sunday morning, hundreds of Filipino men swinging bolos charged out of their tents and the local Catholic church, surprising the American contingent sitting down to breakfast in the mess hall. A few Americans fought their way down to the beach and paddled away in dugouts, but the rest perished. The guerrillas captured a hundred rifles, twenty-five thousand rounds of ammunition, and a great deal of food and equipment. The next day, the navy sent gunboats that shelled the town into oblivion, and the army then sent in a four-thousand-man force to crush resistance on Samar.[67]

General Adna R. Chafee, the commander in Manila, wired "Hell Roaring Jake" Smith, the rough old Indian fighter, and placed him in charge of the punitive expedition, to get results and get them fast. In turn, Smith assigned Major Littleton W. T. Waller, commander of the 6th Marine Brigade, to clear out the southern portion of Samar, an area of about six hundred square miles. "I want no prisoners," Smith orally instructed Waller in front of several other officers. "I wish you to kill and burn, the more you kill and burn the better you will please me. I want all persons killed who are capable of bearing arms in actual hostilities against the United States." Rather shocked by this command to commit war crimes, Waller enquired, "I would like to know the limit of age to respect sir? Persons of ten years and older are those designated as being capable of bearing arms?" To which Smith replied, "Yes." Weeks later, when Waller was setting up his expedition in the field, Lieutenant J. H. A. Day arrived from Smith's headquarters, entered his office, and put a sheet of paper before Waller on which was written in an elegant hand a paraphrase of Sherman's pledge to Georgians before he marched through their state in 1864: "The interior of Samar must be made a howling wilderness." Puzzled by the note, Waller asked Day, "Who gave you this?" Day replied, "General Smith. Those are his instructions."[68]

Whatever he thought of direct orders to slaughter civilians as well as guerrillas, Waller was full of his own martial energy. Wanting his men to avenge their comrades who had been murdered at Balangiga, he promoted the most vigorous action. He warned his brigade, "Place no confidence in the natives and punish treachery immediately with death." In this spirit Waller set off on December 28 with fifty-six Marines and thirty-five Filipino porters and scouts, marching across the southern end of Samar through almost impassable jungle. Soon supplies ran short, and many of the men fell violently ill. On January 2 Waller divided his command, leaving the sickest behind while other contingents pushed back to their base camp. By the time the last group made it out of the jungle, on January 19, eleven of the marines had died or disappeared. Suffering from a malarial fever of 105 degrees, and acting on information Lieutenant Day had extracted from one of the porters by beating him severely, Waller ordered that eleven of the porters and scouts be executed.[69]

At his subsequent court-martial, Waller was found not guilty of any crime; soon he was welcomed back to the United States as a war hero, though he spent the remainder of his military career under a cloud, as the higher authorities privately believed that he had acted rashly and exercised poor judgment on Samar. But the rank and file of the Marine Corps treated Waller's march as one of the greatest feats in its proud history: in future years, when any member of that expedition entered a Marine mess hall, everyone present would stand, snap to attention, and chant, "Stand, gentlemen, he served on Samar."[70]

For his part, because of his incontrovertibly illegal genocidal orders, Smith was tried and convicted of "Conduct to the prejudice of good order and military discipline." The court's mild sentence was that Smith was "to be admonished by the reviewing authority." On July 12, 1902, reviewing the sentence in Washington in the bright light cast by the recently concluded Senate hearings, Secretary of War Elihu Root concluded that Smith's punishment was too light. In instructing Waller as he did, Root wrote, Smith had been "guilty of intemperate, inconsiderate, and violent expressions, which, if accepted literally, would grossly violate the humane rules governing American armies in the field, and if followed would have brought lasting disgrace upon the military service of the United States." Smith had both "signally failed . . . not to incite his subordinates to acts of lawless violence," and to define the appropriate limits on their conduct. Root urged Roosevelt to retire Smith from the service immediately. Agreeing that senior officers had a special task to "keep a moral check" over more junior officers who might feel provoked to "acts of cruelty, and that "loose and violent talk is always likely to excite to wrong doing those among his subordinates whose wills are weak or whose passions are strong," Roosevelt cashiered Smith.[71]

Several other officers were convicted of war crimes on Samar. In 1903 the Secretary of War packaged these court-martial records together and sent them to the Senate as proof that the army was taking war crimes seriously and was acting against the worst malefactors. Yet even in his condemnation of Smith, Root had sought to separate the immoral and illegal orders of one misguided general from a policy of genocide on the part of the army as a whole. There had been several criminal actions but no pattern of war crimes ordered from above, Root insisted. Smith had been guilty of giving rash orders, but they had not been followed—they had never become standard procedure. Luckily for Root and the army, by this time Filipino resistance had almost entirely collapsed; the war crime story soon lost its visibility in the newspapers and in Congress.

It is not clear whether the terrorism used in the American counter-insurgency on places like Samar was necessary to crush the Filipino war effort. With a huge, decentralized, and essentially disorganized political system, with poor equipment and bad military training and strategy, with a revolutionary élan that had not spread widely among the people and had dissipated through internal divisiveness and revulsion at the brutality the guerrillas used against the civilian population, the guerrillas may have been as much responsible for their defeat as American armed success.[72]

And what were the costs in lives lost, leaving aside physical and mental wounds, and lives wildly disrupted? Most historians estimate that between 16,000 and 20,000 Filipino soldiers were killed in battle, although how many men went missing in action is unclear. As for civilians, the most carefully considered figure is that about 775,000 died out of a civilian population estimated at somewhere between 7 million and 10 million.[73]

Ken de Bevoise offers a careful and stunning analysis of war-related mortality rates for the Philippines in *Agents of Apocalypse*. In addition, Glenn A. May has dug deeply into the experience of Batangas, one of the hardest hit provinces during the war. According to May's analysis, death rates soared in 1902 during the period when the American army forced civilians into concentration camps and destroyed most of the food crops in the region. In addition, between 75 and 90 percent of the cattle died by warfare or rinderpest. According to American army surgeons, most of the camps were squalid and unsanitary, with dead animals, manure, and other filth often dumped near the fresh-water supplies. Malnourishment characterized camp life as well, as did vast overcrowding. Under these conditions opportunistic diseases proliferated. Deprived of cattle on which to feed, malarial mosquitoes fed on humans, whose death rates increased because of their physical weakness. Measles, dysentery and other enteric diseases, and, worst of all, the cholera epidemic that swept Asia at this time devastated this province and many other war zones. One cannot simply subtract cholera-related deaths from war-related deaths because an already sickly population, when uprooted by war, was far more likely to succumb to disease. Moreover, it seemed clear to the American medical authorities at the time that no one could trust the estimates of the number of deaths occurring during epidemics. One post commander on Batangas, known as a careful record keeper, estimated that "not more than one fourth" of cholera deaths were being reported, while the ranking American army surgeon believed that "it is probable in the whole archipelago not more than one fifth of the cholera cases are now being reported." The army's official estimate was that between 1896 and 1902, the population on the island of Batangas dropped by more than 90,000, from

332,456 to 241,721, or 27 percent. It is likely that de Bevoise's estimate of 2.5 million civilian deaths for the islands as a whole during this period—that is, between 25 and 40 percent of the population—is on the conservative side, including as it does almost incredible childhood mortality rates throughout the islands.[74]

If these figures are even approximately accurate, American terrorist war practices produced one of the greatest war-related human catastrophes in history. But beyond these figures, it is probable that hundreds of thousands of deaths were never reported, and many of these were also caused by war. Just as opportunistic disease killed millions of American Indians over the long course of their guerrilla war, epidemics accelerated by crowding, malnutrition, unsanitary conditions and demoralization, so too was this the case in the Philippines. Combat fatalities were a relatively small part of the story of mass death.

And yet military domination was central to the suppression of the Philippines, and this meant using as much terrorist force as necessary to break Filipino morale permanently, not merely defeat the Filipinos in battle. Although most of the population had submitted to American dominion by 1902, the heavily Muslim southern portions of the islands continued to resist, as they had earlier fought Spanish rule. In 1906 the leading figures of the Moro community declared a holy war against the Americans. To meet this threat, General Leonard Wood, in charge of American military forces in the Philippines, took a two-track course: negotiation and conquest. When some of the Moro people refused to surrender, Wood assembled an expeditionary force of 790 soldiers, and pursued some 600 to 1,000 Moros, who retreated and fortified themselves inside the dormant volcano of Bud Dajo. On March 5, the Americans circled their mountain howitzers around the lip of the volcano and then fired down into the Moros gathered below, including women and children. The following morning, the American troops made a bayonet charge into the pit. In the battle, 21 American soldiers were killed and 75 wounded, while all but 6 of the Moros were killed.

When news of the killing of hundreds of women and children became public, Wood told the press there was "no wanton destruction of women and children in the fight, though many of them were killed by force of necessity because the Moros used them as shields in hand-to-hand fighting." Receiving news of the battle, President Roosevelt cabled Wood on March 10, "I congratulate you and the officers and men of your command upon the brilliant feat of arms wherein you and they so well upheld the honor of the American flag."[75]

In a savage essay written a few days later, Mark Twain commented that this "would not have been a brilliant feat of arms even if Christian America, represented by its salaried soldiers, had shot them down with Bibles and the Golden Rule instead of bullets." Twain withheld publication of this essay until after his death, fearing his language would be considered too incendiary.[76]

The horror gradually disappeared from public memory. Terrorism in the form of war crimes had served American expansion and civilization; then it was covered up and forgotten.[77]

Coda

Taken together, these five case studies of terrorism in late-nineteenth-century America amount to a counternarrative of American national development, a story characterized by extreme political violence at crucial junctures. It is a history of domination rather than the progressive unfolding of democracy and freedom. These cases illustrate deep patterns, both ideological and behavioral: terrorism colored many of the powerful and contradictory qualities of American state formation during its most crucial phase.

Although I have concentrated in this volume on the second half of the nineteenth century, the structures explored provide templates for understanding later terrorist interactions. As I am a subjective human being living in the early twenty-first century, it is inevitable that my lens on history will have been constructed during my lifetime and reconstructed in the post–September 11, 2001, world. Certainly, powerful new events have impelled me to seek out the deeper patterns of terrorism in the American experience. Terrorism did not begin in 2001, and it is intrinsic, not extrinsic, to American history as a whole.

Were this intended as an exhaustive synthesis of the history of terrorism in the United States, I would have composed another, much lengthier book. But it is my hope that *In the Name of God and Country* will inspire other historians to continue this much larger task.[1]

The conservative historian Richard Hofstadter pointed out in his 1970 documentary collection on violence, composed in response to urban riots in the 1960s and the underground terrorism that was increasing at that time, that various state and quasi-state authorities had killed workers in more than seven hundred labor disputes in American history. No historian has been able to quantify the actual numbers killed over the centuries; as was the case after the Haymarket, no one counted workers' deaths. Although he decried the actions of such terrorist groups as the Weathermen, Hofstadter concluded, when he considered the application of political violence in American history, that "after all, the greatest and most calculating of killers is the national state, and this is true not only in international wars, but in domestic conflicts."[2]

The white Christian paramilitary terrorism of the Mississippi White Liners, and the revolutionary and reactionary interchange at the Haymarket, helped shape the political violence of the next several decades. Local terrorist outbursts with national implications had long characterized American race relations as well as class conflict. Between 1880 and 1930, more than 3,300 African Americans were lynched, although the total number cannot be determined, and other means of domination were even more frequently employed, such as threats, beatings, economic and social ostracism, and driving blacks from the community, means that Leon Litwack discusses in his magnificent *Trouble in Mind: Black Southerners in the Age of Jim Crow.* In the early twentieth century, race "riots" generally consisted of white rampages into segregated black neighborhoods. Between 1900 and 1920, there were major invasions that led to the deaths of numerous African Americans in New York; Philadelphia; Wilmington, North Carolina; Springfield, Ohio; Springfield, Illinois; Atlanta; Greensburgh, Indiana; East Saint Louis, Illinois; Houston; Tulsa; Washington, D.C.; Charleston, South Carolina; and Longview, Texas. In Chicago, in August 1919 one white participant at a community association meeting declared, "If we can't get them out any other way, we are going to put [the niggers] in with the bolshevicki, and bomb them all," and indeed, in a concerted and organized campaign, dozens of bombings followed the two weeks of rioting that began on July 27, in which 23 black men and boys and 15 whites were killed, 342 blacks and 195 whites were wounded, and thousands of African Americans were burned out of their homes.[3]

In many of these lynchings and "riots," the police and local and state authorities were complicit by acts of omission and at times commission, and almost never were white rioters later charged with crimes, particularly in the South. In the United States Senate, southern senators repeatedly killed antilynching legislation through filibuster. Although there were dissenting voices, the senators, the police and local authorities, and the rioters and lynchers were all expressing the general will of white society, and all these modes of reinforcing the segregation system were, in effect, standard social practices of caste domination. The election of Barack Obama notwithstanding, American race relations remain troubled, characterized by extreme violence and the extensive use of prison for young black men. Much of the African American lower class is still engaged in a seemingly perpetual violent embrace with the police, a situation that has many ramifications for the policing and governing of American society.

In her recent in-depth study *The Dark Side: The Inside Story of How the War on Terror Turned into a War on American Ideals,* Jane Mayer, a journalist with the *New Yorker,* synthesizes what is termed here "reactionary terrorism" that the Bush administration developed in response to the attacks of September 11. Henceforth suspected terrorists were to be treated, Mayer writes, neither as prisoners of war nor as criminal defendants but as "illegal enemy combatants" outside the law who were to be captured, interrogated, and disposed of by any means necessary, at the Executive's discretion. This led to a new, extralegal regime that, according to former Vice President Dick Cheney, "guarantees that we'll have the kind of treatment of these individuals that we believe they deserve."[4]

In practice, Bush administration policies contradicted not only the Geneva Conventions but also the 1984 Convention Against Torture that Americans had taken the lead in drafting. Interrogation overruled due process in this state terrorist regimen, Mayer argues, and standard practices included systematic degradation, sleep deprivation, and torture such as water-boarding (formerly known as the water cure). The attorney general's office concluded that the Executive branch had the constituted authority, using a "national and international version of the right of self-defense," to order extreme measures, including torture.[5]

Did standard practice include killing defenseless prisoners? Mayer analyses the post–September 11 Special Access Program authorized by the president and supervised by the Pentagon—a rapid deployment military force authorized to use lethal force worldwide that operated under the motto "Grab whom you must; Do what you must." These death squads abduct and hide away suspected enemies, whom they call ghost detainees, not merely at Guantánamo Bay but in clandestine prisons called black sites in at least eight other countries, where the prisoners are subjected to torture, permanent imprisonment, or death. In his January 28, 2003, State of the Union Address, President Bush boasted, "More than 3000 suspected terrorists have been arrested in many countries. Many others have met a different fate. Let's put it this way: they are no longer a threat to our friends and allies."[6]

One June 28, 2004, in *Hamdi v. Rumsfeld,* archconservative Supreme Court justice Antonin Scalia, joining an 8–1 majority that ruled part of this

Bush administration policy unconstitutional, proclaimed that "indefinite im-prisonment at the will of the Executive [strikes at] the very core of liberty." But it is far from certain that the closing of Guantánamo Bay and the black sites will lead to disclosure of the full range of these coordinated state terrorist practices.[7]

Indeed, we are just learning about the systematic uses of death squads in the Vietnam War. As was the case of Abu Ghraib in the Iraq War, the massacre at My Lai was far from an exception to standard military practice. The distinguished German historian Bernd Griener, using previously little-examined American military records, disclosed in *War Without Frontiers: The USA in Vietnam* that clandestine American death squads systematically killed tens of thousands of Vietnamese civilians, 90 percent of whom had no proven links to the enemy armed or civilian forces. Neither have we learned the extent of such practices by American forces and their reactionary-terrorist surrogates during the long Cold War, a pattern Naomi Klein analyzes, par-ticularly in Latin America, in *The Shock Doctrine*. And so we can move backward in search of long-term patterns, basic structures of violent political domination, back to the growth period for these practices in the late nine-teenth century.[8]

The ways in which terrorist exchanges operate at home help guide the ways they work abroad. The terrorizing of other races or classes at home creates patterns of thinking that shape confrontations with alien others else-where. Given that ideological construct, when one unpacks the notion of "war," one quickly peels away the patina of "civilized warfare" and arrives at terrorism as the more common form of organized mutual human destruction.

Terrorism provokes terrorism in a cyclical and reciprocal manner—the War on Terror as a concept is falsely one-sided. As George W. Bush enunci-ated it soon after September 11, the United States was engaging a new enemy, in "a war unlike any other." Such engagements are in fact not new or unique—all such asymmetrical wars devolve in practice into Terrorism on Terrorism. In *every* colonial war, terrorist means, including torture and the massacre of unarmed civilians, become standard procedure, both licensed by authorities—more often covertly than overtly—and covered up by them.

The ideological justification for state terrorism during colonial warfare resides in the general forms set earlier in American history, beginning as early as the first colonial wars against the Indians on the North American conti-nent. To today's soldiers, Iraqis are non-Christian "sand niggers," another debased foreign "race," and for the U.S. political leadership, the avowed national task is to use all necessary military means to bring freedom, justice, and democracy to this downtrodden people—these remain universalistic values embodied by the nation and ready for export anywhere in the world. American soldiers are sent to impose these values, resistance to which is generalized as insurgencies by terrorist minorities.

When an American president let slip the word *Crusade* early in the current Iraq war, he expressed the usually muted Christian sensibility that underlies American values as they pertain to foreign enemies. Many have taken to describing that elusive and diffuse enemy as "Islamofascism," spelling out the essential nature of the enemy other who is said to hate our essence—defined as freedom, liberty, and respect for individual inviolability. Beneath the linguistic surface, this collection of American values diametrically opposed to Islamofascism could be called "Christodemocracy." But Americans are not given to analysis of the ways in which they utilize Christianity and universalistic republican values as weapons of engagement in terrorist exchanges.

In this book I have tried to analyze some of the means by which this pattern of domination was built, to look at the core of terrorism in the construction of modern American society at home that was later carried with the army abroad. Terrorism as interchange is nothing new, and it is fundamental to the structure of the American state: even if freedom is the ultimate goal, total domination is often the means of establishing the ground of freedom for one's own kind. Defending freedom places security over liberty for all—when reaction confronts social threats it has an impact on all Americans. The fears induced in the American population by reactionary terrorism mute dissent and corrode freedom while punishing revolutionary terrorists and anyone else swept up in the web of accusation.

Such a disillusioned and realist history of American involvement in terrorism, which spills into violent repression of other races and classes at home and war crimes abroad, may prove challenging to many readers. Whether Americans will be able in the future to create a less dualistic and warlike, a more self-examining, complex, and peaceful, alternative framework remains to be seen, but they will never do so unless they are willing to ask discomforting questions about the meanings of the terrorism that flows through the deepest currents of American history.

Note on Terms

Defining terrorism is akin to searching for the Holy Grail. Understandably, most of the immense literature on terrorism focuses on fairly recent events, and almost all the scholarship can be found in journalism and social science writing in the fields of political science, sociology, psychology, and anthropology. Every social scientist opens his or her study with, at the least, a chapter on definitions. Clearly, widespread disagreement characterizes this field; definitional conflicts appear inextricable for scholars coming to terms with such a diffuse and threatening phenomenon.

Curiously, at a minimal level, however, there *is* a widespread consensus about the literal, uninterpreted core of terrorist actions. To condense and paraphrase many of these single-sentence definitions, "Terrorism is violence or the threat of violence used in pursuit of political aims." Even more succinctly, terrorism has been defined simply as a synonym for political violence. Generally, but not always, such definitions include the psychological corollary that those engaged in terrorism deliberately and systematically create and exploit fear.

But the obvious and necessary follow-up questions lead us into theoretical quagmires where agreement ceases. When getting down to actual cases, most social scientists find simple definitions highly unsatisfactory because of their lack of specificity. In the use of political violence, who is a terrorist and who is not? Which violent activities count as terrorist? Where does "war" or "crime" end and "terrorism" begin? (Or are such categories inevitably blurred?) There is no agreement on the answers to these basic questions. Furthermore, in nearly every text such tendentious inquiries lead directly to another even more fundamental issue: How do we understand the morality of terrorist activities?

As the English psychologist Andrew Silke wrote, "Terrorism is a fiercely political word . . . both incredibly alive and dishearteningly legion. As a term, it is far too nimble a creature for social science to be able to pin it down in . . . a reliable manner, and the result has been frustrating and unending debate in order to reach an accepted demarcation of the boundaries of the word."[1] Writers, and for that matter readers, all of whom are bound to be in turmoil over the horrors of our times, approach terrorism from their individual political and moral perspectives, using the definition that best suits their own vantage point. If there is another issue on which students of terrorism can reach minimal consensus it is that *terrorism* is a pejorative word, loaded with deeply held beliefs in the identities of the parties of good versus evil—"us" versus "them." Definitions of *terrorism* invariably depend on who is making them, and they are freighted emotionally as much as intellectually. In practice there is no clear neutral ground from which to define the term.

Given their political position, those in power necessarily deal with terrorism as a violent incursion by outsiders against the society they are protecting. Thus, the FBI defines terrorism as "the unlawful use of force or violence against persons or property to intimidate or coerce a government, the civilian population, or any segment thereof, in furtherance of political or social objectives." Similarly, the Department of Defense defines terrorism from the vantage point of the state, which, it assumes, enjoys a monopoly on lawful violence: "Terrorism is the calculated use of violence or the threat of violence to inculcate fear, intended to coerce or intimidate governments or societies as to the pursuit of goals that are generally political, religious or ideological."[2]

Most citizens tend to identify with their governments, especially in more democratic societies, and undoubtedly share this official point of view. They believe that the people in power are defending them, and license these people to take appropriate measures, including violent and even illegal ones, although governments cannot count on long-term acquiescence with illegal activities. They agree that terrorism is a moral evil visited upon their society and that terrorists are heinous outsiders attacking innocent civilians. They believe that the democratic polity is the moral society under siege. Thus, for example, Paul Johnson, the right-wing political historian who defines terrorism as a simple dualism, the attack of evil upon good, employs highly freighted language close to that used by the Bush administration. Terrorism, Johnson writes, is "the deliberate, systematic murder, maiming, and menacing of the innocent to inspire fear in order to gain political end. . . . Terrorism is intrinsically, necessarily evil and wholly evil."[3]

Such simplistic, outraged definitions do not merely blend description with moralizing but license calls for concerted, often violent, and proactive responses to the terrorists. As Richard Rubenstein wrote two decades ago, "To call an act of political violence terrorist is not merely to describe it but to judge it. Descriptively 'terrorism' suggests violent action by individuals or small groups. Judgmentally, it implies illegitimacy."[4] And threatening, illegitimate forces must be crushed.

The faith that "they" are utterly evil and that "our leaders" are invariably good can lead to blindness about the moral nature of state behavior, actions that one could argue are terrorist. The criminologist Grant Wardlaw puts the matter acutely when he writes, "Attempts at definition often are predicated on the assumption that some classes of political violence are justifiable whereas others are not. Many would label the latter as terrorist whilst being loathe to condemn the former with a term that is usually used as an epithet." Seen thus, the issue can become, Which side has the political and social standing needed to make its epithet stick, despite whatever political violence it may employ against the enemy? There is a general presumption that nation-states are rational actors, Wardlaw writes, while the "individual terrorist actor by contrast is portrayed as irrational . . . cowardly and illegitimate. . . . This reification [of the state], and the legitimacy of official terrorism allows individual terrorism to be condemned as morally repugnant, and official terrorism . . . either not to be recognized at all or accepted as severe, but necessary."[5]

If ordinary citizens feel sufficiently besieged, they will accept, whether consciously or not, a double standard about the use of political violence, what Jason Franks, an international-relations expert, calls the "legitimate/illegitimate dualism that constructs non-state violence as terrorism while state violence is deemed to be legitimate." Following this line of reasoning from legitimate state violence, one arrives at the conclusion that, as William Perdue argues, "Ultimately, terrorism is a label of defamation, a means of excluding those so branded from human standing," the better, of course, to eliminate them. "Paradoxically, then, the very label of terrorism has of itself assumed a terrifying power."[6]

Moral absolutism about the legitimate/illegitimate dualism of non-state versus state actors becomes muddied when scholars step back to address the issue of state terror in a more detached way. Even if one argues that in general, or at least in democratic societies, states can use some forms of political violence in legitimate ways, this faith cannot justify all state uses of political violence. Some states, most social scientists agree, can be considered users of terrorism; indeed, some are "regimes of state terror," as Eugene Walter puts it in his seminal study, *Terror and Resistance*. But Walter's terrorist regime was the Zulu state of the eighteenth and nineteenth centuries, which he defines in his subtitle as "primitive."[7]

Most case studies of state terror focus on totalitarian regimes, such as that of Argentina in 1976–83, which was responsible for the disappearance of thirty thousand Argentine civilians; the South African apartheid regime of the late twentieth century; or rogue states such as Libya (until recently, when it was taken off the Bush administration list of terrorist states). Obviously, the Nazi, Stalinist, and Maoist states were regimes where terrorism was openly construed as central to class struggle and class and racial warfare. But for most analysts there are obvious terrorist regimes, controlled by leaders so despicable and anti-democratic that they can be unequivocally placed on the illegitimate side of the terrorist divide. Despite the fact that they are defined as states, the "axes of evil"—whether during World War II, the Cold War, in the Bush administration's definition of 2002—have placed themselves outside the human family and have to be treated as imminent threats to be combated covertly or through invasion.

What if one comes closer to home? This is where the political intensity of defining terrorism truly heightens. Perdue analyzes the counterrevolutionary Contras of Nicaragua as an example of the United States exercising "surrogate terrorism." And even closer to home, Robert Goodin has analyzed the War on Terror as terrorist in its own right because, he believes, the United States is "acting with the intention of instilling fear of violence for sociopolitical purposes"—his definition of terrorism. Fear-mongering in itself constitutes terrorism from the vantage point of citizens overwhelmed by incessant "warnings" of terrorist attacks, Goodin argues. "Instilling terror circumvents people's reasoning capacity," leading to panic or "cowed" states, thus "undermining" the collective and individual "capacity for autonomous self-government." Goodin argues that the greatest public danger of the War on Terror is that it can produce a terrorist state that, like the United States under the Bush administration, suspends basic constitutional rights to fight fire with fire, or, in short, resorts to terrorism as morally and legally sanctioned government practice in a war against terrorism.[8]

Goodin's basic identity is with the rational, independent citizen and groups of free citizens who exist, in a Jeffersonian or libertarian manner, prior to and outside the state, and who to remain free must always stand vigilantly against abuses of state power. This traditional American political stance, grounded in a detached and individualistic social morality, leads to a definition of terrorism in which the players in terrorist conflicts are all engaged in a struggle, and both sides destroy freedom. They are mutually engaged in terrorism.

Goodin points to the necessity of merging the analysis of actions with that of reactions, the material with the psychological, when examining the psychological impacts that can result from the activities of state as well as anti-state actors. Wardlaw works state terrorism and psychological impacts into his rather sophisticated if unwieldy definition: "Political terrorism is the use, or threat of use, of violence by an individual or group, whether acting for or in opposition to established authority, when such action is designated to create extreme anxiety and/or fear-inducing effects in a target group larger than the immediate victims with the purpose of coercing that group into acceding to the political demands of the perpetrators."[9] This seems to be the most satisfactory available definition, but it is static while history is dynamic.

Once one erases conventional boundaries between non-state and state terrorism, simplistic divisions between those who are good and those who are evil become blurred. Similarly, the definition of terrorism widens to embrace a range of forms of violence that contain political intents and consequences. In her argument calling for definitional rigor, the political scientist Martha Crenshaw demonstrates instead that a broad definition has more explanatory power than the narrow one she favors. She writes, "Defining terrorism becomes particularly troublesome when it occurs against a background of extensive violence. We cannot assume that it is discontinuous with collective political violence. Even the best scholarly intentions may not suffice to distinguish terrorism from protest, guerrilla warfare, urban guerrilla warfare, subversion, criminal violence, paramilitarism, communal violence, or banditry . . . or terrorism in particular from political violence."[10]

Exactly. I believe that discussing terrorism as overlapping forms of political violence reveals more than eliminating or delimiting violent political activities in the name of theoretical clarification. Action meets reaction in violent terrorist exchanges, whether on the streets during insurrectionary engagements or as an element of warfare, both of which I analyze in this book.

Terrorism is indeed graphic action in the service of political demands, but it also can be seen as a process, an exchange rather than a thing. While discussing definitional frameworks is useful, viewing terrorism through dynamic narrative enriches analysis. The five case studies in this book plumb the meanings of various brutal activities intended to coerce larger political changes, even within war itself. Furthermore, when seeking to develop an interactive definition for terrorism, we must move more closely into the mentality of the actors. To this end it is necessary to describe their actions and motivations as they themselves conceive of them, to put aside one's repugnance in order to try to taste the allure of terrorism. This is not to excuse terrorists but to understand them better as human beings—even as they deny the humanity of their enemies. Attaining that level of detachment is perhaps the largest mental and moral block to making a fuller analysis of terrorism possible.

Beneath the ideological and psychological surface, Richard Falk has written, fundamentalist terrorists seek a transformed world, "and are prepared to risk everything to realize their vision." I would add that although most terrorists, and not just religious-fundamentalist terrorists, seek to appear to be rational actors, all tend toward what Falk calls a mind-set "dominated by its melodramatic preoccupation with the destruction of evil. It rejects self-doubt, ambiguity, human solidarity, moral and legal inhibition, constitutionalism. It is a law unto itself, and the bearer of some 'higher morality' to be established later on."[11]

Melodrama is the key concept here, melodrama that is religious as well as political, apocalyptic about the coming end time and the need to help shape the cosmic explosion personally. Wardlaw calls this sensibility the "ecstatic element" of terrorism, with the exercise of terror producing emotional results in the terrorist that become a primary motivating force.[12]

One of the most helpful modern studies of terrorism, Mark Juergensmeyer's *Terror in the Mind of God: The Global Rise of Religious Violence*, insists that "theatrical displays of violence" rather than conscious strategy making create the deep structures of terrorist mentalities. Terrorists act on a symbolic rather than merely a literal level, seeking to portray cosmic truths through graphic and easily understandable actions, creating not merely tactical moves but dramatic performances. True to the traditional role of religion, religion-based terrorists perform public rituals to enact their beliefs, to force their grand agenda on the world. To further this point Juergensmeyer quotes the novelist Don DeLillo, who has written that terrorism is the "language of being noticed."[13]

For terrorists, Juergensmeyer argues, theirs is an all or nothing struggle, a cosmic engagement, conducted in the world rather than subsequent to it. The struggle occurs at a point of crisis during which individual actors take on themselves the task of performing the action that can make the difference in moving from hopelessness to victory, not necessarily in real time, but certainly in sacralized cosmic time. Whatever destruction terrorist acts produce, the perpetrators believe that they can achieve immortality on earth and sainthood in heaven.[14]

To achieve cosmic victory, the terrorist needs an evil foe, for, as Juergensmeyer writes, "one cannot have a war without an enemy," and that enemy needs to be satanized to be clearly identified. Terrorists assert their superior moral power by "belittling and humiliating" their foes, changing them into subhumans on whom they can commit atrocities without compunction. Terrorist attacks on the dehumanized other are acts of "empowerment," engaged in with the "exuberance of the hope that the tide of history will eventually turn their way." (They can strike a blow at the "Great Satan" just as those fighting them can eliminate "Evil-Doers.") Even should they die in committing their terrorist acts, "victory is at hand." They are soldiers in the great cause of world cleansing, even if their battles are unwinnable in ordinary military terms, and their victories, such as they are, have been "purchased at an awful cost."[15]

Although Juergensmeyer eschews analysis of state terrorism, dealing only with individual and small groups of terrorists, his mode of analyzing terrorist process can also be applied to activities of states, where many of the same energies are called forth in the name of purging evil through politically violent means. The dynamics of terrorist politics can be elucidated further when one sees them as social enactments created by colliding parties. Even if one party is the initial aggressor, the other counter-aggresses in reaction. This is both a physical conflict and a conflict of basic values. The opposing parties understand each other; they are mirroring each other's enraged and self-righteous dualism, working out opposing versions of a shared discourse. Terrorist discourse is always highly charged, religiously as well as politically. When girding for combat or engaging in it, a terrorist cannot afford detachment from this emotionally moralistic loading.

Terrorism can best be understood as a shared process that includes "us" not merely as innocent victims but as participants, even if we did not initiate the combat. Terrorists can be "we" as well as "they," particularly when we call for punishment of "them" as a form of retribution. As themselves citizens of threatened societies, scholars have great difficulty standing outside the process sufficiently to see the larger dialectical patterns, but that should be their goal.

Terrorism, then, is not one thing but a many-valenced process, best examined as a set of actions and reactions arising between conflicting parties. All these agents engage in political violence with self-righteous justification because they are able to conceptualize those they terrorize as an other outside and inimical to their world. Understanding the ideological and psychological contexts of physical violence is crucial to interpreting terrorist acts. Those engaged in the interchange of terrorism are arguing over basic moral and social beliefs; they are conducting a violence-grounded campaign to protect deeply held political and religious values. When outsiders attack, the state acts in kind, in retaliation for a threat to what state actors see as their God-given right to maintain their own hegemony. Ironically, the revolutionary terrorist act only reinforces the state's notion of alien otherness that produces a reactionary retaliatory terrorism in retribution.

Notes

Introduction

1. Adelbert Ames to his wife, October 12, 1875, quoted in Richard N. Current, *Three Carpetbag Governors* (Baton Rouge: Louisiana State University Press, 1967), 89–90.

2. The discussion in the following note is based on these texts: Paul Berman, *Terror and Liberalism* (New York: Norton, 2003); Richard Clutterbuck, *Terrorism and Guerrilla Warfare* (New York: Routledge, 1990); Richard Falk, *Revolutionaries and Functionaries: The Dual Face of Terrorism* (New York: Dutton, 1988); Michael Fellman, *Inside War: The Guerrilla Conflict in Missouri During the American Civil War* (New York: Oxford University Press, 1989); Jason Franks, *Rethinking the Roots of Terrorism* (Basingstoke, U.K.: Palgrave, 2006); Robert E. Goodin, *What's Wrong with Terrorism?* (Cambridge: Polity, 2006); Fred Halliday, *Nation and Religion in the Middle East* (London: Saqi, 1988); John Horgan, *The Psychology of Terrorism* (London: Routledge, 2005); Mark Juergensmeyer, *Terror in the Mind of God: The Global Rise of Religious Violence*, 3rd ed. (Berkeley: University of California Press, 2003); William E. Perdue, *Terrorism and the State: A Critique of Domination Through Fear* (New York: Praeger, 1989); Richard E. Rubenstein, *Alchemists of Revolution: Terrorism in the Modern World* (New York: Basic, 1987); Phil Scranton, ed., *Beyond September 11: An Anthology of Dissent* (London: Pluto, 2002); Andrew Silke, ed., *Terrorists, Victims and Society: Psychological Perspectives on Terrorism and Its Consequences* (Chichester, U.K.: Wiley, 2003); Jeffrey A. Sulka, *Death Squad: The Anthropology of State Terror* (Philadelphia: University of Pennsylvania Press, 2000); Charles Townshend, *Britain's Civil Wars: Counterinsurgency in the Twentieth Century* (London: Faber and Faber, 1986); Townshend, *Political Violence in Ireland: Government and Resistance Since 1848* (Oxford: Clarendon, 1983); Townshend, *Terrorism: A Very Short Introduction* (Oxford: Oxford University Press, 2002); Eugene Victor Walter, *Terror and Resistance: A Study of Political Violence, with Case Studies of Some Primitive African Communities* (New York: Oxford University Press, 1969); Grant Wardlaw, *Political Terrorism: Theory, Tactics, and Counter-Measures*, 2nd ed. (London: Cambridge University Press, 1989); David J. Whittaker, ed., *The Terrorism Reader* (London: Routledge, 2001); Paul Wilkinson, *Terrorism Versus Democracy: The Liberal State Response* (London: Frank Cass, 2001).

3. Grotius and Ascham are discussed in Jill Lepore, *The Name of War: King Philip's War and the Origins of American Identity* (New York: Random House, 1999), 88, 107–11, 121.

4. Lawrence H. Keeley, *War Before Civilization* (New York: Oxford University Press, 1996), 87.

5. For a rich and sophisticated treatment of this cultural clash see in particular Edmund S. Morgan, *American Slavery, American Freedom: The Ordeal of Colonial Virginia* (New York: Norton, 1975), 3–107.

6. Lepore, *Name of War*, 73, 105, 108, 113, 120–21 (emphasis added). Also see Peter Silver, *Our Savage Neighbors: How Indian War Transformed Early America* (New York: Norton, 2008). For another vivid analysis drawn from an extremely bloody French and Indian raid on Deerfield, Massachusetts, in 1704, see John Demos, *The Redeemed Captive: A Family Story from Early America* (New York: Knopf, 1994).

7. Matthew C. Ward, *Breaking the Backcountry: The Seven Years' War in Virginia and Pennsylvania, 1754–1765* (Pittsburgh: University of Pittsburgh Press, 2003), 55–56, 239, 256–57. Also see Fred Anderson, *Crucible of War: The Seven Years' War and the Fate of Empire in North America, 1754–1766* (New York: Knopf, 2000), 612.

8. These examples are drawn from Sung Bok Kim, "The Limits of Politicization in the American Revolution: The Experience of Westchester, New York," *Journal of American History* 80 (December 1993): 868–89; Catherine S. Crary, *The Price of Loyalty: Tory Writings from the Revolutionary Era* (New York: McGraw-Hill, 1973), 188–89, 236; and Harry M. Ward, *The American Revolution: Nationhood Achieved, 1763–1788* (New York: St. Martin's, 1995), 259–72, an excellent succinct analysis of the Loyalists that includes a useful bibliography.

CHAPTER 1. John Brown

1. Frederick Law Olmsted, *A Journey in the Back Country* (New York: Mason Brothers, 1860), 70–93. I have condensed the narrative that was excerpted in Willie Lee Rose, ed., *A Documentary History of Slavery in North America* (New York: Oxford University Press, 1976), 297–99.

2. Quoted in Franklin B. Sanborn, *The Life and Letters of John Brown* (Boston: Roberts Brothers, 1885), 131.

3. John Brown to Henry L. Stearns, July 15, 1857, quoted in Zoe Trodd and John Stauffer, eds., *Meteor of War: The John Brown Story* (Maplecrest, N.Y.: Brandywine, 2004), 38–39. This excellent collection contains many of the important letters and documents concerning Brown. Brown's letter and many other Brown primary materials are also reprinted in four less accessible places: Louis Ruchames, ed., *A John Brown Reader* (New York: Abelard-Schuman, 1959); Sanborn, *Life and Letters of John Brown*; Richard J. Hinton, *John Brown and His Men* (1894: New York: Arno Press, 1968); and Oswald Garrison Villard's superb biography *John Brown* (Boston: Houghton Mifflin, 1910).

4. John Brown to his father, August 11, 1832, quoted in Richard O. Boyer, *The Legend of John Brown* (New York: Knopf, 1973), 249.

5. John Brown to My Dear Afflicted Wife & Children, November 8, 1846; Brown to Mary, November 29, 1846, in Trodd and Stauffer, *Meteor of War*, 52–53.

6. Brown to his family, May 28, 1839, quoted in Stephen P. Oates, *To Purge This Land with Blood: A Biography of John Brown*, 2nd ed. (Amherst: University of Massachusetts Press, 1984), 44. For a succinct and insightful analysis of Brown's spiritual activism, see John Stauffer, *The Black Hearts of Men: Radical Abolitionists and the Transformation of Race*

(Cambridge: Harvard University Press, 2002), 118–23. In addition, among the vast Brown literature, Robert E. McGlone, *John Brown's War Against Slavery* (New York: Cambridge University Press, 2009), is a deeply researched and thoughtful analysis of Brown's personality and actions.

7. Biographical fragment from John Brown, Jr., undated but probably concerning events around 1831, in Sanborn, *Life and Letters of John Brown,* 92–93 (emphasis in the original).

8. Brown to Hon. J. R. Giddings, June 22, 1848, in Ruchames, *John Brown Reader,* 65.

9. John Brown," Sambo's Mistake" (1848), in Trodd and Stauffer, *Meteor of War,* 55–58.

10. Brown, "Words of Advice to the Branch of the United States of Gileadites," January 15, 1851, in Trodd and Stauffer, *Meteor of War,* 77–79. The league was named after Gideon's warrior band in the Old Testament, three hundred men winnowed from thirty-two thousand when tested for bravery by God.

11. W. A. Phillips, "Three Interviews with Old John Brown," *Atlantic Monthly* (December 1879), reprinted in Ruchames, *John Brown Reader,* 218; George Gordon, Lord Byron, "Childe Harold's Pilgrimage," canto 2, stanza 75. On the frequent radical abolitionist use of this particular quotation, and on Byron more generally as the model romantic revolutionary, see Stauffer, *Black Hearts of Men,* 60–62, 66, 85, 113, 150–51, 187.

12. Thomas Wentworth Higginson, "Physical Courage," *Atlantic Monthly* (September 1858): 728–37. For a thorough discussion of Brown, Higginson, and the theory of redemptive violence, see Jeffery Rossbach, *Ambivalent Conspirators: John Brown, the Secret Six, and a Theory of Slave Violence* (Philadelphia: University of Pennsylvania Press, 1982), 182–209.

13. Quoted in Sanborn, *Life and Letters of John Brown,* 117, 122 (emphases in the original).

14. John Brown, "A Declaration of Liberty by the Representatives of the Slave Population of the United States of America," in Hinton, *John Brown and His Men,* 638–39.

15. John Brown, "Articles of Enlistment and By-Laws of the Kansas Regulars, made and established by their commander, Kansas Territory, AD 1856," in Sanborn, *Life and Letters of John Brown,* 287–90; Brown to Augustus Wattles, April 8, 1857, ibid., 391.

16. Phillips, "Three Interviews with Old John Brown," 210.

17. Villard, *John Brown,* 153–57.

18. Jason Brown's conversation is ibid., 165; Brown to Dear Wife and Children, Everyone, June 1856, in Trodd and Stauffer, *Meteor of War,* 85–88. For a range of primary documents on the massacre, see Trodd and Stauffer, *Meteor of War,* 84–95, and Ruchames, *John Brown Reader,* 189–218. All the biographies have full discussions of the massacre. In many ways the fullest, based on the most primary research, are the oldest: Sanborn, *Life and Letters of John Brown,* 247–282, and Villard, *John Brown,* 148–88.

19. For a brilliant analysis of this group see Stauffer, *Black Hearts of Men.*

20. Katherine Mayo, "Brown in Hiding and in Jail," in Ruchames, *John Brown Reader,* 234–40.

21. The clearest descriptions of this plan came from a letter from Hugh Forbes, a treacherous associate, to the New York *Herald* published October 27, 1859, and the testimony of Richard Realf, one of Brown's disciples, to a congressional committee in 1860; they are reprinted in Villard, *John Brown,* 231–32, 285–86. The Provisional Constitution is reprinted in Trodd and Stauffer, *Meteor of War,* 109–22.

22. Quoted in Villard, *John Brown*, 275.

23. John Brown, "Old Browns Farewell to The Plymouth Rocks, Bunker Hill Monuments, Charter Oaks, and Uncle Thoms Cabbins," in Ruchames, *John Brown Reader*, 106.

24. John Brown to Franklin B. Sanborn, February 24, 1858, in Sanborn, *Life and Letters of John Brown*, 444.

25. Frederick Douglass, *Life and Times of Frederick Douglass* (1893), reprinted in Frederick Douglass, *Autobiographies* (New York: Library of America, 1994), 757–60.

26. For a compact and clear discussion of the raid, see Oates, *To Purge This Land with Blood*, 274–302.

27. Brown to My Dear Friend E. B. of R. I., November 1, 1859, in Ruchames, *John Brown Reader*, 129.

28. For this alternative version of tactics not taken, I draw on Villard, *John Brown*, 427.

29. John Brown's Interview with Senator James M. Mason, Congressman Clement L. Vallandingham, and Others, October 18, 1859, reprinted in Trodd and Stauffer, *Meteor of War*, 123–29.

30. *The Life, Trial and Execution of Captain John Brown* (1859; reprint New York: Da Capo, 1969), 56–95, quotations at 62, 64–65, 75, 94–95.

31. From a speech Wendell Phillips gave in New York, December 15, 1859, quoted in Trodd and Stauffer, *Meteor of War*, 135

32. Henry David Thoreau, "A Plea for Captain John Brown," in Thoreau, *Anti-Slavery and Reform Papers* (Montreal: Harvest House, 1963), 74.

33. Quoted in David S. Reynolds, *John Brown: Abolitionist* (New York: Knopf, 2005), 384.

34. Brown to My Dear Devoted Wife, November 10, 1859, in Villard, *John Brown*, 540; Brown to Dear Brother Jeremiah, November 12, 1859, in Trodd and Stauffer, *Meteor of War*, 142.

35. Brown to Rev. H. C. Vaill, November 15, 1859, in Trodd and Stauffer, *Meteor of War*, 143.

36. Brown to Rev. James. W. McFarland, November 23, 1859, ibid., 150. For another comparison to Paul, see Brown to Heman Humphrey, November 25, 1859 (153).

37. Brown to Dear Wife and children, Every One, November 8, 1859, ibid., 141; Charlestown *Independent Democrat*, November 22, 1859, quoted in Villard, *John Brown*, 545.

38. Brown to My Dearly beloved Wife, Sons: & Daughters, every one, November 30, 1859, in Trodd and Stauffer, *Meteor of War*, 157.

39. Brown to Mrs. George L. Stearns, November 29, 1859, ibid., 156–57. For a useful analysis of the origins of the legend of Brown's kissing of the black child see Benjamin Quarles, *Allies for Freedom: Blacks on John Brown* (1974; New York: Da Capo, 2001), 120–21.

40. Note composed by John Brown, December 2, 1859, in Trodd and Stauffer, *Meteor of War*, 159.

41. Thomas Wentworth Higginson to Louisa Higginson, November 5, 1859, quoted in Rossbach, *Ambivalent Conspirators*, 219. Also see Paul Finkelman, "Manufacturing Martyrdom: The Antislavery Response to John Brown's Raid," in Finkelman, ed., *His Soul Goes Marching On: Responses to John Brown and the Harpers Ferry Raid* (Charlottesville: University of Virginia Press, 1995), 41–66.

42. Ralph Waldo Emerson, "Courage," lecture given at Tremont Temple Boston, November 8, 1859, quoted in Ruchames, *John Brown Reader*, 12, and Reynolds, *John Brown:*

Abolitionist, 366, 369; Theodore Parker to Francis Jackson, November 24, 1859, quoted in Boyer, *Legend of John Brown*, 17. Also see Emerson's address at Salem, January 6, 1860, in Trodd and Stauffer, *Meteor of War*, 219–23.

43. William Lloyd Garrison, Speech at Tremont Temple, December 2, 1859, in Villard, *John Brown*, 560.

44. Thoreau's journal, quoted in Sanborn, *Life and Letters of John Brown*, 503; Thoreau, "Plea for Captain John Brown," 45, 65, 71.

45. Rev. M. D. Conway, Cincinnati, December 4, 1859, quoted in Ruchames, *John Brown Reader*, 281; Wendell Phillips "Burial of John Brown," December 8, 1859, ibid., 283. Also see Phillips, "The Lesson of the Hour," November 1, 1859, and "The Age and the Man," Lecture in Lawrence, Kansas, January 20, 1860, in Trodd and Stauffer, *Meteor of War*, 133, and his speech in New York, December 15, 1859, in Richard Scheidenhelm, ed., *The Response to John Brown* (Belmont, Calif.: Wadsworth Publishing, 1972), 61–75.

46. J. Stella Martin, Speech at Tremont Temple, December 2, 1859, in Quarles, *Allies for Freedom*, 25–31.

47. Charles H. Langston to the *Cleveland New Dealer*, November 18, 1859, ibid., 11–19; Reynolds quotes the Melodeon speech in *John Brown: Abolitionist*, 407–8. Also see Daniel C. Littlefield, "Blacks, John Brown, and a Theory of Manhood," in Finkelman, *His Soul Goes Marching On*, 67–97.

48. Salmon P. Chase to Joseph H. Barrett, editor of the Cincinnati *Gazette*, in Ruchames, *John Brown Reader*, 249.

49. William H. Herndon to Charles Sumner, December 10, 1860, quoted in Charles Joyner, "'Guilty of the Holiest Crime': The Passion of John Brown," in Finkelman, *His Soul Goes Marching On*, 317.

50. Abraham Lincoln, Speech at Elwood, Kansas, December 1, 1859, and Speech at Leavenworth, Kansas, December 3, 1859, in Roy P. Basler, ed., *The Collected Works of Abraham Lincoln* (New Brunswick: Rutgers University Press, 1953), 3:496, 502.

51. Abraham Lincoln, Address at Cooper Institute, New York, February 27, 1860, ibid., 3:542.

52. Speech of Theodore Tilton in Philadelphia, December 2, 1859, in Ruchames, *John Brown Reader*, 272–75; Phillips, speech in New York, December 15, 1859, in Scheidenhelm, *Response to John Brown*, 60–75. See also Charles O'Conor, Speech at the New York Conservatory of Music, December 19, 1859, in Scheidenhelm, *Response to John Brown*, 111–27.

53. *Dred Scott V. Stanford*, 19 How. 393 (1857).

54. Governor Henry A. Wise, Message to the Virginia Legislature, December 5, 1859, in Scheidenhelm, *Response to John Brown*, 132–53.

55. See Peter Wallenstein, "Incendiaries All: Southern Politics and the Harpers Ferry Raid," in Finkelman, *His Soul Goes Marching On*, 149–73.

56. *Mobile Daily Register*, October 25, 1859; *Richmond Enquirer*, October 25, 1859; *Savannah Republican*, quoted in the *Liberator* on November 11, 1858, in Villard, *John Brown*, 500.

57. Amanda Virginia Edmonds Diary quoted in Elizabeth Varon, *We Mean to Be Counted: White Women and Politics in Antebellum Virginia* (Chapel Hill: University of North Carolina Press, 1998), 160.

58. *De Bow's Review* (January and May, 1860), 542–49, quoted in Oates, *To Purge This Land with Blood*, 323.

59. *Report of the Joint Committee of the General Assembly of Virginia on the Harpers Ferry*

Outrages, January 26, 1860, quoted in Villard, *John Brown,* 567; Speech of Robert Toombs, January 12, 1860, quoted ibid., 565–56.

60. Florida Committee on Federal Relations, quoted in Reynolds, *John Brown: Aboli-tionist,* 423–24.

61. Ibid., 434.

62. South Carolina, "Declaration of the Causes of Secession," December 20, 1860; *New Orleans Daily Crescent,* November 13, 1869; Mary Boykin Chesnut, Diary entry for November 8, 1860, all quoted in Joyner, " 'Guilty of the Holiest Crime,' " 327.

63. Abraham Lincoln, Second Inaugural Address, March 4, 1865, in Basler, *Collected Works of Lincoln,* 8:332–33.

CHAPTER 2. Terrorism and Civil War

1. [Francis W. Lieber], War Department General Orders No. 100, Washington, April 24, 1863, quoted in Michael Fellman, *Inside War: The Guerrilla Conflict in Missouri During the American Civil War* (New York: Oxford University Press, 1989), 83.

2. William Tecumseh Sherman, *Memoirs,* 2nd ed. (1886; New York: Penguin, 2000), 608–9; Sherman is quoting Psalms III: 10. For a comparative analysis of what he calls the "profoundly interactive" nature of terrorism in civil war, see Stathis N. Kalyvas, "The Paradox of Terrorism in Civil War, *Journal of Ethics* 8 (2004): 97–138, and Kalyvas, *The Logic of Violence in Civil War* (Cambridge: Cambridge University Press, 2006).

3. Sherman to Henry Halleck, September 4, 1864, in *The War of the Rebellion: A Compilation of the Official Records of the Union and the Confederate Armies* (hereafter cited as *Official Records*), 127 vols. (Washington, D.C.: Government Printing Office, 1880–1901), ser. 1, vol. 38, pt. 5, p. 794; John Bell Hood to Sherman, September 9, 1864, *Official Records,* ser. 1, vol. 39, pt. 2, p. 414, Sherman to James M. Calhoun et al., September 12, 1864, in *Official Records,* ser. 1, vol. 39, pt. 2, p. 503, all quoted in Michael Fellman: *Citizen Sherman: A Life of William T. Sherman* (New York: Random House, 2000), 180–88; many of these documents and much other Sherman correspondence are reprinted in Brooks D. Simpson and Jean V. Berlin, eds., *Sherman's Civil War: Selected Correspondence of William T. Sher-man, 1861–65* (Chapel Hill: University of North Carolina Press, 1999).

4. Sherman to Calhoun et al., September 12, 1864, 503.

5. Sherman to Halleck, October 18, 1864, Sherman to George Thomas, October 20 and October 29, 1864, Sherman to Ulysses S. Grant, November 6, 1864, all in *Official Records,* ser. 1, vol. 39, pt. 3, pp. 377–78, 659–61.

6. Quoted in Fellman, *Citizen Sherman,* 217–18, 215.

7. Sherman to Halleck, December 11, 1864, quoted in Simpson and Berlin, *Sherman's Civil War,* 669; Sherman to Halleck, December 11, 1864, Sherman to Grant, December 18, 1864, Sherman to Halleck, December 24, 1864, all in *Official Records,* ser. 1, vol. 44, pp. 701–2, 741–43, 798–800; Henry H. Slocum to My Dear Cal, January 6, 1865, J. Howland Papers, New York Historical Society, quoted in Joseph Glatthaar, *The March to the Sea and Beyond* (New York: New York University Press, 1985), 79.

8. Simpson and Berlin, *Sherman's Civil War,* 776; Fellman, *Citizen Sherman,* 223, quotation at 231; Marion Brunson Lucas, *Sherman and the Burning of Columbia* (College Station: Texas A & M University Press, 1976).

9. All these quotations, are from Everard H. Smith's superb "Chambersburg: Anat-

omy of a Confederate Reprisal" in *American Historical Review* 96 (April 1991): 432–55, which provides a thoughtful analysis of the "dark carnival" of the raid.

10. Gerald F. Linderman, *Embattled Courage: The Experience of Combat in the American Civil War* (New York: Free Press, 1987), 200.

11. Phillip Shaw Paludan, *Victims: A True Story of the Civil War* (Knoxville: University of Tennessee Press, 1981), 73, 97.

12. Richard B. McCaslin, *Tainted Breeze: The Great Hanging in Gainesville, Texas, 1862* (Baton Rouge: Louisiana State University Press, 1994), 60–83, 143–46.

13. Edward E. Leslie, *The Devil Knows How to Ride: The True Story of William Clarke Quantrill and His Confederate Raiders* (New York: Random House, 1994), esp. 237, 276–79, 327–29. For a larger discussion of this theater of war, see Fellman, *Inside War.*

14. Gregory J. W. Urwin, ed. *Black Flag over Dixie: Racial Atrocities and Reprisals in the Civil War* (Carbondale: Southern Illinois University Press, 2004),

15. Thomas A. DeBlack, *With Fire and Sword: Arkansas, 1861–1874* (Fayetteville: University of Arkansas Press, 2003), 113; Anne J. Bailey, "A Texas Cavalry Raid: Reaction to Black Soldiers and Contraband," and Gregory J. W. Urwin, "'We Cannot Treat Negroes . . . as Prisoners of War': Racial Atrocities and Reprisals in Civil War Arkansas," in Urwin, *Black Flag over Dixie*, 29, 135. Also see George S. Burkhardt, *Confederate Rage, Yankee Wrath: No Quarter in the Civil War* (Carbondale: Southern Illinois University Press, 2007).

16. Urwin, "'We Cannot Treat Negroes,'" 142–43.

17. J. Tracy Power, *Lee's Miserables: Life in the Army of Northern Virginia from the Wilderness to Appomattox* (Chapel Hill: University of North Carolina Press, 1998), 136–38; Weymouth T. Jordan, Jr., and Gerald W. Thomas, "Massacre at Plymouth: April 20, 1864," in Urwin, *Black Flag over Dixie*, 168. The estimate of 265 murdered black soldiers comes from the careful research of Bryce A. Suderow, who notes that the ratio of blacks killed to wounded was about 423 to 757, or 1 to 1.8, while in the Civil War for all Union troops, the ratio was 1 to 4.8. Using that comparison, one can deduce that if a unit suffered 757 wounded, it would usually have sustained 158 deaths in combat, rather than 423, by which he derives the approximation of 265 black Union troops killed while surrendering. See Suderow, "The Battle of the Crater: The Civil War's Worst Massacre," in Urwin, *Black Flag over Dixie*, 208.

18. Albert Castel, "The Fort Pillow Massacre: An Examination of the Evidence," in Urwin, *Black Flag over Dixie*, 93

19. Jordan and Thomas, "Massacre at Plymouth," 153, 171–74.

20. Bailey, "Texas Cavalry Raid," 20, 24; David J. Coles, "'Shooting Niggers Sir': Confederate Mistreatment of Union Black Soldiers at the Battle of Olustee," in Urwin, *Black Flag over Dixie*, 75, 74.

21. Coles, "'Shooting Niggers Sir,'" 76.

22. Jordan and Thomas, "Massacre at Plymouth," 167–68; Urwin, "We Cannot Treat Negroes," 150n43.

23. For a full documentary presentation and analysis of the African American military experience during the Civil War, see Ira Berlin et al., *Free at Last: A Documentary History of Slavery, Freedom, and the Civil War* (New York: Free Press, 1992), and Michael Fellman, Lesley J. Gordon, and Daniel E. Sutherland, *This Terrible War: The Civil War and Its Aftermath* (New York: Longman's, 2003), 141–67.

24. Simpson and Berlin, *Sherman's Civil War*, 701, 727. For a full discussion of Sherman on the subject of black soldiers see Fellman, *Citizen Sherman*, 149–70.

25. Joseph T. Glatthaar, *The March to the Sea and Beyond: Sherman's Troops in the Savannah and Carolinas Campaigns* (New York: New York University Press, 1986), 57.

26. Urwin, "We Cannot Treat Negroes ," 143–46.

27. Fellman, Gordon, and Sutherland, *This Terrible War*, 164–65; Urwin, "Introduction: Warfare, Race, and the Civil War in American Memory," in Urwin, *Black Flag over Dixie*, 9.

28. Fellman, *Inside War*, xv.

29. Ibid., 27.

30. Ibid., 25–26.

31. Ibid., 58, 59.

32. Ibid., 59, 79.

33. Ibid., 54.

34. Ibid., 76, 77.

35. Ibid., 80, 78, 80.

36. Ibid., 77 (emphasis mine).

37. Ibid., 83, 123–24.

38. Ibid., 82, 92, 123.

39. George Crook, *General George Crook: His Autobiography* (1887), quoted in Kenneth W. Noe, "Exterminating Savages: The Union Army and Mountain Guerrillas in Southern West Virginia, 1861–62," in Kenneth W. Noe and Shannon H. Wilson, eds., *The Civil War in Appalachia: Collected Essays* (Knoxville: University of Tennessee Press, 1997), 87.

40. General Orders No. 100, quoted in Fellman, *Inside War*, 83–84.

41. Fellman, *Inside War*, 122.

42. Ibid., 133.

43. Noe, "Exterminating Savages," 107; Fellman, *Inside War*, 188.

44. Fellman, *Inside War*, 186.

45. On the aesthetics of destruction in combat see J. Glenn Gray, *The Warriors: Reflections on Men in Battle* (New York: Harper and Row, 1970).

46. Fellman, *Inside War*, 137, 139.

47. Ibid., 148.

48. Ibid., 160–61.

49. Ibid., 161, emphasis in the original.

50. Ibid., 165, 183–84.

51. Ibid., 151–52.

52. Bodwell's diary is in the archives of the Kansas Historical Society; these quotations are in my *Inside War*, 189–92.

53. Fellman, *Inside War*, 265–66. Sanborn was quoting 2 Samuel 23:3 (King James Version).

54. John Wilkes Booth, quoted in David S. Reynolds, *John Brown: Abolitionist* (New York: Knopf, 2005), 397–98, 477–79. Emphasis in the original.

55. These passages are quoted in the compelling final chapter of Lisa Tendrich Frank, "To 'Cure Her of Pride and Boasting': The Gendered Implications of Sherman's March" (Ph.D. diss., University of Florida, 2001), 228–30.

CHAPTER 3. Blood Redemption

1. Testimony of Alzina F. Haffa and Florence E. Haffa, *Mississippi in 1875: Report of the Select (Senate) Committee to Inquire into the Mississippi Election of 1875*, 2 vols. (Washington, D.C.: Government Printing Office, 1876), vol. 1, pp. xv–xix, 491. Henceforth, these volumes will be cited as Senate Hearings. Volume 1 contains "Report" (iii–cxi) and "Testimony" (1–1020); volume 2 continues "Testimony" (1021–1819), followed by "Documentary Evidence" (1–173).

2. Testimony of Margaret Ann Caldwell, Jackson, June 20, 1876, Senate Hearings, 435–40.

3. Townsend is quoted and South Carolina secession analyzed in Stephanie McCurry, *Masters of Small Worlds: Yeoman Households, Gender Relations, and the Political Culture of the Antebellum South Carolina Low Country* (New York: Oxford University Press, 1995), 277–304. Also see Steven A. Channing, *Crisis of Fear: Secession in South Carolina* (New York: Norton, 1970), and, more generally, David M. Potter, *The Impending Crisis: 1848–1861* (New York: Harper and Row, 1976).

4. Testimony of Reuben Davis, Senate Hearings, 1053–71.

5. These quotes are drawn from Vernon Lane Wharton, *The Negro in Mississippi, 1865–1890* (New York: Harper and Row, 1965), 184. Wharton's book, originally published in 1947, with certain political limitations, was for its time a remarkably incisive study of the nature of black rule in the Mississippi and contains the sharpest single analysis of the White Line movement of 1875.

6. Charles Sumner's letter to black leaders of July 29, 1872, is quoted in David Blight, *Race and Reunion: The Civil War in American Memory* (Cambridge: Harvard University Press, 2001), 128; emphasis in the original. Blight provides the seminal study of the political abandonment of efforts for racial justice in the name of sectional reconciliation. The other quotations are drawn from William Gillette, *Retreat from Reconstruction, 1869–79* (Baton Rouge: Louisiana State University Press, 1979), 301.

7. See Wharton, *Negro in Mississippi*, 157.

8. For a succinct analysis of the Alcorn Republicans and the subsequent Radical Republican regime, see Warren Ellem, "The Overthrow of Reconstruction in Mississippi," *Journal of Mississippi History* 54 (May, 1992): 175–201. Although insightful concerning the shifts in Republican politics, Ellem tends to blame internal division in the party exclusively for its downfall, giving scant consideration to brutally effective terrorism of the White Line campaign of 1875.

9. See Allen W. Trelease, *White Terror: The Ku Klux Klan Conspiracy and Southern Reconstruction* (New York: Harper and Row, 1971), 287–91, 410–413.

10. Ellem, "Overthrow of Reconstruction in Mississippi," 189.

11. Eric Foner, *Reconstruction: America's Unfinished Business, 1863–1877* (New York: Harper and Row, 1988), 563.

12. Ibid., 535, Ellem, "Overthrow of Reconstruction in Mississippi," 191.

13. Testimony of J. D. Vetner, Senate Hearings, 158–220; see also the testimony of E. H. Stiles, ibid. We are fortunate here to have the conflicting testimony of both the white Republican sheriff and the White Liner who drove him from office.

14. Testimony of E. L. Webber, Senate Hearings, 1571.

15. "Report," Senate Hearings, lxxxvii.

16. Testimony of T. M. Miller, Senate Hearings, 670.

17. Testimony of W. D. Brown, Senate Hearings, 705.

18. Testimony of P. C. Powell and Eli Hunt, Senate Hearings, 883, 890.

19. Testimony of Derry Brown, Senate Hearings, 630.

20. Testimony of W. W. Edwards, Testimony of M. G. Bennett, Senate Hearings, 1356, 1386–87.

21. Deposition of A. H. Silvey, Senate Hearings, 365.

22. Gary is quoted in a brilliant essay by Stephen Kantrowitz, "One Man's Mob Is Another Man's Militia: Violence, Manhood and Authority in Reconstruction South Carolina," in Jane Dailey, Glenda Elizabeth Gilmore, and Bryant Simon, eds., *Jumpin' Jim Crow: Southern Politics from Civil War to Civil Rights* (Princeton: Princeton University Press, 2000), 67–87 (78). Tolbert is quoted in Richard Zuczek, *State of Rebellion: Reconstruction in South Carolina* (Columbia: University of South Carolina Press, 1996), 54.

23. Testimony of Kenner James, Testimony of G. S. Bedwell, Senate Hearings, 1589, 1651.

24. Wharton, *Negro in Mississippi*, 190; William C. Harris, *The Day of the Carpetbagger: Republican Reconstruction in Mississippi* (Baton Rouge: Louisiana State University Press, 1979), 648; George C. Rable, *But There Was No Peace: The Role of Violence in the Politics of Reconstruction* (Athens: University of Georgia Press, 1984), 147–48.

25. Wharton, *Negro in Mississippi*, 191; Vicksburg *Monitor*, quoted in Rable, *But There Was No Peace*, 155–56. Emphasis in the original

26. For a prescient analysis of the shift of the Mississippi press in 1875 see Wharton, *Negro in Mississippi*, 183; Brandon *Republican*, July 1 and 16, 1875, quoted in William Bland Whitley, "Precious Memories: Narratives of the Democracy in Mississippi, 1865–1915" (Ph.D. diss., University of Florida, 2004), 61–84; Canton *Mail*, quoted in Wharton, *Negro in Mississippi*, 183.

27. Testimony of J. W. Robbins, Testimony of John T. Harrington, Senate Hearings, 1205, 227

28. Testimony of Harrington, 225.

29. Testimony of W. B. Cunningham, Senate Hearings, 839.

30. Testimony of Henry Kerneghan, Senate Hearings, 1246–47.

31. Testimony of George Glenn, Senate Hearings, 899–900.

32. See James C. Cobb, *The Most Southern Place on Earth: The Mississippi Delta and the Roots of Regional Identity* (New York: Oxford University Press, 1992), 66.

33. Testimony of Henry Kerneghan, Senate Hearings, 1248.

34. W. Scott Poole, "Religion, Gender, and the Lost Cause in South Carolina's 1876 Governor's Race: 'Hampton or Hell!'" *Journal of Southern History* 68 (August 2002): 588–89.

35. W. H. Stiles to Governor Adelbert Ames, Port Gibson, October 30, 1875, James W. Lee to Ames, Aberdeen, October 23, 1875, in "Documentary Evidence," Senate Hearings, 22–23, 67.

36. Testimony of Green Foster, Senate Hearings, 863–65.

37. Testimony of J. W. Lee, Senate Hearings, 1025, 1030.

38. Testimony of Lex Brame, Senate Hearings, 254–55.

39. Testimony of Henry Kerneghan, Testimony of J. W. Caradine, Senate Hearings, 1245, 241.

40. Testimony of John T. Harrington, Senate Hearings, 226.

41. Testimony of P. C. Powell, Senate Hearings, 883–85.

42. Testimony of M. G, Bennett, Testimony of Alfred Black, Senate Hearings, 1389, 1583.

43. Address published in Jackson *Pilot* and Jackson *Times*, October 4, 1875, quoted in Harris, *Day of the Carpetbagger*, 683.

44. Testimony of Robert Gleed, Senate Hearings, 790–93.

45. Testimony of H. R. Ware, Senate Hearings, 1220, 1225.

46. Testimony of Derry Brown, Senate Hearings, 625–35.

47. Whitley, "Precious Memories," and Poole, "Religion, Gender, and the Lost Cause," provide excellent and thorough discussions of the dynamics of white-supremacy rallies. For more on such ceremonials of racial solidarity, see Jean Baker, "The Ceremonies of Politics: Nineteenth-Century Rituals of National Affirmation," in William J. Cooper, Michael F. Holt, and John McCardell, eds., *A Master's Due: Essays in Honor of David Herbert Donald* (Baton Rouge: Louisiana State University Press, 1985), 161–78, and Lawrence Powell, "Reinventing Tradition: Liberty, Place, Historical Memory and Silk-Stocking Vigilantism in New Orleans Politics," *Slavery and Abolition* 20 (March, 1999): 127–48.

48. Testimony of J. W. Robbins, Senate Hearings, 1199.

49. John W. Kyle, writing in 1912, quoted in Wharton, *Negro in Mississippi*, 186.

50. Natchez *Democrat*, quoted in Whitley, "Precious Memories," 146–47. Whitley provides a thorough and insightful discussion of White Line rallies throughout his excellent dissertation, particularly at pages 145–56.

51. Jackson *Weekly Clarion*, October 6, 1875, Oxford *Falcon* (November 24, 1875), both quoted in Whitley, "Precious Memories," 155–56; Kantrowitz, "One Man's Mob," 71.

52. Testimony of H. R. Ware, Senate Hearings, 1220; Yazoo *Democrat*, n.d., quoted in "Documentary Evidence," Senate Hearings, , 164.

53. Oxford *Falcon*, n.d., quoted in Whitley, "Precious Memories," 156. Most religious figures supported the white-supremacy campaign, some with fervor, some with reservations about the use of violence, though few criticized it in any direct way. See Charles Reagan Wilson, *Baptized in Blood: The Religion of the Lost Cause, 1865–1920* (Athens: University of Georgia Press, 1980), H. Shelton Smith, *In His Image but . . . .: Racism in Southern Religion, 1780–1910* (Durham: Duke University Press, 1972), and John Lee Eighmy, *Churches in Cultural Captivity: A History of the Social Attitudes of Southern Baptists*, rev. ed. (Knoxville: University of Tennessee Press, 1987).

54. All these quotes about the evangelical nature of South Carolina Redeemers are found in Poole, "Religion, Gender, and the Lost Cause," 585–86.

55. Ibid., 577; Zuczek, *State of Rebellion*, 173–74.

56. Alfred Brockenbrough Williams, quoted in Poole, "Religion, Gender, and the Lost Cause," 573, 591.

57. Testimony of W. E. Kelley, Senate Hearings, 280–82.

58. Pierrepont, quoted in Foner, *Reconstruction*, 560–61; also see Richard N. Current, *Three Carpetbag Governors* (Baton Rouge: Louisiana State University Press, 1967), 88–89.

59. Adelbert Ames to his wife, October 12, 1875, quoted in Current, *Three Carpetbag Governors*, 89–90.

60. Harris, *Day of the Carpetbagger*, 672.

61. For the full text of this agreement see "Report," Senate Hearings.

62. Kantrowitz, "One Man's Mob," 78.

63. Wharton, *Negro in Mississippi*, 196–97.

64. "Documentary Evidence," Senate Hearings, 37–38, 144–45.

65. Rable, *But There Was No Peace*, 161.

66. Current, *Three Carpetbag Governors*, 91–92.

67. Wharton, *Negro in Mississippi*, 200; Harris, *Day of the Carpetbagger*, 708–9.

68. Wharton, *Negro in Mississippi*, 202.

69. Judge Chrisman's comment is from the Port Gibson *Reveille*, September 19, 1890, quoted ibid., 206.

70. For an understanding of the rhetoric and practice of white supremacy see Joel Williamson, *The Crucible of Race: Black-White Relations in the American South Since Emancipation* (New York: Oxford University Press, 1984). Williamson is convincing on the radical rhetoric of the post-1889 period but, in my opinion, far less complete or satisfactory on the Redeemers. The introduction of the periodization of southern history that divides the post-1876 period into a "conservative" Redeemer movement followed by a "radical" racist regime after the mid-1880s owes most to C. Vann Woodward, *The Strange Career of Jim Crow*, 2nd ed. (New York, Oxford University Press, 1966). For the fullest and by far the most compelling treatment of the dark ages of American race relations see Leon F. Litwack, *Trouble in Mind: Black Southerners in the Age of Jim Crow* (New York: Knopf), 1998). Litwack begins with the post-1889 period.

71. Robert Wallace Shand, "Journal" (n.d.), quoted in Zuczek, *State of Rebellion*, 159.

72. Testimony of George T. Cook, Senate Hearings, 1045–49. Between 1873 and 1875, Monroe County, where blacks outnumbered whites 14,000 to 8,631, went from a 170-vote Republican majority to a 1,067-vote Democratic majority.

CHAPTER 4. The Haymarket

1. Testimony of Samuel Fielden, August 7, 1886, *Illinois v. August Spies et al.* Trial Transcript, 349 (hereafter cited as Trial Transcript), reprinted in the Haymarket Affair Digital Collection (hereafter HADC), Chicago Historical Society (hereafter CHS); Paul Avrich, *The Haymarket Tragedy* (Princeton: Princeton University Press, 1984), 197–214. Also valuable, in addition to Avrich's fine account, is James Green, *Death in the Haymarket: A Story of Chicago, the First Labor Movement, and the Bombing That Divided Gilded Age America* (New York: Pantheon, 2006), from which (5–6) some data in these paragraphs are drawn.

2. Quoted in Avrich, *Haymarket Tragedy*, 216–17.

3. Quoted in Green, *Death in the Haymarket*, 192–93, 201.

4. *Philadelphia Record*, Pittsburgh *Commercial Gazette*, *Albany Journal*, all quoted in Philip M. Katz, *From Appomattox to Montmartre: Americans and the Paris Commune* (Cambridge: Harvard University Press, 1998), 174.

5. Burke A. Hinsdale, ed., *The Works of James Abram Garfield*, 2 vols. (Boston, 1883), vol. 2, p. 549, quoted in Katz, *From Appomattox to Montmartre*, 161; *Chicago Daily News*, January 14, 1886, quoted in Bruce C. Nelson, *Beyond the Martyrs: A Social History of Chicago's Anarchists, 1870–1900* (New Brunswick, N.J.: Rutgers University Press, 1988), 7.

6. *Chicago Tribune*, January 16, 1872, quoted in Carl Smith, *Urban Disorder and the Shape of Belief: The Great Chicago Fire, the Haymarket Bomb, and the Model Town of Pullman* (Chicago: University of Chicago Press, 1995), 103.

7. Quoted in Avrich, *Haymarket Tragedy*, 219.

8. Quoted ibid., 176.

9. Nelson, *Beyond the Martyrs*, 102–26. Nelson, whose research is painstaking and sensible, develops various counts between 751 and 861; he was able to identify 666 by name. As these groups had fluid memberships, more precise figures seem unlikely to be determined.

10. The Pittsburgh Manifesto has been widely reprinted, and it can be found in the HADC, CHS. Albert Parsons included it in his autobiography, reprinted in Philip S. Foner, ed., *The Autobiographies of the Haymarket Martyrs* (New York: Humanities, 1969), 38–42.

11. William Holmes, "Anarchism," *The Alarm*, November 1, 1884; autobiography of Parsons in Foner, *Autobiographies of the Haymarket Martyrs*, 45.

12. Nelson, *Beyond the Martyrs*, 172; Parsons, "Anarchy vs. Religion," *The Alarm*, November 28, 1885.

13. Quoted in Avrich, *Haymarket Tragedy*, 112–13.

14. Parsons, column in *The Alarm*, November 29, 1884. Elsewhere, Parsons cited verses from Acts 4 and 5, Matthew 10–41, and Mark 11:15–19; see, for example, his broadside "An Appeal to the People of America," September 21, 1887, CHS.

15. William Holmes, "Advice to Workingmen," *The Alarm*, April 3, 1886.

16. *Arbeiter-Zeitung*, January 2 and June 20, 1885, reprinted in the Trial Evidence Book, People's Exhibits 98 and 126, *Illinois vs. August Spies et al.*, HADC, CHS (translation by Martin Kitchen).

17. Avrich analyzes the Autonomists in his chapter "The Intransigents," *Haymarket Tragedy*, 150–59.

18. Lucy E. Parsons, "To Tramps: The Unemployed, the Disinherited, the Miserable," *The Alarm*, October 4, 1884, emphasis in the original.

19. "Assassination," *The Alarm*, April 18, 1885.

20. "Dynamite: The Protection of the Poor Against the Armies of the Rich," *The Alarm*, December 6, 1884, which quoted from Sheridan's report.

21. "The Butchers of Men," *The Alarm*, November 15, 1884; [?] Lizius, "Dynamite," *The Alarm*, February 21, 1885; Gorsuch, "The War Cry," *The Alarm*, February 7, 1885. All this material made its way into the state's case against the anarchists and can be found in "The Haymarket Affair Digital Collection" at the CHS Web site: http://www.chi cagohistory.org/hadc/index.html.

22. *The Alarm*, May 2, 1885. Also accessible at "Haymarket Affair Digital Collection."

23. *Arbeiter-Zeitung*, April 30 and May 1, 1886, reprinted as People's Exhibits 93 and 94, Trial Transcript, HADC, CHS (translation by Martin Kitchen).

24. August Spies, *Arbeiter-Zeitung* broadside, May 3, 1886, and poster, May 4, 1886, CHS (translation by Martin Kitchen).

25. Deposition of Otto S. Favor, November 7, 1887, quoted in Governor John P. Altgeld, "Reasons for Pardoning Fielden, Nebbe and Schwab" (Chicago, June 26, 1893), 6–8, reprinted in HADC, CHS. The following examples of the empanelling of jurors are all taken from this document; a complete court record can be found in Trial Transcript, HADC, CHS.

26. Testimony quoted in Altgeld, "Reasons for Pardoning Fielden, Nebbe and Schwab," 13–14, 18, 26–27.

27. For a full account of the trial, including the quotations from Grinnell and Gary, see Avrich, *Haymarket Tragedy*, 260–78; juror, quoted in Green, *Death in the Haymarket*, 229.

28. Swing, quoted in the *Chicago Times,* May 10, 1886, quoted in Green, *Death in the Haymarket,* 200.

29. Charles Carroll Bonney, "The Present Conflict of Labor and Capital" (Chicago: Chicago Legal News Company, 1886), copy in CHS.

30. Rev. Frederick A. Noble, DD, "Christianity and the Red Flag: A Sermon Preached at the Union Park Congregational Church of Chicago," May 9, 1886, copy in CHS.

31. Quoted in Katz, *From Appomattox to Montmartre,* 185; Avrich, *Haymarket Tragedy,* 220.

32. Powderly and *Knights of Labor* editorial, quoted in Avrich, *Haymarket Tragedy,* 220.

33. All these images are reproduced in HADC, CHS.

34. Notes taken by Albert Parsons during his trial, pp.6–7, Albert R. Parsons Papers, Wisconsin State Historical Society.

35. Testimony of Albert Parsons, August 9, 1886, Trial Transcript, HADC, CHS.

36. Testimony of Samuel Fielden, August 6 and 7, 1886, Trial Transcript, HADC, CHS.

37. Autobiographies of Adolph Fischer and August Spies in Foner, *Autobiographies of the Haymarket Martyrs,* 88, 65; Parsons to Lucy Parsons, August 20, 1886, quoted in Avrich, *Haymarket Tragedy,* 323.

38. Autobiography of August Spies, 71.

39. Adolph Fischer to Paul Bulian, July 27, 1886, published in *Freiheit,* August 28, 1886, quoted in Avrich, *Haymarket Tragedy,* 358; Abe Isaak, Jr., "The Chicago Martyrdom," *Free Society,* November 8, 1903, quoted ibid., 385.

40. Parsons to William Holmes, May 22, 1886, published in *Free Society,* November 5, 1899, quoted in Avrich, *Haymarket Tragedy,* 248; Parsons quoted in Chicago *Daily News,* May 9, 1886, quoted in Avrich, 244; Parsons to the *Chicago Tribune,* November 4, 1887.

41. Spies quoted in *Chicago Tribune* and *Chicago Times,* August 21, 1886, quoted in Avrich, *Haymarket Tragedy,* 287; autobiography of August Spies, 63.

42. Fischer to George Francis Train, quoted in *The Alarm,* January 14, 1888; Fischer quoted in Avrich, *Haymarket Tragedy,* 289; "Remember John Brown," October 31 [1887], poster in the Wisconsin Historical Society; John Brown, Jr., to Franklin B. Sanborn, November 7, 1887, in Louis Ruchames, "John Brown, Jr., and the Haymarket Martyrs," *Massachusetts Review* 5 (Summer, 1964): 765–68.

43. Lingg quoted in Avrich, *Haymarket Tragedy,* 411. Avrich describes Lingg's suicide on 375–78.

44. On Powderly see ibid., 448–49; Ely quoted ibid., 222; Whitlock quoted in Green, *Death in the Haymarket,* 199.

45. William Dean Howells to the Editor of the Tribune, November 6, 1887, quoted in Kenneth S. Lynn, *William Dean Howells: An American Life* (New York: Harcourt, Brace, Jovanovich, 1971), 290–91; Howells to George William Curtis, August 18, 1887, Curtis to Howells, September 23, 1887, quoted in Avrich, *Haymarket Tragedy,* 303.

46. William M. Salter, "What Shall Be Done with the Anarchists? A Lecture Before the Society for Ethical Culture of Chicago," Grand Opera House, October 23, 1887, pamphlet in CHS.

47. "The Law Vindicated—Four of the Chicago Anarchists Pay the Penalty of Their Crime," *Frank Leslie's Illustrated Newspaper,* November 19, 1887.

48. Howells to William M. Salter, November 24, 1887, quoted in Howard A. Wilson, "William Dean Howells' Unpublished Letters About the Haymarket Affair," *Journal of the Illinois State Historical Society* 55 (Spring 1963): 5–19 (15); Howells, "A Word to the Dead," quoted in Avrich, *Haymarket Tragedy*, 404. Evidently, Howells intended these remarks for a memorial volume to the Haymarket anarchists that was never published.

49. Chicago *Times*, January 16, 1889, quoted in Richard Schneirov, *Labor and Urban Politics: Class Conflict and the Origins of Modern Liberalism in Chicago, 1986–97* (Urbana: University of Illinois Press, 1998), 278.

50. Karl Polanyi and Jane Addams, quoted ibid., 289, 290. Schneirov makes useful connections between middle-class responses to the Haymarket affair and the development of the social gospel and muckraking movements, which led after 1900 to Progressivism (though Schneirov does not discuss the Progressives). I argue in the next chapter that modern forms of state terror also grow from conflicting responses by others in that same class. On Pullman, see Green, *Death in the Haymarket*, 294–97. For the growth of increasingly self-confident middle-class reformism in labor relations see Robert H. Wiebe's two classic books, *Businessmen and Reform: A Study of the Progressive Movement* (Cambridge: Harvard University Press, 1962) and *The Search for Order, 1877–1920* (New York: Hill and Want, 1967).

51. Altgeld, "Reasons for Pardoning Fielden, Nebbe and Schwab," 49.

52. Chicago *Tribune*, June 28, 1893, quoted in Harry Barnard, *Eagle Forgotten: The Life of John Peter Altgeld* (New York: Duell, Sloan and Pearce, 1938), 241. Both cartoons, by Victor, appeared in the New York magazine *The Judge*, on July 15 and July 28, 1893.

CHAPTER 5. The Philippines War

1. Millet in *Harper's Weekly*, May 13, 1901, quoted in Richard Slotkin, *Gunfighter Nation: The Myth of the Frontier in Twentieth-Century America* (New York: Athenaeum, 1992), 110.

2. Hill testimony, Thoburn testimony, *Affairs in the Philippine Islands: Hearings Before the Committee on the Philippines of the United States Senate*, Senate Document 331, 57th Congress, 1st Session, 3 vols. (Washington: Government Printing Office, 1902), vol. 3, pp. 2439, 2669, 2705. These hearings ran from January 31 to June 26, 1902. The transcript is divided into three volumes paginated consecutively: volume 1, 3–848; volume 2, 849–1968; volume 3, 1969–2984. Further citations will be to *Hearings* followed by the page number.

3. Smith quoted in Stuart Creighton Miller, *"Benevolent Assimilation": The American Conquest of the Philippines, 1899–1903* (New Haven: Yale University Press, 1982), 95; Roosevelt quoted in Slotkin, *Gunfighter Nation*, 106; King quoted in Mark D. Van Ells, "Assuming the White Man's Burden: The Seizure of the Philippines, 1898–1902," *Philippine Studies* 43 (1994): 612.

4. Sherman quoted in Michael Fellman, *Citizen Sherman* (New York: Random House, 1995), 264; for the Fetterman and Sand Creek slaughters, see Fellman, *Inside War: The Guerrilla Conflict in Missouri During the American Civil War* (New York: Oxford University Press, 1989), 213, and Richard White, *"It's Your Misfortune and None of My Own": A History of the American West* (Norman: University of Oklahoma Press, 1991), 90.

5. White, *"It's Your Misfortune and None of My Own,"* 109–13; Robert M. Utley, *Frontier Regulars: The United States Army and the Indian, 1866–1891* (New York: Macmillan, 1973), 133.

6. McKinley, quoted in Miller, *"Benevolent Assimilation,"* frontispiece, emphasis added.

7. Rudyard Kipling, "The United States and the Philippine Islands, 1899," *McClure's Magazine* (February 1899).

8. Albert J. Beveridge, "In Support of American Empire," January 9, 1900, *Congressional Record,* 56th Congress, 1st Session (Washington, D.C.: Government Printing Office, 1900), 704–12.

9. Charles S. Olcott, *The Life of William McKinley,* 2 vols. (Boston: Houghton Mifflin, 1916), vol. 2, pp. 109–111. Olcutt's source was the *Christian Advocate* of January 22, 1903. Olcott refers to the meeting, which occurred on November 21, 1899, as "a well-authenticated interview." His footnote states that his account came from "a report of the interview written by General James F. Rusling, and confirmed by the others who were present." Robert H. Ferrell urges caution in accepting Rusling's version, however, as he used similar language when describing an 1863 interview with Abraham Lincoln just before Gettysburg; see Ferrell, *American Diplomacy: A History,* 3rd ed. (New York: Norton, 1975), 367–69.

10. Olcott, *Life of McKinley,* vol. 2, p. 111.

11. William McKinley, State of the Union Address, 1899, http://www.presidency.ucsb.edu/sou.php.

12. William McKinley, Second Inaugural Address, March 4, 1901, http://www.presidency.ucsb.edu/sou.php.

13. Taft quoted in Andrew J. Birtle, "The U.S. Army's Pacification of Marinduque, Philippine Islands, April 1900–April 1901," *Journal of Military History* 61 (April 1997): 255.

14. William Howard Taft testimony, *Hearings,* 64–65.

15. Ibid., 70, 74, 77.

16. Ibid., 74, 76.

17. Ibid., 322, 406, 411.

18. Robert P. Hughes testimony, ibid., 563, 645–46, 548–49, 636, 638, 642.

19. Hughes diary for February 6 and 8, 1899, quoted in Brian McAllister Linn, *The Philippine War, 1899–1902* (Lawrence: University Press of Kansas, 2000), 64.

20. Elwell S. Otis testimony, *Hearings,* 739, 830–31.

21. Arthur L. Wagner testimony, ibid., 2858–59.

22. A Lester Haslett testimony, ibid., 1742–43.

23. James M. Thoburn testimony, ibid., 2669–77, 2690–91.

24. Arthur MacArthur testimony, ibid., 868–71, 1383, 1918–19.

25. Ibid., 1952–57.

26. Louis W. Koenig, *Bryan: A Political Biography of William Jennings Bryan* (New York: Putnam's, 1971), 292.

27. William Jennings Bryan, "The Paralyzing Influence of Imperialism," *Official Proceedings of the Democratic National Convention Held in Kansas City, Mo., July 4, 5, and 6, 1900* (Chicago, 1900). For two thorough discussions of Bryan and the Philippines issue, see Koenig, *Bryan,* 288–94, 325–31, and Paolo E. Coletta, *William Jennings Bryan,* 3 vols. (Lincoln: University of Nebraska Press, 1964–70), 1:232–37, 263–89.

28. [Peter Finley Dunne], "Expansion," in *Mr. Dooley in the Hearts of His Countrymen* (Boston: Small Maynard, 1899), 3–7. Also see "The Philippine Peace," in *Observations by Mr. Dooley* (New York: Russell, 1906), and several essays by Dunne reprinted in Elmer Ellis, ed., *Mr. Dooley at His Best* (New York: Archon, 1969), 59–77.

29. Twain quoted in *New York World,* October 6, 1900, and *New York Herald,* October

15, 1900, reprinted in Jim Zwick, ed., *Mark Twain's Weapons of Satire: Anti-Imperialist Writings on the Philippine-American War* (Syracuse: Syracuse University Press, 1992), 3–5 (emphasis added).

30. Mark Twain, "To the Person Sitting in Darkness" (1901), ibid., 22–39.

31. Schurz, quoted in Robert L. Beisner's compelling *Twelve Against Empire: The Anti-Imperialists,1898–1900* (New York: McGraw-Hill, 1968), 22–23, 27.

32. Godkin, quoted ibid., 73, 76, 78.

33. "Ministers' Meeting of Protest Against the Atrocities in the Philippines," Tremont Temple, Boston, May 22, 1902, pamphlet, photocopy in the collection of the author.

34. Charles Francis Adams and William James, quoted in Beisner, *Twelve Against Empire*, 44–47, 235.

35. George F. Hoar quoted ibid., 160–62.

36. Both songs are compiled in Joseph L. Schott, *The Ordeal of Samar* (Indianapolis: Bobbs-Merrill, 1964), 65, 155. Krags became the standard rifle only well into the war, but that does not undercut the general point of the song.

37. *Army and Navy Journal* 38 (November 11, 1899): 259, as quoted in Michael C. Robinson and Frank N. Schubert, "David Fagan: An Afro-American Rebel in the Philippines," *Pacific Historical Review* 44 (February 1975): 68.

38. Quoted in Linn, *Philippine War*, 117; quoted in Richard E. Welch, "American Atrocities in the Philippines," *Pacific Historical Review* 43 (May 1974): 233–53 (253).

39. Quoted in Slotkin, *Gunfighter Nation*, 115; quoted in Van Ells, "Assuming the White Man's Burden," 619.

40. Quoted in Slotkin, *Gunfighter Nation*, 115.

41. Quoted in Van Ells, "Assuming the White Man's Burden," 618. More generally, see Miller, *"Benevolent Assimilation,"* 176–218. I have discussed guerrilla hunting in Missouri during the American Civil War as "blood sport," in *Inside War*, 176–84.

42. George Osborn to his parents, January 15, 1900, quoted in Russell Roth, *Muddy Glory: America's 'Indian Wars' in the Philippines, 1899–1935* (West Hanover, Mass.: Christopher Publishing House, 1981), 54, emphasis in the original.

43. William J. Gibbs testimony, *Hearings*, 2296–97.

44. MacArthur testimony, ibid., 1943.

45. Mark H. Evans testimony, ibid., 2890, 1535.

46. Charles Riley testimony, ibid., 1529–37; see 1538–41 for another description of the same incident.

47. D. J. Evans testimony, ibid, 2062–65; Leroy Hollock testimony, ibid., 1971; testimony, ibid., 2304, 2601.

48. Ibid., 1537–39, 1730, 1766, 1971,1975, 2062, 2256–58, 2304; for Brownell's testimony, see Letter from the Secretary of War, "Trials or Courts-Martial in the Philippine Islands in Consequence of Certain Insurrections," 57th Congress, 2nd Session (Washington, D.C.: Government Printing Office, 1903), Senate Document 213, page 85.

49. Grover Flint testimony, *Hearings*, 1769–83.

50. *Hearings*, 1979.

51. Quoted in Glenn Anthony May, *Battle for Batangas: A Philippine Province at War* (New Haven: Yale University Press, 1991), 147–49.

52. *Hearings:* on whipping see 2061, 2236–37; on the loaded pistol, 1733; on the confinement of a woman prisoner, 2244–47; on the burning with cigars, 2260; on ducking, 2883–91.

53. Seiward J. Norton testimony, ibid., 2066; Hollock testimony, ibid., 2900.

54. George D. Boardman testimony, ibid., 2328; Edward J. Davis testimony, ibid., 1735.

55. *Hearings*, 2787.

56. MacArthur testimony, ibid.,1927–32.

57. Richard J. O'Brien testimony, ibid., 2550–58.

58. *Hearings*, 1444–59. In another deposition, sworn in Manila on July 25, 1899, Private Donald Thorne of the same Kansas regiment testified that he saw Captain Bishop of that unit emptying his revolver into the bodies of two wounded captives. This was the regiment commanded by Frederick Funston, the Kansas politician and soldier who gained fame for leading the daring raid that captured Emilio Aguinaldo. For a time, Funston was considered suitable for the national Republican ticket before he talked too freely about his military methods. See Thomas W. Crouch, *A Leader of Volunteers: Frederick Funston and the 20th Kansas in the Philippines, 1898–99* (Lawrence, Kans.: Coronado, 1984).

59. Hollock testimony, *Hearings*, 1972–73, 1982–83, 2254.

60. Wagner testimony, ibid., 2847–65.

61. *Hearings*, 2877–78; the best analysis of the conditions of these camps is in May, *Battle for Batangas*, 262–67.

62. A thorough description of this process is found in Brian McAllister Linn, *The U.S. Army and Counterinsurgency in the Philippine War, 1899–1902* (Chapel Hill: University of North Carolina Press, 1989), 154–59. In this context and more generally, see Glenn A. May, "Was the Philippine-American War a 'Total War'?" in Manfred F. Bomcke, Roger Chickering, and Stig Forster, eds., *Anticipating Total War: The German and American Experiences, 1871–1914* (New York: Cambridge University Press, 1999), 437–57. On disease see the astute and careful study by Ken de Bevoise, *Agents of Apocalypse: Epidemic Disease in the Colonial Philippines* (Princeton: Princeton University Press, 1995), 12–13, and passim.

63. See, for example, the reports from the *Washington Post* about a supposed slaughter reprinted in *Hearings*, 2264. On smaller atrocities see Miller, *"Benevolent Assimilation,"* 188–95.

64. Norton testimony, *Hearings*, 2905.

65. Boardman testimony, ibid., 2331.

66. Gibbs testimony, ibid., 2308, 2320–21.

67. For an excellent analysis of the Balingiga massacre and the entire campaign in Samar, see Linn, *Philippine War*, 306–21. Also see Schott, *Ordeal of Samar*, though his detailed reconstruction of events on the island is both illuminated and limited by the credence he lends to the recollections of American participants, many interviewed fifty years after the events.

68. Schott, *Ordeal of Samar*, 71–72, 98.

69. Ibid., 73, Linn, *Philippine War*, 317–18.

70. Joel D. Thacker, "Stand, Gentlemen, He Served on Samar" (1945), distributed from the Marine Corps University Library Headquarters, U.S. Marine Corps, Washington D.C., http://www.scuttlebuttsmallchow.com/samar.html.

71. Letter from the Secretary of War, 3–7.

72. Much of this argument is advanced in Glenn A. May, "Why the United States Won the Philippine-American War, 1899–1902," *Pacific Historical Review* 52 (1983): 353–77.

73. de Bevoise, *Agents of Apocalypse*, 13.

74. Glenn A. May, *Battle for Batangas: A Philippine Province at War* (New Haven: Yale University Press, 1991), 262–67, 273, 283; de Bevoise, *Agents of Apocalypse*, 12.

75. For the Moro massacre, see Mark Twain "Comments on the Moro Massacre,

March 10 and 14, 1906" (unpublished), in Zwick, *Twain's Weapons of Satire*, 172–73. Also see Christine Gibson, "American Troops Killing Muslims: A Massacre to Remember," *American Heritage.com*, http://www.americanheritage.com/places/articles/web/200603 08-moro-my-lai-leonard-wood-theodore-roosevelt-philippines-sulu-juramentado-manila-pershing.shtml.

76. Twain, "Comments on the Moro Massacre," 168–78.

77. For an intense analysis of the Philippine war as a race war, set in the context of the entire period of American sovereignty over the islands, see Paul A. Kramer, *The Blood of Government: Race, Empire, and United States, and the Philippines* (Chapel Hill: University of North Carolina Press, 2006).

Coda

1. A superb reference work that presents substantial essays and useful bibliographies on the topics covered in this coda, and on violence in American history more generally, is Ronald Gottesman, ed., *Violence in America: An Encyclopedia*, 3 vols. (New York Scribner's, 1999). For a recent collection of vivid documents on a wide sweep of social violence in American history, see Christopher Waldrep and Michael Bellesiles, eds., *Documenting American Violence: A Sourcebook* (New York: Oxford University Press, 2006).

2. Richard Hofstadter, "Reflections on Violence," in Hofstadter and Michael Wallace, eds., *American Violence: A Documentary History* (New York: Knopf, 1970), 6, 11, 19–20, 39–40.

3. Leon F. Litwack, *Trouble in Mind: Black Southerners in the Age of Jim Crow* (New York: Knopf, 1998). On Chicago, see the classic book by William M. Tuttle, Jr., *Race Riot: Chicago in the Red Summer of 1919* (1970; rpt. Urbana: University of Illinois Press, 1996). The quotation is on page 180.

4. Jane Mayer, *The Dark Side: The Inside Story of How the War on Terror Turned into a War on American Ideals* (New York: Doubleday, 2008), 7.

5. Ibid., 52.

6. Ibid., 139, 148, 150.

7. Ibid., 301.

8. Bernd Griener, *War Without Frontiers: The USA in Vietnam* (London: Bodley Head, 2009). For an intense study of one elite force dedicated to killing Vietnamese civilians—let loose "in Indian Country"—as they put it at the time, see Michael Sallah and Mitchell Weiss, *Tiger Force: A True Story of Men and War* (New York: Little, Brown, 2006). Naomi Klein, *The Shock Doctrine: The Rise of Disaster Capitalism* (New York: Metropolitan, 2007).

Note on Terms

1. Andrew Silke, preface to Silke, ed., *Terrorists, Victims and Society: Psychological Perspectives on Terrorism and Its Consequences* (Chichester, U.K.: Wiley, 2003), xv.

2. Quoted in David J. Whittaker, ed., *The Terrorism Reader* (London: Routledge, 2001), 3.

3. Johnson quoted ibid.

4. Richard E. Rubenstein, *Alchemists of Revolution: Terrorism in the Modern World* (New York: Basic, 1987), 17.

5. Grant Wardlaw, *Political Terrorism: Theory, Tactics, and Counter-Measures*, 2nd ed. (London: Cambridge University Press, 1989), 4, 7–8.

6. Jason Franks, *Rethinking the Roots of Terrorism* (Basingstoke, U.K.: Palgrave, 2006), 3; William E. Perdue, *Terrorism and the State: A Critique of Domination Through Fear* (New York: Praeger, 1989), 4.

7. Eugene Victor Walter, *Terror and Resistance: A Study of Political Violence, with Case Studies of Some Primitive African Communities* (New York: Oxford University Press, 1969), 7.

8. Perdue, *Terrorism and the State*, 181–204; Robert E. Goodin, *What's Wrong with Terrorism?* (Cambridge: Polity, 2006), 78, 105, 157–58.

9. Wardlaw, *Political Terrorism*, 16.

10. Martha Crenshaw, "Terrorism in Context" (1995), quoted in Whittaker, *Terrorism Reader*, 12–13.

11. Richard Falk, *Revolutionaries and Functionaries: The Dual Face of Terrorism* (New York: E. P. Dutton, 1988), 93.

12. Wardlaw, *Political Terrorism*, 54

13. Mark Juergensmeyer, *Terror in the Mind of God: The Global Rise of Religious Violence*, 3rd ed. (Berkeley: University of California Press, 2003), 141.

14. Ibid., 186.

15. Ibid., 189.

Index